DATE			

Second Edition

THE
BIOLOGIC
AGES
OF MAN

From Conception through Old Age

DEVELOPED AT THE UNIVERSITY OF WASHINGTON
SCHOOL OF MEDICINE

Edited by

DAVID W. SMITH, M.D.

Professor of Pediatrics,
University of Washington School of Medicine

EDWIN L. BIERMAN, M.D.

Professor of Internal Medicine,
University of Washington School of Medicine

NANCY M. ROBINSON, Ph.D.

Associate Professor of Psychiatry and Behavioral
Sciences, University of Washington School of Medicine

W. B. SAUNDERS COMPANY

Philadelphia • London • Toronto

W. B. Saunders Company: West Washington Square
                         Philadelphia, PA   19105

                         1 St. Anne's Road
                         Eastbourne, East Sussex BN21 3UN, England

                         1 Goldthorne Avenue
                         Toronto, Ontario M8Z 5T9, Canada

Library of Congress Cataloging in Publication Data

Smith, David W   1921 (Sept. 24)-

The biologic ages of man.

1. Aging.   2. Growth.   I. Bierman, Edwin L., joint
   author.   II. Robinson, Nancy M., joint author.
   III. Washington (State). University. School of Medicine.
   IV. Title.

QP84.S468 1978   612.6   77–16963
ISBN 0–7216–8409–2

THE BIOLOGIC AGES OF MAN   ISBN   0-7216-8409-2

Last digit is the print number: 9   8   7   6   5   4   3   2

CONTRIBUTORS

JEFF ALTMAN, M.D.

Clinical Instructor, Department of Family Medicine, University of Washington School of Medicine; Staff Physician, Student Health Center, University of Washington, Seattle.

EDWIN L. BIERMAN, M.D.

Professor of Medicine, University of Washington School of Medicine; Head, Division of Metabolism and Gerontology, University Hospital and Veterans Administration Hospital; Attending Physician, Harborview Medical Center and Veterans Administration Hospital, Seattle.

SHERREL L. HAMMAR, M.D.

Chairman and Professor, Department of Pediatrics, University of Hawaii School of Medicine; Chief of Pediatrics, Kauikeolani Children's Hospital, Honolulu.

WILLIAM R. HAZZARD, M.D.

Associate Professor of Medicine, University of Washington School of Medicine; Attending Physician, Harborview Medical Center, University Hospital, Seattle.

ELAINE D. HENLEY, M.D.

Clinical Professor of Medicine, University of Washington School of Medicine; Attending Physician, University Hospital; Associate Director, Student Health Center, University of Washington, Seattle.

ALAN W. HODSON, M.D.

Professor, Department of Pediatrics; Head, Division of Neonatal Biology, University of Washington School of Medicine, Seattle.

VANJA A. HOLM, M.D.

Assistant Professor, Department of Pediatrics, University of Washington School of Medicine; Attending Physician, Clinical Training Unit, Child Development and Mental Retardation Center, University of Washington, Seattle.

MRS. MYRTLE LARSON

Ventura, California.

JANET H. MURPHY, M.B.C.H.B.

Assistant Professor, Department of Pediatrics, Division of Neonatal Biology, University of Washington School of Medicine, Seattle.

CAROLINE E. PRESTON, M.A.

Associate Professor, Department of Psychiatry and Behavioral Sciences, Division on Aging, University of Washington School of Medicine, Seattle.

NANCY M. ROBINSON, Ph.D.

Associate Professor, Department of Psychiatry and Behavioral Sciences, University of Washington School of Medicine; Discipline Head, Psychology/Education, Clinical Training Unit, Child Development and Mental Retardation Center, University of Washington, Seattle.

CLIFFORD J. SELLS, M.D.

Associate Professor, Department of Pediatrics, University of Washington School of Medicine; Director, Clinical Training Unit, Child Development and Mental Retardation Center, University of Washington, Seattle.

DAVID W. SMITH, M.D.

Professor, Department of Pediatrics; Head, Dysmorphology Unit, University of Washington School of Medicine, Seattle.

MORTON A. STENCHEVER, M.D.

Chairman and Professor, Department of Obstetrics and Gynecology, University of Washington School of Medicine, Seattle.

RICHARD P. WENNBERG, M.D.

Associate Professor, Department of Pediatrics; Director, Neonatal Medicine, University of California School of Medicine, Davis.

DAVID E. WOODRUM, M.D.

Associate Professor, Department of Pediatrics, Division of Neonatal Biology, University of Washington School of Medicine, Seattle.

PREFACE

The purpose of this text is to provide an integrated portrayal of human life from conception through old age. The changing nature of the life situation, the common disorders, and the needs for health maintenance are considered for each of the seven biologic ages of man. Initial presentations on the biology of growth, the biology of aging, and preparation for new life, in addition to a concluding consideration of death and dying are presented to provide an even more comprehensive view of life.

This primary book was designed to offer a basic framework of knowledge about the whole human being at all ages. The student should be able to interweave into this framework the in-depth knowledge on particular organ systems, diseases, and disorders. Beyond being of value in the basic learning process, this approach may enhance the likelihood that the health professional will view any health disorder in the total context of the life stage of the patient.

DAVID W. SMITH, M.D.
EDWIN L. BIERMAN, M.D.
NANCY M. ROBINSON, Ph.D.

ACKNOWLEDGMENTS

Mary Ann Sedgwick Harvey deserves very special thanks and acknowledgment for her contributions as editorial assistant in the development of this book. Her combination of high intellect, hard work, and a practical approach coupled with an element of confidence and a spirit of optimism have not only contributed to the formation of this book but have made it a more pleasant task for the editors and authors.

Mrs. Phyllis Wood of the University of Washington Department of Medical Illustration drew the illustration on the cover, as well as many of those, including charts, within the text. The assistance of the University of Washington Medical Photography group is also acknowledged. We also thank Jan Norbisrath, Medical Illustrator with the Department of Obstetrics and Gynecology of the University of Washington, for her contributions to Chapter Five.

The library research of Mrs. Lyle Harrah is greatly appreciated, particularly with regard to Chapters One, Three, and Four.

CONTENTS

INTRODUCTION

Life is an ever-changing process, a moving picture rather than a series of snapshots. Projection of each frame of a motion picture may be useful in analyzing details of the whole film. In this volume we have attempted such a sequential analysis, beginning with the origin of life, conception, and ending with the final event, death. The most meaningful interpretation of these chapters will be made by the reader who resynthesizes the contents into the continuum of events which is life. And the optimal application of this knowledge by the thoughtful health professional will require a comparison between the general characterization of life sketched in this volume and the particular patient whose life is under examination. For the individual human being with a unique set of internal and external environmental circumstances is still the central figure in the effective delivery of health care.

WILLIAM R. HAZZARD

This second edition has been extensively revised with the addition of sections on The Young Adult, Death and Dying, and Some Overviews of Life. A major change has been the inclusion of a cohesive approach to the psychological and behavioral sections throughout the book, provided by Dr. Nancy M. Robinson.

THE BIOLOGIC AGES—A PICTORIAL OVERVIEW

MYRTLE LARSON

Editor's Comment:

The ten photographs which follow present a brief overview of the life stages of one individual, Mrs. Myrtle Larson, from early childhood to her present age of 81 years. Mrs. Larson (a very healthy individual) is the mother of Mrs. Phyllis Wood, the illustrator of this book. The photographs and the accompanying text were most graciously supplied by Mrs. Larson. It is hoped that this pictorial biography, with its revealing age-related changes, will provide the reader with a more human perspective toward *The Biologic Ages of Man.*

Age 2 years I was born in 1896 in Juneau, Alaska. We moved to Skagway, where my father died when I was four years old. He died of a ruptured appendix. My mother left me with some friends when she went to the hospital and I can still remember how hard I cried and could not be consoled. His obituary said he was a loving and indulgent father.

We had been to Europe for six months the year before he died and my parents had gone to a fortuneteller—maybe on a lark (they were good church people)—and my father was told he would be killed the next year by a gray-haired man with a knife. Although he may not have believed it, he bought more life insurance.

He was in agony with the ruptured appendix and was operated on in the middle of the night by a gray-haired doctor; his own doctor was out of town. There was no penicillin in 1901.

Age 6 years My mother's first interest was always my sister and myself. After my father's death we moved to Seattle, where we lived on a lake. We had a rowboat and would row all around the lake. I later was on the women's crew at the University of Washington.

Age 11 years My mother married again when I was eleven. We were always good friends, but my stepfather never had anything to say about my upbringing. My mother never forgot her great love for my father.

At this age I fell from a teeter-totter at school and dislocated my left shoulder, and a doctor pulled it back in place.

Age 14 years My adolescence was quite normal with lots of activity, including tennis. I began to think I was smarter than my mother, which, of course, I wasn't. She was kind and gentle.

I had my teeth straightened when I was in High School. I also had my tonsils removed, after having them clipped twice at 5 and 10 years of age, in the old-fashioned way.

Age 21 years This was taken on board a cruise ship to Juneau, where I visited friends and climbed to the top of Mount Juneau with young friends.

On the way back to Seattle my fiancé met the boat in Vancouver. He soon left for overseas, World War I. He returned a second lieutenant. Half of his machine-gun battalion had been killed. We were married March 10, 1920.

Age 30 years We always wanted children, and our first child, a daughter, was born a year and three months after we were married; another daughter, Phyllis, two years and four months later, and then a son, four years and two months later.

We always enjoyed our children.

Age 44 years I was busy—golf at the Country Club, president of our Orthopedic Guild for the Children's Orthopedic Hospital, Ladies of Kiwanis, et cetera.

Age 49 years Our 25th wedding anniversary. My husband always encouraged me in everything I did—generous in every way.

One Christmas I had pleurisy.

Age 69 years We moved to California in 1960. My husband died in 1967. He was in the hospital a year and three months. I visited him every day.

My throat had bothered me off and on since our move to California, apparently related to some nodules of tonsil which were left over when my tonsils were removed. There was some concern as to whether these nodules were a tumorous growth. I had x-rays taken and never did find out if my nodules looked O.K. or not. My internal medicine doctor wanted me to have my throat operated on by the same surgeon who had performed a gastric resection and also a hernia operation on my husband. I said, "Shouldn't I see a throat specialist?" He said, "What did you come to me for?" Needless to say, I didn't have the operation. This was ten years ago. I knew what he was going to say afterwards if I'd had it done—"Aren't we lucky it wasn't malignant?"

Age 76 years In 1972, all of a sudden, my back acted up—it killed me to get up or sit down. I finally got a doctor (most doctors here won't take a new patient). He took several x-rays, gave me some medicine, and the next day I was fine again. Did he help me or did it run its course?

One thing we don't like is when the first thing a doctor says is, "How old are you?" He might as well say, "Don't you know you have to start having something that's going to kill you?"

We have to keep our sense of humor and enough money so we can be independent.

We know death is a part of living, or rather the end of living, and I try to keep it that way—and live while I live.

I have just returned from three days at Disneyland with my son and grandchildren.

I swim half an hour every day in the large heated pool here at the apartment and end up with five minutes in the 108° whirlpool. I golf one day a week and enjoy an occasional trip to Las Vegas and the horse races.

Age 80 years This picture of me with my granddaughter was taken on my 80th birthday. This last year, off and on, I have had a slight temperature of 99° to 99.6°F. I have had all the tests including heart, lung x-rays, blood culture, etc. Everything comes out okay. My blood pressure the other day was 130 over 62.

I drive my car and keep as active as I care to and like the year-round mild climate here in California.

I have nine grandchildren.

1

Biology of
Growth

DAVID W. SMITH

The unicellular organism is able to utilize its entire genome, and multiplies immortally at a rate which is dependent upon the environment. The multicellular organism evolves from a single cell with a programmed system of constraints on development and growth. Constraints are placed on the portion of the genome which will be active in a particular cell type, thus accounting for differentiation. There are also constraints on the rate of cell division of specific cells, thereby regulating cell number and growth. These control mechanisms normally carry the organism through a harmoniously channeled sequence of development. The rate of this process and thereby the time required to achieve the mature adult form is variable. The stage an individual is in at a particular time may be referred to as "biologic age."

BASICS OF GROWTH

Control over Mitotic Rate. Though cell size plays a role, the rate of growth of the whole individual or of a given organ tissue is most fundamentally determined by mitotic rate, and thereby cell number. Studies of strains of large versus small rabbits demonstrated a higher mitotic rate and thereby a greater cell number in the large rabbit. Breeding studies with these strains of large and small rabbits indicate that the difference in mitotic rate and thereby size is the effect of many genes. Precisely how the control is exerted is unknown. There appear to be specific factors which affect the mitotic rate and thereby cell number and size for particular organ tissues. One such factor is implied for the liver. Removal of part of the liver will result in an increased mitotic rate of the remaining liver cells, with a return toward the usual liver size and DNA content within a few weeks. This effect appears to be mediated by a humoral protein factor. The hypothesis is that individual liver cells produce and project a particular protein into the circulation which, when accumulated in adequate amount, has an antimitotic effect on the liver cells in general. This type of humoral negative feedback mechanism would tend to keep the liver size proportionate to the whole individual during growth, since it would require more of the factor to maintain the same plasma level as the circulation expands. A similar negative feedback of a tissue-specific antimitotic factor has been implied for growth control of the kidney and spleen. The question has been raised whether these factors might be the same which confer organ tissue antigen specificity. On the other hand, there have been indications of tissue-specific factors which enhance growth. One example is the nerve growth factor which specifically stimulates growth in sympathetic ganglia.

In summary, the control over growth is most fundamentally a control over mitosis and thereby cell number. There appear to be general factors relating to total body mitotic rate and size, and specific humorally transmitted factors which affect mitotic rate and thereby size in particular tissues.

Critical Periods in Growth and Development. The most critical period in the development of the whole individual or in the growth of a particular organ tissue is during the time of the most rapid cell divisions. Most organ tissues go through the developmental stages shown in Figure 1–1 and are most susceptible to permanent residual alterations in growth during the period of rapidly increasing cell numbers. The critical period will thereby vary in different organs according to the timing and dura-

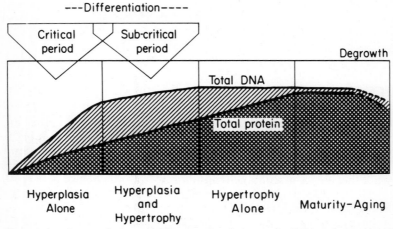

Figure 1–1 Stages of organ development in relation to the DNA and protein content. The earlier stages are the more critical ones in terms of permanent residua arising from problems during that period. (Adapted from Winick, M.: Fetal nutrition and growth processes. Hosp. Pract. *34*:33, May, 1970.)

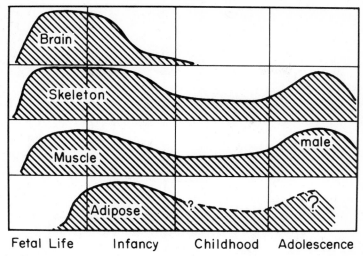

Fetal Life   Infancy   Childhood   Adolescence

Figure 1–2   Critical periods of increasing cell number for several organ tissues.

tion of accelerated mitotic rate for that tissue. Figure 1–2 depicts the critical periods for some tissues.

Normal Growth

Fetal Growth

THE MAJOR ERA OF MATERNAL INFLUENCES ON GROWTH.   Each biologic age has its particular growth characteristics. Fetal growth is heavily dependent upon the mother, and birth weight is influenced by maternal size since the uterus has a constraining influence on growth during late fetal life. This is exemplified in Figures 1–3 and 1–4. Ideally, birth size should be interpreted in relation to the size of the mother, as shown in Figure 1–5. This is also evident for human twins and triplets, who grow at a normal pace until about 30 weeks of gestation and thereafter tend to grow at a slower than usual pace. Once the combined weight of fetal twins exceeds about 4 kilograms there is a restraint on further growth, as shown in Figure 1–4.

The placenta has achieved most of its growth in cell number by 32 weeks' gestation, and its enlargement thereafter is mainly due to cellular hypertrophy. In time the placenta may become a limiting factor in fetal growth.

Following the advent of adipose tissue at 7 to 8 fetal months there is a doubling of weight in the last 2 months of fetal life.

Infancy

THE ERA OF CHANGING GROWTH RATE.   The faster late fetal growth rate of the male as compared to that of the female in length, weight, and head growth continues for 3 to 6 months after birth, as shown for length In Figure 1–6. Thereafter, there is no appreciable sex difference in

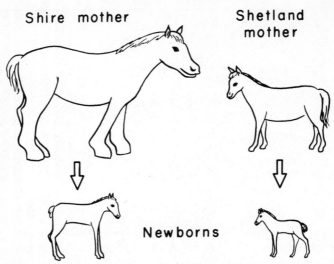

Figure 1–3 Influence of maternal size on the offspring of a cross between a small Shetland stallion and a large Shire mare (left) and a Shire stallion with a Shetland mare (right). Though the genetic situation is the same, the offspring of the larger mother is distinctly bigger. (Adapted from Hammond, J.: Growth in size and body proportions in farm animals. In Zarrow, M. X.: Growth in Living Systems. New York, Basic Books, Inc., 1961, p. 321.)

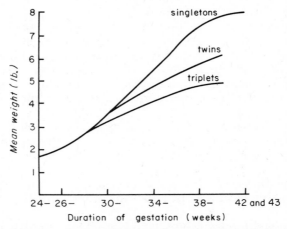

Figure 1–4 The mean fetal weights of singletons as compared to twins and triplets. While the initial growth rate is the same, the combined size of the twins or the triplets leads to early uterine constraint and slowing of growth. (Adapted from Bulmer, M. G.: The Biology of Twinning in Man. Oxford, Clarendon Press, 1970.)

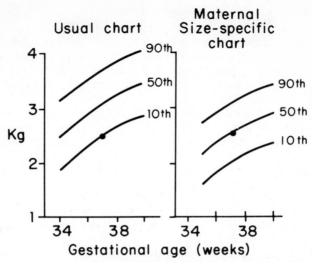

Figure 1–5 The weight of a 5 pound newborn baby, born of a 4-foot, 11-inch, 88-pound mother, plotted on a usual growth grid to the left and on one which is specific for the maternal size on the right. (Adapted form Winick, M.: Biological correlations. Am. J. Dis. Child. *120:* 416, 1970. The standards on the right are from Thomson, A. M. *et al.*: The assessment of fetal growth. J. Obstet. Gynec. Brit. Comm. *75:*903, 1968.)

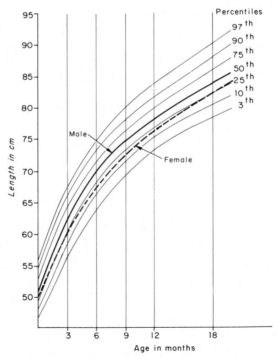

Figure 1–6 Mean and percentiles for the linear growth of male infants and mean for female infants, derived from longitudinal growth values of 90 middle-class white babies. The rate of growth of the males is more rapid than that of the females during the first 3 to 6 months. (From Smith, D. W., Harvey, M. A. S., Rogers, J. E., Greitzer, L. G., and Skinner, A. L.: Unpublished observations.)

growth rate until the advent of adolescence. This early acceleration of male growth may be the consequence of testosterone, which is produced in levels up to 250 ng per 100 ml in the serum of the infant male in the first few postnatal months. Thereafter the serum testosterone values are low in both sexes until adolescence.

After birth, the infant shifts from a growth rate that is predominantly determined by maternal factors to one that is increasingly related to his own genetic background as reflected by midparental size. As a consequence, for about two thirds of normal infants, the linear growth rate shifts during the first year. Infants who are relatively small at birth but whose genetic background tends toward larger size begin their acceleration toward the new growth channel soon after birth. Those who are relatively large at birth but whose genetic background tends toward smaller size usually begin their deceleration into a lower growth channel at several months of age.

During this period the individual is generally obese and by 1 year is 50 per cent longer than at birth and about three times as heavy. Toward the latter part of the first year, there is a gradual diminution in growth rate, accompanied by a reduction in the degree of adiposity. By 18 months to 2 years, the older infant has reached the more consistent growth rate of childhood.

Childhood

THE ERA OF STABLE GROWTH.   The child grows at a fairly consistent rate of 5 to 7.5 cm yearly. As shown in Figures 1–7 and 1–8, there is a gradual deceleration of linear growth rate and an acceleration of weight gain in the period between infancy and adolescence. The major period of brain growth is then over, and lymphoid tissue has achieved its greatest size in proportion to the individual. Adiposity is relatively less in mid-childhood but often increases in the few years before adolescence.

Adolescence

THE ERA OF SEX HORMONE–INDUCED SHIFTING GROWTH.   (See Figs. 1–7 and 1–8.) At a given biologic age, which correlates roughly with the

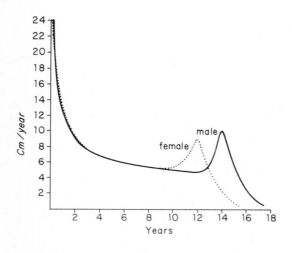

Figure 1–7 Individual velocity curves for length and height for males and females. Note the comparable deceleration in the rate of growth from infancy until the onset of adolescence. (Adapted from Tanner, J. M., Whitehouse, R. H., and Takaishi, M.: Standards from birth to maturity for height, weight, height velocity, and weight velocity. British children, 1965. Arch. Dis. Child. 41:613, 1966.)

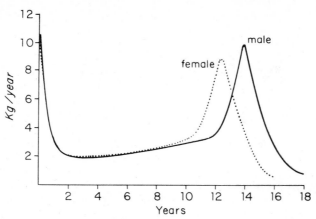

Figure 1–8 Individual velocity curves for weight for males and females. Note the similar gradually increasing rate of weight gain from 2 years of age until adolescence. (Adapted from Tanner, J. M., Whitehouse, R. H., and Takaishi, M.: Standards from birth to maturity for height, weight, height velocity, and weight velocity. British children, 1965. Arch. Dis. Child. 41:613, 1966.)

level of osseous maturation ("bone age"), the hypothalamic gonadotropin releasing centers are no longer suppressed by the very small amounts of androgen or estrogen produced during childhood. The amount of gonadotropin (especially luteinizing hormone) rises gradually over a period of years. This results in a slow increase in the levels of sex hormones, which signals the start of adolescence. The acceleration of linear growth gradually increases, with a peak growth velocity about 2 to 3 years after the advent of adolescence.

The *female* matures more rapidly than the male throughout childhood and begins adolescence 2 years earlier, at the average age of 10 years. Menarche occurs at approximately 13 years, after which there may be continued slow growth up to the age of 16 years.

The *male* matures more slowly than the female, and his rate of growth and maturation is less predictable. Thus, there is greater variability in the male in the age at which adolescence begins and in its progression. The onset is heralded by gonadotropin-induced enlargement of the testes at about 9 to 12 years. Testosterone, a potent androgen, allows for enlargement of the penis, skin changes such as acne, apocrine sweating, and development of pubic, axillary, and facial hair. Shoulder breadth is increased, and facial and bone structure is enlarged. The vocal cartilage expands, and the voice deepens. The number and strength of muscle cells are almost doubled, which results in improved coordination and a relative decrease in the amount of adipose tissue. Owing to these changes, athletic prowess correlates better with osseous maturation ("bone age") than with chronologic age, since the fast maturer achieves adolescent changes before the slow maturer. Most linear growth has been achieved by the age of 18 years, with an average total of one cm in further growth taking place between 18 and 21 years. Cessation of linear growth occurs first in the distal parts (the hands and feet), then in the legs, the trunk, and the shoulder girdle.

Adulthood

CONTINUED GROWTH WITH INCREASING DETERIORATION (DE-GROWTH). The epiphyses of the limbs become ossified and thereby cease their linear growth by about 16 years in girls and 18 years in boys. There is about a 2 per cent increase in length thereafter, however, into the mid-20s. This is mostly accounted for by continued vertebral growth. From 30 to 45 years, stature remains stable while adiposity increases. Thereafter, there is an insidious degrowth in height. The breadth of bones in the face, the skull, and the metacarpals may increase, however, even into the 60s, and the ears may continue to lengthen into the 80s!

Changes in Proportion with Growth

One of the most dramatic changes in proportion is that of the head to the body. This is a consequence of the early growth of the brain, which has already reached two thirds of the adult size by early childhood, as compared to the prolonged growth period for most of the rest of the body. Thus, at two months of fetal life, the brain is 20 per cent of the body weight; by birth it is 12 per cent, by 10 years 6 per cent, and by 16 years it is only 3 per cent.

The limbs grow faster than the trunk from early fetal life until at least mid-adolescence. Thus, measured from the upper level of the pubic ramus to the medial base of the heel, the ratio of the upper to the lower segment is 1.7 at birth, 1.0 at 10 years of age, and 0.9 in adolescent boys of 14 years. Thereafter the long bones ossify and stop growing owing to the effects of sex hormones, but the continued growth of the trunk results in an adult ratio of 1.0. The trunk constitutes 75 per cent of body mass in the infant and 67 per cent in the child. As previously mentioned, the hips increase in breadth in the female owing to the effects of estrogen, and in the male testosterone causes the shoulders to increase in breadth and the bones to become broader.

Growth occurs earlier in the distal part of the leg than in the proximal segment. The foot is half its adult size by 1½ years, whereas the femur does not achieve half its adult size until 4 years. Accelerated growth of the feet is one of the earliest and most sensitive indicators of the advent of adolescence, and it usually precedes and predicts the adolescent growth spurt. The feet achieve their final size one to two years before the remaining leg bones have stopped growing. Thus, the feet mature more rapidly than the long bones of the leg.

Growth of Specific Tissues and Their Assessment

Following are some pertinent comments on the development of particular tissues and the means of assessing their growth. There is one critical point relative to growth assessment: *Always* compare the individual to the immediate genetic background *first*, before comparing the individual to general population standards. For example, Figure 1–9 shows the growth curves of two normal girls in relation to the mean stature of their parents. Growth charts are being developed which are

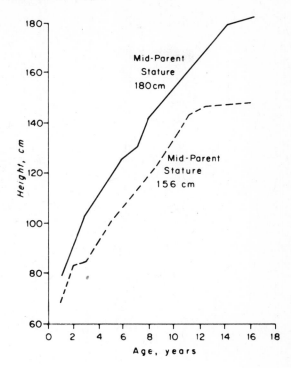

Figure 1–9 Linear growth of two normal girls one from tall (solid line) and one from short (broken line) parentage. (Adapted from Garn, S. M., and Rohmann, C. G.: Interaction of nutrition and genetics in the timing of growth and development. Pediatr. Clin. North Amer. *13*:356, 1966.)

specific for the mean size of the parents and these will be most helpful. Height (length until 18 months), weight, and head circumference are the more usual measurements obtained. These are plotted on standard percentile curves in order to determine not only the relative percentile but also the *rate of growth* of the individual. A *change* in growth rate, as in Figure 1–10, may be an important sign in a number of disorders. Alternatively, the growth may be plotted and interpreted in standard deviations (SD's) from the mean. The 3rd and 97th percentiles are close to 2 SD's below and above the mean.

Skeleton. The skeletal system has a prolonged critical period during which cell numbers are increasing at the epiphyseal plate and in the subperiosteal areas. Skeletal growth is reflected in stature, measured as length during infancy and standing height thereafter. Length should be obtained with the knees straight, and height should be taken with the heels and head against a wall and a right-angle device placed on top of the head to ensure accurate reading of the measurement. The pace of linear growth is an excellent feature to follow in order to detect any change in *growth rate,* which may signify a problem.

Skeletal tissues not only provide the best gauge of general growth progress through stature but also give us our best approximation of biologic age. This can be crudely assessed by facial bone development, utilizing height of the nasal bridge, prominence of the malar eminences, and relative size of the mandible for an overall indication of how old the

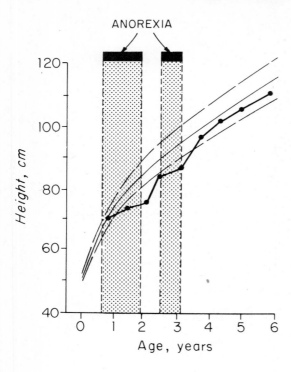

ANOREXIA

Figure 1–10 Decelera-
tion during periods of caloric
insufficiency followed by catch-
up growth toward normal after
adequate nutritional intake.
(Adapted from Prader, A., Tanner, J. M., and Harnack, G. A.:
Catch-up growth following illness or starvation. J. Pediatr.
62:646, 1963.)

child looks. When indicated, skeletal roentgenograms can be utilized to
assess "bone age" by contrasting the findings for mineralization of secondary centers of ossification and advancing bony form to age-related
standards. Prior to 3 months, views of the knee and foot are most
helpful. Thereafter, a roentgenogram of the hand and wrist is the single
most helpful area for evaluation, though some clinicians prefer to obtain
roentgenograms of additional centers. Figure 1–11 shows the changes in
the hand and wrist at 4 and 6 years, as an example. Bone age is a crude
assessment; at 2 years of age there is a normal range of variability of 1
year and at 10 years of age the variability is 2 years. However, it is still the
best indicator of biologic age which we have at the present time, as
indicated by the fact that bone age correlates more closely with the
advent of adolescence than does chronologic age or height age. (Height
age is the age for which the individual's height represents the 50th
percentile.) Thus a 13-year-old with a bone age of 8 years would not be
expected to reach the advent of adolescence for several years at least.
Bone age determination may be helpful as an index of biologic age in
growth problems and in determining whether an older child with no
signs of adolescence has reached the *biologic age* of adolescence or not.
During infancy, a lag in osseous maturation may be evident in the
calvarium by unusually large fontanels for age, in the absence of increased intracranial pressure.

    Brain.   The critical period for brain growth and development ex-
tends into infancy, as shown in Figure 1–12. The brain is growing at a

very rapid pace at the time of birth and on through the first year, and increases threefold in weight during infancy. Although most of the neurones are present at birth, a major addition of glial cells occurs at 1 to 3 months. Most of the myelination process, the responsibility of the glial cells, occurs during the first year. Axone networks, critical to function, are also developing. The functional consequences of this rapid brain growth are reflected in the orderly progression of advancing performance during this time. Brain growth is almost complete by 2 years, the organ being about 80 per cent of adult size by that age.

The best present assessment of brain size is head circumference, which correlates well with DNA content of the brain and thereby with cell number in the brain. The measurement is taken as the widest occipital-frontal circumference. Head circumference should be followed serially as a gauge of the rate of brain development, and plotted on normal head-size charts. A slow rate should raise concern about a prob-

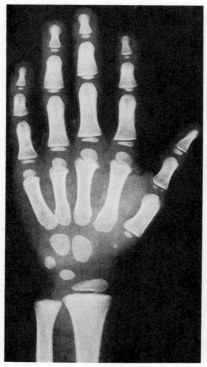 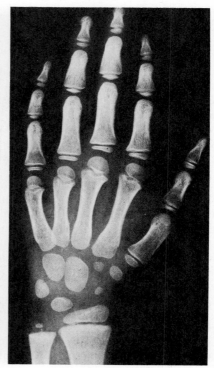

4 years   6 years

Figure 1–11 Roentgenograms of the hand and wrist at the 4- and 6-year age in males. The advancement in mineralization of secondary centers of ossification and in bony form during this biologic age allows for some discrimination of "bone age," crude though it may be. (Adapted from Greulich, W. W., and Pyle, S. I.: Radiographic Atlas of Skeletal Development of the Hand and Wrist. 2nd ed. Stanford, Calif., Stanford University Press, 1959.)

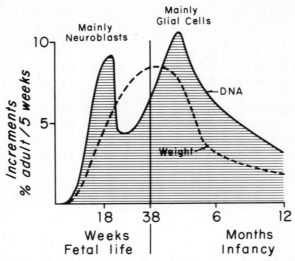

Figure 1–12 Brain rates of addition of new DNA (new cells) and fresh weight during the critical period of brain growth and development. (Adapted from Dobbing, J.: Undernutrition and the developing brain. Am. J. Dis. Child. *120*:411, 1970.)

lem in brain development. Again, it is important first to compare the child's head size to that of the parents before further evaluating a child with an unusual head size. You may find that the head size of one of the parents is similarly unusual.

Lymphoid Tissue. The amount of lymphoid tissue is proportionately greatest in childhood and decreases with adolescence. Thus the tonsils which look relatively large at 6 years of age may not appear so at 14 years.

Facial Growth and Dentition. Figure 1–13 shows facial growth and Figure 1–14 depicts the development of the deciduous and permanent dentition. Teeth are developing from 5 months of fetal age. Deciduous teeth begin erupting at about 5 to 8 months, and all 20 are usually erupted by 2 years. The relative "underbite" may change in time as the mandible "catches up" to the maxilla in growth. The permanent dentition begins erupting around 6 to 7 years. The teeth most commonly missing are the third molars and the upper lateral incisors. Dental maturation is a poor index of biologic age.

Adipose Tissue. The fetus is 0.5 per cent fat in the first half of gestation. At around 7 months of fetal life adipose tissue begins to develop and the fetus progresses from 3.5 per cent fat at that age to 16 per cent fat by birth. The child continues to be obese through infancy, then tends to slim out until the preadolescent age, when some children again become mildly obese. With adolescence, girls maintain a mild obesity and boys tend to lose it under the effects of androgen. As regards cell number, fat cells continue to be added during infancy and childhood. It has now been shown that most obese individuals have excess fat cells and the question is being raised as to whether overfeeding during

Text continued on page 16

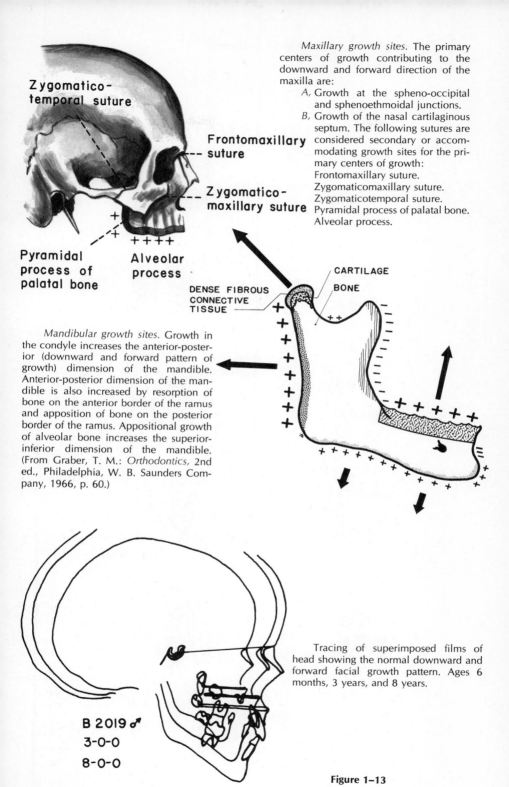

Zygomatico-temporal suture

Frontomaxillary suture

Zygomatico-maxillary suture

Pyramidal process of palatal bone

Alveolar process

DENSE FIBROUS CONNECTIVE TISSUE

CARTILAGE

BONE

Maxillary growth sites. The primary centers of growth contributing to the downward and forward direction of the maxilla are:

A, Growth at the spheno-occipital and sphenoethmoidal junctions.

B, Growth of the nasal cartilaginous septum. The following sutures are considered secondary or accommodating growth sites for the primary centers of growth:
Frontomaxillary suture.
Zygomaticomaxillary suture.
Zygomaticotemporal suture.
Pyramidal process of palatal bone.
Alveolar process.

Mandibular growth sites. Growth in the condyle increases the anterior-posterior (downward and forward pattern of growth) dimension of the mandible. Anterior-posterior dimension of the mandible is also increased by resorption of bone on the anterior border of the ramus and apposition of bone on the posterior border of the ramus. Appositional growth of alveolar bone increases the superior-inferior dimension of the mandible. (From Graber, T. M.: *Orthodontics,* 2nd ed., Philadelphia, W. B. Saunders Company, 1966, p. 60.)

B 2019 ♂
3-0-0
8-0-0

Tracing of superimposed films of head showing the normal downward and forward facial growth pattern. Ages 6 months, 3 years, and 8 years.

Figure 1–13

DECIDUOUS DENTITION

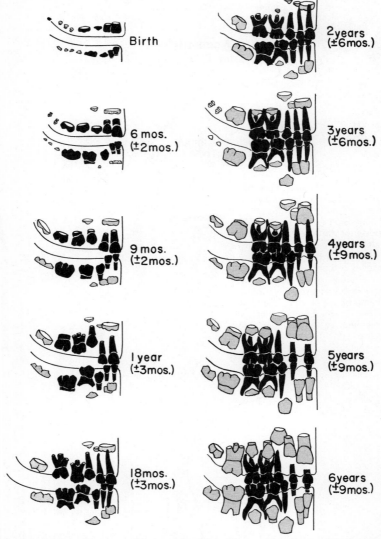

Figure 1–14 Development of human dentition. Black = deciduous teeth: gray = permanent teeth. (From Schour et al.: *Atlas of the Mouth*. Copyright by the American Dental Association. Reprinted by permission. Modified by Graber, T. M.).

Illustration continued on opposite page.

MIXED DENTITION PERMANENT DENTITION

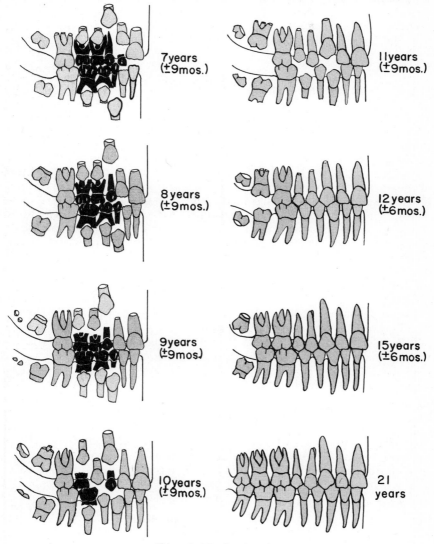

7years
(±9mos.)

8years
(±9mos.)

9years
(±9mos.)

10years
(±9mos.)

11years
(±9mos.)

12years
(±6mos.)

15years
(±6mos.)

21
years

Figure 1–14 *Continued.*

early life can increase the number of fat cells and thereby the liability towards obesity at a later age.

Muscle.   Muscle cells are multinucleate, and the number of nuclei continues to increase throughout childhood, being slightly higher in boys than in girls. Under the effects of androgen the adolescent male doubles the number of nuclei, and his muscle cells also hypertrophy. As a consequence, strength almost doubles, and coordination usually improves. Athletic prowess in teenagers relates better to bone age than to chronological age, again reflecting the correlation between bone age and biologic age of adolescence.

The Phenomenon of Catch-up Growth

During childhood, correction of the cause of a growth deficiency problem may be followed by "catch-up" growth toward the size that would have been attained if the lag had not occurred. The capacity for catch-up growth after a period of induced growth deficiency seems to be limited during early fetal life. For example, temporary undernutrition of the suckling rat, comparable in maturation to a 4 to 5 month human fetus, was not followed by significant catch-up growth. A similar period of undernutrition for the older weanling rat was followed by virtually complete catch-up growth when adequate nutrition was again provided. Thus, it has been suggested that there may be a critical period during which the number of cells sets the stage for future growth. Growth deficiency prior to that time, as in the weanling rat, permanently affects the cell number and the ultimate size of the individual. At a later stage, however, when the control system has been set at a higher level, the same deficiency would be followed by nearly complete restitution of the cell number and the size of the individual.

Such a situation is implied for the human. Most babies who are unduly small for gestational age do not show catch-up growth. This is true, for example, in prenatal growth deficiency secondary to chronic alcoholism in the mother (the fetal alcohol syndrome). When removed from the cause of growth deficiency at birth, these babies do not show catch-up growth. A baby with prenatal growth deficiency due to uterine constraint, such as one of twins, may show catch-up growth after birth, however. When the growth deficiency is of postnatal onset, there may be dramatic catch-up growth following correction of a variety of secondary growth deficiency disorders. Figure 1–15 shows an example.

Secular Changes in Growth and Maturation

In 1876 an astute English physician noted that "the factory child of 9 years weighs as much as one did at 10 years in 1833 — each age has gained one year in 40 years." This phenomenal trend has continued during the past 100 years. A century ago males reached final height attainment at 23 years and girls had menarche at 17 years. Since then

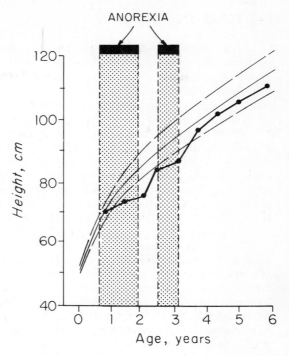

Figure 1–15 Deceleration during periods of caloric insufficiency followed by catch-up growth toward normal after adequate nutritional intake. (Adapted from Prader, A., Tanner, J. M., and Harnack, G. A.: Catch-up growth following illness or starvation. J. Pediatr. 62:646, 1963.)

each generation has matured more rapidly, entering adolescence six months to 1 year sooner, and each generation has been about one inch taller than the preceding one. Thus we are maturing about 25 per cent faster today than 100 years ago. Intelligence quotients at age 11 years are also distinctly higher. It is not possible to state whether this latter phenomenon is a direct corollary of the faster pace of maturation or whether it is related to the fact that head circumference and thereby brain size has also increased.

Since children of today are more mature and taller than those of the previous generation at the same chronologic age, past growth standards are not wholly appropriate for the present generation. Unfortunately, adult society and educational systems have generally failed to keep step with this advancing pace of maturation in terms of curriculum, age of college entrance, age of employment, and, in a more general sense, the age at which an individual is treated as an "adult."

The reason for this dramatic change is unknown. Better nutrition and relative lack of serious childhood disease are major considerations. Increased outbreeding with consequent "hybrid vigor" has been conjectured. Regardless of cause, animal studies imply that the more rapidly a species matures, the shorter is the life span. Thus, some of the evidence of earlier aging (such as atherosclerosis) in recent generations may be partially related to the more rapid pace of biologic aging in the earlier stages of life.

FACTORS IN GROWTH

The basic capacity for growth and for pace of maturation are polygenic determinations, with at least some of the genes being on the X and Y chromosomes. Thus, the most common causes of small stature in well-fed children represent the lower end of the normal polygenic spectrum for statural size and maturational rate, respectively, as summarized in Table 1–1.

Given an adequate genetic endowment, with cells which have a normal capability for growth, there are a host of factors which must be functioning adequately or be available in order to allow for the innate growth capacity. Besides those problems discussed below, these include: intestinal absorption and utilization of nutrients; chronic cardiac, respiratory, or renal disorders; certain metabolic and chronic infectious diseases; and central nervous system and emotional disorders.

Nutrition

The most common worldwide cause of growth deficiency is malnutrition. Because of deficiency in energy or other nutrient resources there is a slowing in the pace of growth and maturation. This is most evident for adipose tissue, muscle, and skeletal growth. However, one of the gravest concerns is malnutrition which occurs during the critical period of increasing brain cellularity. Studies on rats have clearly shown a permanent residual deficit of brain size and cellularity, with compromised brain function, secondary to malnutrition during the period of increasing brain cellularity. The findings in the human are similar; in the wake of prenatal and early infancy malnutrition there may be a permanent deficit in head circumference, brain DNA (cell) content, and subsequent intellectual performance. Hence adequate nutrition is critical to normative growth and development, especially during the periods of increasing cell number for a particular organ tissue.

Hormones

Testosterone and Other Androgens. Testosterone, the most potent of the androgens, allows for an increase in muscle cell number and size as well as for an increase in bone mass, with accelerated epiphyseal cartilaginous linear growth. Broadening of the shoulders also occurs. Androgens accelerate osseous maturation more rapidly than linear

TABLE 1–1 FEATURES OF FAMILIAL SMALL STATURE
VERSUS FAMILIAL SLOW MATURATION

	Familial Small Stature	Familial Slow Maturation
Frequent family history of	Short stature	Late adolescence
Size at birth	Normal	Normal
Growth during childhood	Slow	Slow
Maturational rate	Normal	Slow
Onset of adolescence	Normal age	Late onset
Final height attainment	Usual age, short	Late age, normal
General evaluation	Otherwise normal	Otherwise normal

growth, however, and hence bring the individual more rapidly to the stage of final height attainment. Thus, though testosterone and other androgens have profound effects on growth, they do not appear to be growth hormones in the sense that they increase the ultimate stature of the individual.

ESTROGENS.   Estrogens accelerate the lateral growth of the pelvis and thereby widen the hips, at the same time accelerating the pace of osseous maturation without affecting linear growth as profoundly as testosterone. Thus, the female reaches final height attainment sooner than the male and has less of an adolescent growth spurt.

PITUITARY GROWTH HORMONE AND SOMATOMEDIN. Pituitary growth hormone has a primary action on cell metabolism and affects the utilization of amino acids, glucose, and free fatty acids. Its predominant effect on linear growth is exerted through the stimulation of soma-tomedin production, apparently from the liver. Somatomedin enhances the rate of mitosis in cartilage cells at the epiphyseal plate, thereby affecting linear growth. This is accomplished without undue acceleration of osseous maturation; hence, somatomedin may be considered a growth hormone.

THYROID HORMONE.   Thyroid hormone is essential for normal energy metabolism to facilitate growth after birth. It should not be considered a growth hormone, since excess thyroid hormone results in only mild acceleration of linear growth with moderate acceleration of osseous maturation, both at the expense of a dangerous increase in metabolic rate.

Hopefully, this section will have provided the reader with a feeling for the dynamic nature of the process of growth and development. At no stage is the individual static; hence the evaluation of a given individual at a particular moment in time must always be viewed in relation to the past and future in terms of both interpretation and prognostication.

Critical events which occur during growth and development may alter the form and function of the mature individual. But once having attained that mature form, the nature of the individual continues to change in time. For growth and aging are a continuum, the one following upon the other. As you shall see in the next chapter, many aspects of aging tend to be a reversal or loss of the processes involved in growth — a degrowth.

Growth and Behavioral Development

NANCY ROBINSON

Maturation vs. Learning.   Not all the changes one sees during the life span of an individual can be attributed to biological growth, of course. Behavioral changes and even a number of physical changes can be attributed to a rich interplay of experience and physiological "ripening." Behavioral changes which occur mainly as a result of experience are said to be a product of *learning,* whereas those depending mainly on biological development are said to be a product of *mat-*

uration. Beginning in infancy, we can see the interaction of these two sets of factors. No one could possibly deny the importance of the learning which takes place throughout life. It is equally true that many behavioral changes reflect a kind of individual biological time clock which, within broad limits of experience, cannot easily be tampered with. For example, the ages of walking and of uttering the first word do not vary much across cultures and seem highly dependent on maturation. Other behaviors which are also highly dependent on central nervous system function, such as age of reaching for objects, are known to be markedly affected by the level of stimulation an infant experiences, with either over- or understimulation tending to delay emergence of the skill. What we see, then, is a complex interplay, which in any individual may be very difficult to unravel. The separation of physical and psychological features in health and illness becomes even more complex as the child matures.

Continuity Versus Discontinuity in Development. From one point of view, behavioral change is correctly viewed as "growth." There is a progression in size and complexity from the tiny zygote to the adult human being. There are, however, a number of ways in which — superficially, at least — behavioral progress proceeds by discontinuous leaps from one stage or status to another. There is no evidence that development of the central nervous system progresses by stages, although behavior is more rapid in some parts of the physiological system than others at any given time. Even so, behaviorally speaking, the emergence of certain skills seems to permit a quantum jump from one phase to another. The "toddler" seems qualitatively different from the "crawler" and requires different kinds of attention from the parent. We all recognize the "Terrible Twos" stage and, much later, the "menopausal" stage. Throughout the life span, we are accustomed to thinking in terms of stages which are useful in communicating with parents, patients, and others regarding many important life problems. Indeed 10 of the 12 chapters of this book are organized according to life periods, most of which cannot be sharply distinguished from one another on a physiological basis.

Two theorists who have dealt with stage-oriented developmental questions in the behavioral sphere will be mentioned in Chapters 6 through 11. Erik Erikson exemplifies an approach to the developmental life tasks faced by individuals throughout the age span. Jean Piaget has described the rapid emergence of complex cognitive skills which is more or less complete by late adolescence. One should, however, keep in mind that to some extent the concept of life stages lies in the eye of the beholder rather than in the underlying biological substrate.

REFERENCES

Bayer, L. M., and Bayley, N.: Growth Diagnosis. Chicago, University of Chicago Press, 1959.
Blais, M. M., Green, W. T., and Anderson, M.: Lengths of the growing foot. J. Bone Joint Surg., *38-A*:998, 1956.

Falkner, F. (Ed.): Human Development. Philadelphia, W. B. Saunders Company, 1966.

Garn, S. M., and Rohmann, C. G.: Interaction of nutrition and genetics in the timing of growth and development. Pediat. Clin. N. Amer., *13*:353, 1966.

Needham, A. E.: The Growth Process in Animals, Princeton, New Jersey, D. Van Nostrand Company, Inc., 1964.

Smith, D. W.: Growth and Its Disorders. Philadelphia, W. B. Saunders Company, 1977.

Tanner, J. M., Goldstein, H., and Whitehouse, R. H.: Standards for children's height at ages 2–9 years allowing for height of parents. Arch. Dis. Childh., *45*:755, 1970.

Thomson, A. M.: The evaluation of human growth patterns. Am. J. Dis. Child., *120*:398, 1970.

Watson, E. H., and Lowrey, G. H.: Growth and Development of Children. 5th ed. Chicago, Year Book Medical Publishers, 1967.

Winick, M.: Fetal malnutrition and growth processes. Hospital Practice *34*:33, May, 1970.

2

Biology of Aging

EDWIN L. BIERMAN
WILLIAM R. HAZZARD

The process of aging begins with conception and ends with death. The study of this process is the science of gerontology. Because the aging process proceeds gradually and inexorably to death, its study has been until very recently largely neglected by scientists preoccupied either with the more positive processes such as growth and development or with specific, often dramatic disease entities. As a result we know relatively little about aging. What follows, then, is necessarily a highly preliminary summary based on current investigation of possible mechanisms whereby aging may take place.

Why do people die? Apparently individuals do not die "of old age," but of specific disorders or diseases. Therefore one can define "aging" and "senescence" as the underlying process that leads to an increased probability of disease. In simpler terms, aging represents a progressive decline of vigor and resistance with the passage of time. Even if we escape wars, accidents, and diseases, aging proceeds at a rate which differs little from person to person, so that there are heavy odds in favor of dying between the ages of 65 and 80. Some will die sooner, and a few will live into the ninth or tenth decade. However, at the present time there appears to be a virtual limit on the life span, however lucky, robust, and free of disease one remains. If this process of aging were not a factor in our lives, and if we kept throughout life the same resistance to stress, injury, and disease which we had at age 12, it has been estimated by Comfort that half of us alive today might expect to live another 700 years. In point of fact, however, the maximal human life space has rarely been authentically documented to have exceeded 110 years. Recent reports of extreme longevity of Abkasians (residents of the Caucasus) and others reputed to live from 120 to 160 years have been found unacceptable upon critical examination.

THE PROCESS OF AGING

General

The process of aging is easy to demonstrate by examination of mortality curves. If death were a random event, the mortality rate would be constant with time, and the survival curve of such a population would be semi-logarithmic (Fig. 2–1), like that of a radioactive isotope or of water glasses in a cafeteria. The survival curve of a population that exhibits senescence, however, is strikingly different (Fig. 2–1). It shows an initial gradual decline followed by a sharp increase in mortality rate with time so that a rectangular-shaped curve results. Translated into numbers, the probability of dying doubles approximately every eight years. The human population curve clearly shows the impact of the aging process, even in groups which have increased mortality rates due to such devastating infectious diseases as infantile diarrhea and tuberculosis, which are prevalent in underdeveloped countries or in the disadvantaged population in the United States (Fig. 2–2). The conquest of such diseases has resulted in a shift of the survival curve to the typical one of aging by a reduction in the mortality of the younger age groups (Fig. 2–3). This increase in life expectancy, now averaging approximately 70 years at birth (Fig. 2–4), has been due almost entirely to the reduction in mortality from such specific diseases, but this conquest of disease has not appreciably altered maximum life span, which remains at 90 to 100 years. As a result of the reduction in mortality from disease in younger age groups, allowing more people to reach the upper limit, we are left primarily with aging and age-linked diseases in adult clinical practice. Moreover, the proportion of the population in the United States over age 65, which was 10 per cent (20 million) in 1970, is steadily increasing (Figs. 2–5 and 2–6). Thus the medical, sociological, and economic implications of the aging process loom ever larger in our projec-

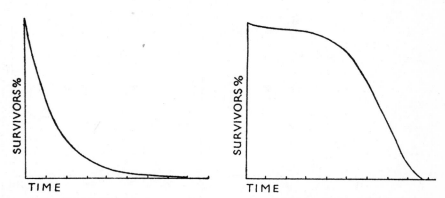

Figure 2–1 *Left:* Survival curve at a constant rate of mortality 50% per unit time. *Right:* Survival curve of a population which exhibits senescence. (From Ageing: The Biology of Senescence, by Alex Comfort. Copyright (©) 1956, 1964 by Alex Comfort. Reprinted by permission of Holt, Rinehart and Winston, Inc.)

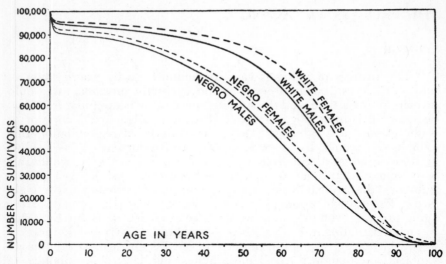

Figure 2–2. Number of survivors per 100,000 live births, by race and sex: United States, 1939–41. (From Ageing: The Biology of Senescence, by Alex Comfort. Copyright (©) 1956, 1964 by Alex Comfort. Reprinted by permission of Holt, Rinehart and Winston, Inc.)

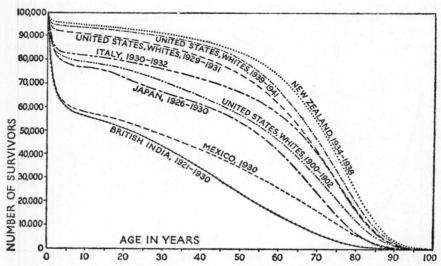

Figure 2–3 Number of survivors out of 100,000 live male births, from life tables for selected countries. (From Ageing: The Biology of Senescence, by Alex Comfort. Copyright (©) 1956, 1964 by Alex Comfort. Reprinted by permission of Holt, Rinehart and Winston, Inc.)

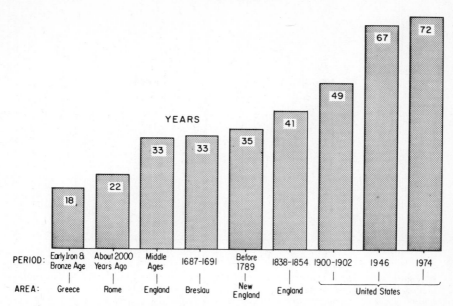

Figure 2–4 Average life expectancy at birth from ancient to modern times. Adapted from Dublin, L. I., Lotka, A. J., and Spiegelman, M.: Length of Life, New York, The Ronald Press Co., 1949, and the U.S. Bureau of the Census, Current population reports, series P-23, No. 43, Some demographic aspects of aging in the United States. U.S. Government Printing Office, Washington, D.C. 1973.

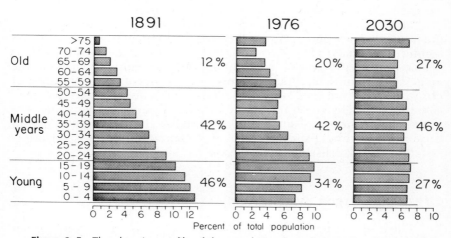

Figure 2–5 The changing profile of the population from demographic figures of U.S. and England. Whereas before the turn of the century almost half of the individuals were below age 20, fifty years hence almost half will be over age 40. Projection based on U.S. census figures assuming a fertility rate of 2.1 children per woman. Adapted from The Graying of America, Newsweek 89:50–65, 1977, and Coni, N., Davison, W., and Webster, S.: Lecture Notes on Geriatrics. Oxford, Blackwell Scientific Publications, 1977.

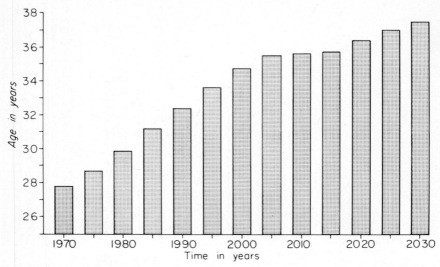

Figure 2–6 The projected rise in the median age of the U.S. population (half the population older, half younger) based on U.S. Census calculations assuming a fertility rate of 2.1 children per woman. Adapted from The Graying of America, Newsweek 89:50–65, 1977.

tions of the future needs of our population. It has been estimated that even if the present leading causes of death (i.e., heart disease, stroke, and cancer) were eliminated successfully, approximately 20 years of additional life expectancy would result, allowing more individuals to reach healthier older ages, but not increasing total life span, thus approaching the theoretical ultimate rectangular longevity curve.

Thus, the human life span appears limited not by disease, but by intrinsic biological aging. Aging is clearly not unique to man but occurs among all animals. The oldest known animal, the Galapagos turtle, has been estimated to reach 175 years of age. Of the mammals, man has the longest life span. Unicellular organisms are probably the only form of life which may not age, since they divide into two new cells and thus could theoretically go on forever. This in itself suggests that aging is in some way a function of multicellular existence. In multicellular organisms, aging occurs at various levels of organization: organs and organ systems; tissues; cells; subcellular particles; and molecules.

Organ and Organ System Aging

The examination of aging at the level of organs and organ systems suggests that many processes begin to decline long before death. Thus their measurement may provide an estimate of the physiological age of an individual, which is a far better index of his rate of aging than his chronological age. Such physiological aging is apparent in man after the age of 30 (Fig. 2–7) and some functions, notably cardiovascular work per-

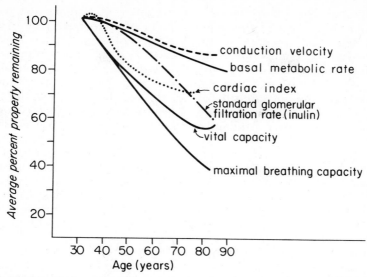

Figure 2–7 Decline in various human functional capacities and physiological measurements with age. (Adapted from Shock, N. W. *In* Strehler, B. L., Ebert, J. D., Glass, H. B., and Shock, N. W.: The Biology of Aging. Washington, D.C., American Institute of Biological Sciences, 1960, p. 22.)

formance and sexual function in males, clearly reach their peak at the end of the adolescent growth period. There is a nearly linear decline in most integrated body functions at the rate of about 1 per cent per year in adult life. In addition, many homeostatic systems which continue to function well at rest may become unable to react to stress and perturbation and thereby become progressively impaired. Examples include regulation of blood pH, blood glucose, and pulse rate, to mention only a few. As a result, older persons are characteristically less effective than young people in meeting environmental challenges and require a longer time to readjust their internal environment after displacements occur. None of these functional decrements appears to be a fundamental cause of the aging process in the whole organism, but rather a result. The impact of these age-linked functional changes on diagnostic criteria for certain diseases is an important problem, which will be discussed in detail in Chapter Eleven. It is sufficient to say that aging is not limited to any organ or system. This suggests that a fundamental feature of the aging process might be apparent in tissues or cells, or even at some lower level of organization.

Tissue and Cellular Aging

Tissue and cellular aging can be examined in three major categories: noncellular material, multiplying cells, and nonrenewing cells.

Much attention has been focused on noncellular interstitial tissue and, in particular, on collagen, the major element of connective tissue in the skin, skeletal, and vascular systems. Clearly, if collagen became altered so that diffusion of metabolites from circulation to cells were impaired, a generalized decrease in organ function with time would be explained. Properties of connective tissue normally change in the direction of increased cross-linking and stiffness and loss of elasticity. Whether these connective tissue changes, though clearly important in such tissues as skin and arteries, are a fundamental factor in the aging process is still unresolved.

Of particular importance in tissues in which cells tend to be nonrenewable, such as nerve and muscle cells, is the loss of cells with time, and a consequent decrease in functioning cell number. For example, all areas of the cerebral cortex lose cells with age, and muscle mass decreases. Although this loss might account for some aspects of functional deterioration, changes must also be taking place in those cells that remain in the body.

An interesting aspect of cellular aging is the accumulation in cells of substances which are not metabolized and may, in fact, be harmful. One such example is a fluorescent pigment called "lipofuscin" or "age pigment," which is deposited in certain tissues of many species, in cells that divide very slowly, such as in brain and heart muscle. This pigment may occupy as much as 5 per cent of the volume of the heart muscle cell in a 70 year old individual. Lipofuscin contains a large amount of lipid, presumably representing auto-oxidation products derived from degenerated cell membranes, possible lysosomes. (Lysosomes are enzyme packets that are responsible for degradation of cell debris; their failure has been implicated in accumulation of cell waste products with aging.) The deposition of age pigment may play some role in the decreased functional capacity of certain cells and tissues with age. Also, a high proportion of elderly individuals have been found at autopsy to have a proteinaceous substance called *amyloid* in their tissues, particularly in brain, heart, and pancreatic islets. This, too, may contribute to functional impairment.

The multiplicity of factors controlling cell replacement and tissue regeneration are also of central interest in an appraisal of the biologic nature of the aging process, since these functional processes decline with time. In tissue culture, human cells do not divide indefinitely but have a finite capacity for division which decreases with the age of the donor. For example, embryonic cells divide about 50 times in culture, those from a 20-year-old divide about 30 times, and cells derived from older donors divide about 20 times. Furthermore, the capacity of cells of a species to divide *in vitro* appears to be related to the maximum life span of that species. *In vivo* transplantation studies in which normal cells are serially transplanted into young hosts also do not survive indefinitely. Thus normal somatic cells have an intrinsic predetermined capacity for division. From fusion studies of isolated nuclei and cytoplasm from young and old cells, it appears that the "clock" that determines proliferative capacity is located in the nucleus.

With regard to subcellular and molecular aging, no characteristic biochemical sign of oldness in cells or molecules has yet been described. However, most of the rather fanciful theories on the nature of the aging process are concerned with molecular interactions within specialized cells. There are theories concerned with the functional deterioration of cells that no longer divide which invoke such processes as exhaustion of irreplaceable enzymes and denaturation of proteins and macromolecules. However, there is no evidence that the gradual decline of overall metabolic rate with age is related to decreased function of existing cells, rather than to a loss of cells from tissues. With the recent remarkable increase in understanding the molecular biology of the genetic apparatus, a variety of theories that relate aging to the genetic message have come into focus. Are there specific "aging" genes or does the organism simply run out of genetic information? A popular argument is that errors in the reading out of the genetic code may be related to the aging process. Thus, if there occurs a progressive accumulation of faulty copying and misspecified proteins (including enzymes) in clonally dividing somatic cells (such as mutation or cross linkages in RNA and DNA), some of the progressive functional deterioration seen in the aging organism might be explained. If a somatic cell were to undergo such changes, it would become a different cell, one which might not perform its original function. Molecular mischief might result in an "error catastrophe." Chromosomal aberrations, which may be a rough index of mutations, do accumulate in mammalian cells such as liver. Indeed, the life span of a species appears to be directly related to its ability to repair damaged chromosomes. Perhaps an aging cell may even represent an alternative to a neoplastic cell.

An interesting theory suggests that aging may represent an autoimmune process. In other words, a mutation or decline in replicative capacity of immunologic cells could produce immune reactions to one's own native tissues and might lead to cell dysfunction and death. Serum autoantibodies to various cellular antigens as, for example, thyroid, stomach, and nuclei, are found with greater frequency in older individuals. Monoclonal gamma globulin "paraproteins" also appear to accumulate with age. Perhaps also involved is the age-related increase in amyloid deposition which has already been noted.

One theory which has few proponents today is the historical hormonal imbalance theory. The early discoverers of hormones, particularly the sex hormones, were fully convinced that they had the key to the prevention of aging. This even led to the therapeutic use of tiger testicle extracts! Unfortunately, such treatment with sex hormones has been ineffective in providing eternal youth. Furthermore, it is well recognized that gonadal senescence, as seen in male castrates or with surgically-induced early menopause in the female, does not result in somatic senescence.

General Factors Affecting Aging

Unknown features of the specific biologic process of aging appear to be inherited. The life spans of identical twins are more similar than those

of fraternal twins. Short life spans seem to be inherited in that a predisposition to a fatal disease like cancer or heart attack may be genetically
determined. The reverse also appears to hold true in that longevity also
seems to be inherited. Parents of centenarians and nonagenarians appear to have lived much longer than parents of individuals dying at an
earlier age. Sex also appears to affect longevity, with the advantage to
the female. This is not confined to the human species but extends to
most animals as well. One theory advanced to explain this phenomenon
has to do with sexual exhaustion. In several species, it is true that the
male dies soon after reproductive activity ceases. There is good evidence
against this idea in the case of man. The mortality figures for clergymen
in England show that Anglican and Protestant clergy had only 70 per
cent of the general male mortality; the mortality of the celibate Roman
Catholic clergy was 105 per cent. It would seem that the virtues of sexual
abstinence as a factor in promoting longevity has been overemphasized.
In contrast to many Western writers, who until quite recently continued
to proclaim the harmful consequences of sexual excess, Indian and
Chinese sages thought that continued sexual activity in man was the way
to eternal youth. Although this may be an extreme view, death rate
figures for the United States appear to show that married persons have a
mortality rate which is one and one-half to two times lower than that of
widowed or divorced persons. Undoubtedly, there are other factors
involved as well.

Alteration of Aging by Experiment and by Disease

Despite our lack of fundamental knowledge about aging, there have
been several approaches to the experimental alteration of the aging
process. One approach proceeds from the concept that life is programmed like a computer so that an organism goes through a fixed sequence of operations involving growth, differentiation, and aging. Under
such circumstances, aging might occur because a program had run out
with no further built-in instructions. As a result, guidance and control
mechanisms would progressively fail, not unlike the progressive failure of
homeostasis which occurs in the aging organism. This has logically suggested that the faster the rate of growth and differentiation, the faster
the aging process. One experimental approach has been to retard the
growth rate by underfeeding. This has led to prolongation of life in
many species. In the classical experiments of McKay, rats were fed diets
deficient in calories but adequate in all other respects for up to three
years. Their growth retardation was associated with a decreased incidence of many chronic rat diseases, and survival well beyond their
usual life span. In a sense they were put into "dietary cold storage" and
thereby kept artificially young. The mechanism of this prolongation of
life with growth retardation is unknown.

However, the reverse experiment, an attempt to accelerate growth
and development by treatment with an agent such as growth hormone,
does not shorten life. Attempts to accelerate aging by other means have
also been relatively unsuccessful. Radiation may be an exception. Expo-

sure to significant amounts of x-radiation shortens life span, but it is not clear whether such radiation results in accelerated aging or chronic toxicity. If one excludes the induction of tumors, cataracts and hair loss, radiation does not alter causes of death but lowers the age at which animals die from them, which is the typical property of the aging process. This continues to be an interesting area of investigation.

One "experiment of nature" may exist in man in the form of an extremely rare disease called adult progeria, or Werner's syndrome, which superficially resembles accelerated aging. People with this disorder present between the ages of twenty and forty with gray hair, thin and atrophic skin, hair loss, a high-pitched squeaky voice, cataracts, skin ulcers, and short stature, In this disorder the most frequent causes of death are related to connective tissue tumors and vascular atherosclerosis. However, many of the features of the aging process, such as collagen changes and age pigment deposition, are not found in this syndrome. Although the mortality curve is shifted earlier in time, there is not a proportional increase in all the causes of death or all the features of the aging process. Therefore, this syndrome is thought to be a caricature of aging, exaggerating the ectodermal features of the aging process but not simply representing premature or accelerated aging. However, cells cultured from these individuals have a marked reduction in their capacity for division. It may be that accelerated aging, if not usually generalized in man, may occur in individual organs and organ systems asynchronously with that of the rest of the body, as, for example, seems to occur in the pre-senile brain syndromes. It is always difficult to separate changes due to disorders of specific tissues and organs from effects of the aging process *per se*.

There is a lack of understanding of the nature of some of the biologic fundamentals of the aging process, its relation to other time-related processes, such as cessation of sexual function, and its relation to growth, tissue organization, and development. If the biological scientist is asked whether human aging is ever likely to be controlled or even influenced, at present he can only answer that until the nature of the processes involved are known, he can make no predictions. But we as health professionals must face, rather than ignore or approach with professional disdain, the clinical consequences of the aging process. Despite some progress from the efforts of social medicine, behavioral medicine, medical science, and rehabilitation professionals, our society at present is finding it difficult to cope with the increased number of people reaching later life without any dramatic change in biologic age. From the social point of view, it must be realized that an increase in longevity which would result from even a limited control of aging might produce a major revolution in social patterns.

Future possibilities for the treatment of aging such as the replacement of young organs for old, the use of drugs that counteract radiation or oxidation effects, and the use of drugs or procedures that counteract antibody-antigen reactions will compound these difficulties, and their use must be weighed in the total social context. Perhaps it might be possible to modify the rate of aging, thus lengthening the period of adult vigor without increasing the ultimate life span or producing an ageless man. Such a modification would present a nearly square survival curve, with its limit short of the century mark. If this situation came to pass, we would have realized one facet of life peculiar to Huxley's *Brave New World,* where people remained apparently young and vigorous until an advanced age and then died quickly at "approximately the usual time."

REFERENCES

Burnet, F. M.: An immunologic approach to aging. Lancet, 2:358, 1970.
Comfort, A.: Ageing: The Biology of Senescence. New York, Holt, Rinehart & Winston, Inc., 1964.
Comfort, A.: The Process of Aging. New York, Signet Science Library, 1964.
Comfort, A.: Test-battery to measure aging rate in man. Lancet, 2:1411, 1969.
Finch, C. E., and Hayflick, L. (eds.): Handbook of the Biology of Aging. New York, Van Nostrand Reinhold Co., 1977.
Goldstein, S.: The biology of aging. N. Engl. J. Med., 285:1120, 1971.
Hayflick, L.: The cell biology of human aging. N. Engl. J. Med., 295:1302, 1976.
Kohn, R. R.: Principles of Mammalian Aging. Englewood Cliffs, New Jersey, Prentice-Hall, 1971.
Leaf, A.: Every day is a gift when you're over 100. National Geographic, 143:93, 1973.
Strehler, B. L.: Time, Cells, and Aging. 2nd Ed. New York, Academic Press, 1978.
Walford, R. L.: The Immunological Theory of Aging. Copenhagen, Munksgaard, 1969.

3

Preparation for New Life

DAVID W. SMITH

The decision to start a new life, to have a child, is the most important one made by the individual relative to the future of mankind. Society is increasingly shifting its perspective toward quality of life rather than quantity of life. Disease and malnutrition, tragic and unwanted, were the major partially limiting factors on population size in the past. The predominant mortality prior to old age was in the first year after birth. Figure 3–1 shows the dramatic reduction in infant mortality from 1915 to 1965. This relative control of disease has increasingly shifted the responsibility for population stabilization to man himself. Today, population stabilization means the average couple having one to two children, and this obviously requires control of reproduction. The means of achieving control are presently available as summarized in Table 3–1. Unfortunately, 44 per cent of births from 1966 to 1970 were unplanned and, of these, one-third were unwanted.

Population stabilization will allow for ever-increasing concern and attention to the quality of life for our children-to-be. The first consideration is to have children who will not be handicapped early in life by problems related to physical and mental development. This concern should begin prior to conception in order to affect some of the major causes of mortality and handicapping morbidity during the early critical period of development. Figure 3–2 shows the major causes of infant death in 1965. Many of these same disorders are the major causes of handicapping morbidity. Most of these deaths and morbidity are due to problems which had their advent prior to birth. For example, the number one cause of infant death and morbidity is being born too soon, prematurity; and the number two cause is problems in morphogenesis, malformation. A significant portion of this mortality and handicapping morbidity is preventable by the concerned preparation for new life prior to conception and throughout the early period of development.

33

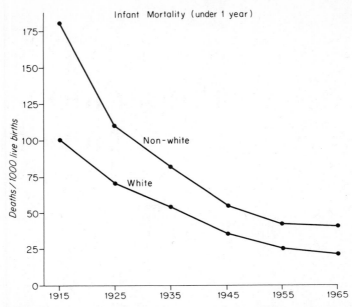

Figure 3–1 Drop in white (400%) and non-white (450%) infant mortality during 50 years in the United States. (Data from United States Public Health Service, National Center for Health Statistics.)

Factors to Consider in the Preparation for New Life

Following are some factors which can affect a new life and which should be considered in the preparation for having a child. Many of these are presented in more detail in Chapter 4.

Maternal Age. The ideal maternal biologic age for reproduction would appear to be from about 18 to 35 years. Prematurity is more common in the very young mother. The neonatal mortality is almost twice as high for babies born of 40- to 45-year-old women and 4 times as high for women beyond the age of 45 years. The likelihood of chromosomal abnormality in the offspring increases progressively beyond the maternal age of 35, as illustrated in Figure 3–3 for the occurrence of 21-trisomy Down syndrome (mongolism).

Paternal Age. The likelihood of a fresh gene alteration (mutation) increases with older paternal age, there being about a tenfold increase in the possibility of the offspring having a fresh mutant gene disorder from the paternal age of 30 to 60 years. Specific disorders due to a single mutant gene include achondroplasia, the Marfan syndrome, the Apert syndrome, acrodysostosis, and certain other rare disorders. Though such conditions are rare in comparison to chromosomal abnormalities (related to older maternal age), their frequency of fresh occurrence is related to older paternal age.

Maternal Nutrition. Ideally, it is advantageous for the woman to be well nourished *prior* to conception and to maintain good nutrition throughout the pregnancy, anticipating a weight gain of approximately 20 to 35 pounds based on her pre-pregnant size. A pattern of weight gain that reaches 10 pounds at 20 weeks' gestation is desirable.

Maternal Medications, Drugs, Alcoholism, Heavy Cigarette Smoking. The potentially deleterious effects of a variety of chemical agents on early development are summarized in Chapter Four, Prenatal Life and the Pregnant Woman. Alcohol intake should be reduced and ideally discontinued *before* a woman becomes pregnant in order to avoid the risk of alcohol exposure to the fetus, a very serious risk if the mother has a heavy alcohol intake. Cigarette smoking should also be reduced and hopefully stopped before pregnancy. Not only is birth size smaller in the offspring of heavy cigarette smokers, but there is a higher frequency of prematurity and a 30 per cent greater incidence of perinatal mortality.

TABLE 3–1   MEANS OF REPRODUCTIVE CONTROL

Method	Action	Comment
Hormonal	Inhibition of ovulation	Most preparations 100% effective
Estrogen		Some major side effects
Progesterone		Reversible means of control
Mechanical		
Intrauterine device	? altered tubal egg transport	97% effective
	? inhibition of ovum implantation	Side effects: Expulsion of device, bleeding, cramps, infection
		Reversible means of control
Other Mechanical		
Coitus interruptus		Low patient acceptance
Jellies; foams	Spermicidal	Reversible means of control
Diaphragm; condom	Mechanical barriers to sperm	
Surgical		
Ligation of vas deferens —male	Mechanical barrier to sperm	No effect on sex hormone production or sexual performance in either sex.
Ligation of Fallopian tubes —female		Permanent means of control
Termination of Pregnancy		
Menstrual extraction immediately following missed period		Little or no anesthesia required; outpatient procedure
Suction curettage prior to 10–12 weeks' gestation		Some form of anesthesia needed; outpatient procedure
Saline induction, late abortion		Increased risk; hospitalization; psychological sequelae; combine with contraceptive advice
Prostaglandin induction		

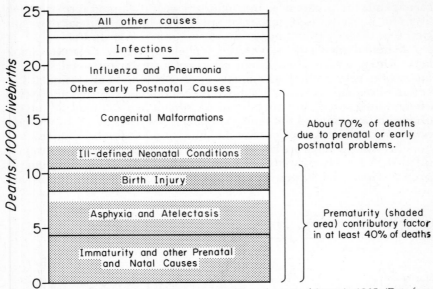

Figure 3–2 Causes of infant (first year) mortality in the United States in 1965. (Data from United States Public Health Service, National Center for Health Statistics.)

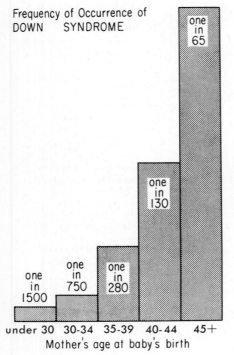

Figure 3–3 Progressive increase in incidence of 21-trisomy Down syndrome during the latter stages of a woman's reproductive life. (Adapted from Mikkelsen, M., and Stone, J.: Human Heredity 20:457, 1970, reproduced with permission.)

If a woman is taking anticonvulsive medication such as hydantoins (Dilantin) or trimethadione (Tridione), these teratogenic agents should ideally be discontinued before pregnancy. Barbiturates should also preferably be discontinued or kept to a low level of dosage. Basically it is safest for the woman to avoid taking any medication about the time of conception and throughout pregnancy unless there is a very strong indication for its usage and the medication is not recognized as being harmful to the developing fetus. Heroin tends to cause fetal growth deficiency and should ideally be discontinued a year or so before pregnancy.

Rh Incompatibility. The prospective parents should know their Rh blood type. Rh sensitization of the Rh-negative mother by an Rh-positive fetus and potential damage to subsequent Rh-positive fetuses can now be prevented, as set forth in Chapter Four.

Maternal Infectious Disease. A serologic test for syphilis should be considered prior to conception, and any active disease at that time or during the pregnancy should be promptly treated. Gonorrhea should be treated, especially prior to delivery, at which time the baby may become infected. A couple should avoid any sexual promiscuity during pregnancy in order to lessen the chance of exposing the fetus or newborn to both syphilis and gonorrhea as well as cytomegalic inclusion disease virus and genital herpes simplex virus, all of which may be transmitted by venereal contact.

All children should be vaccinated against rubella in an effort to prevent the pregnant woman from having contact with, and being infected by, this agent during the first 4 months of gestation, since rubella infection of the fetus is a very serious disease (see Chapter Four).

The pregnant woman should avoid unnecessary contact with domestic cats in order to lessen the likelihood of the fetus being exposed to toxoplasmosis, a protozoan organism which may be carried by the domestic cat.

If the woman has active urinary tract infection, this should be treated prior to conception.

Maternal Hyperthermia. Recent studies have suggested that high fever during the first 4 months of gestation can be teratogenic, especially to the early brain. Hence it would seem wise while pregnant to avoid contact with such infectious diseases as influenza, to seek early treatment for remedial infectious disease such as urinary tract infection and bacterial pneumonia, and to avoid excessive artificial heat such as sauna bathing during pregnancy.

Maternal Noninfectious Diseases or Disorders. Certain maternal disorders create an increased risk of a problem in fetal development. When the disorder can be effectively managed *prior* to conception, this is ideal. When it cannot be managed in such a manner as to reduce the risk to the fetus, then the potential parents should be informed about the risks, to enable them to make an intelligent decision as to having a child. The former category, which can be managed, includes hypothyroidism and hyperthyroidism. The latter category includes heart disease, hypertension, chronic renal disease, and diabetes mellitus. For the woman who has had diabetes mellitus for several years there is an increased risk of miscarriage, stillbirths, and neonatal problems in adaptation, plus a threefold greater than usual risk (6 per cent) of the baby having a malformation problem.

Inheritable Disorders, Genetic Counseling. For families in which there is an individual with a serious genetically determined disorder, the risk for any family member's having an offspring with the same type of disorder should be determined. This determination will enable a couple to take this risk into consideration in the decision to have or not to have children. For a few disorders it is now possible to detect an affected fetus by early amniocentesis (see Chapter Four), allowing for early termination of that pregnancy if the fetus is affected. This method is also applicable to the older mother, who has an increased risk of having a child with a chromosomal abnormality. Amniocentesis and chromosomal studies of the early fetal cells in which there is a serious chromosomal abnormality can indicate the need to have a pregnancy terminated.

Practical Measures in Preparation for New Life

One of the important steps in the preparation for new life is to have a planned pregnancy. Unless a pregnancy is planned the mother usually does not realize she is pregnant until sometime between 3 and 8 weeks after conception. By that time the embryo has passed through, or is in, some of the most critical phases in early development. Without the appreciation that she *is* pregnant the woman is less likely to be practicing fetal preventive medicine and avoiding environmental agents or situations which might be damaging to the embryo and early fetus.

A very important step in preventing early infant mortality and decreasing the frequency of handicapping disorders is to foster the ready availability of termination of unwanted pregnancies. For example, following the liberalized termination of pregnancy in New York state there was a drop in the neonatal (up to 28 days after birth) mortality from 17 per 1000 down to 11 per 1000. About 75 per cent of this remarkable fall in early mortality was attributed to a *decrease* in prematurity as a consequence of an *increase* in early termination of unwanted pregnancies.

Ideally, it would be advantageous for most of the foregoing information to become general public knowledge, and for each new life to start as a *wanted* individual whose prospective parents have prepared for the event prior to conception and throughout the period of pregnancy. This preparation should include a preconceptual evaluation of the couple for Rh typing and determination of any risk of offspring having a serious genetically determined disorder when such a disorder is present in one or more family members. The prospective mother should be evaluated for the presence of any nutritional deficiency, active infectious disease, or metabolic disorder which might compromise the early development of a fetus. Remediable disorders should be treated *prior* to conception. For nonremediable disorders, the couple should understand the potential risk to the woman in becoming pregnant, as well as the risk to the fetus. All women should be informed of the optimal maternal life situation for the fetus during pregnancy and for preparation for childbirth. Such measures will do more to reduce infant mortality and handicapping morbidity than any therapeutic measures instituted after birth.

By these means the preparation for new life could achieve the goal of enhancing the quality of life for each new individual.

Psychosocial Life Situation
NANCY ROBINSON

If one were to write a scenario for an optimal pregnancy, the basics would surely include:

1. Healthy parents, especially a well-nourished mother of optimal childbearing age (18 to 35 years), one not depleted by bearing too many children, closely spaced;

2. A stable home capable of promoting the health and psychosocial development of the child;

3. Parents who actively, mutually, and responsibly want the child and look forward to bringing up a distinctive, growing person;

4. An effective social support system — an extended family and/or a circle of friends, and an integrated network of services and resources to complement the parents' primary roles.

In fact, American society does little to assure that anything like this scenario will ensue. The past decades have clearly wrought some social changes which bode well for the birth of healthy children. Among such changes are the increased availability of contraceptives (which are, however, better utilized by older than younger women), smaller family size, health and nutritional programs for mother and child, and a rise in the general standard of living. Many other changes, however, make it more difficult for prospective parents to play their roles well. For example, changes in social roles leave many women conflicted about motherhood in the context of a career. Changes in sexual practices have increased the exposure of young people to the risk of pregnancy (many teenagers obtain contraceptives only after a pregnancy has occurred) and to venereal disease as well. Nuclear family structure decreases children's exposure to infants and reduces their opportunities to acquire childrearing skills.

American teenagers are at risk for what amounts to an epidemic of pregnancies and rampant social problems. Of the 21 million people in the United States aged 15 to 19 years fully 11 million are thought to be sexually active. More than a million teenage women become pregnant each year, approximately 10 per cent, yet two thirds of these pregnancies are unwanted. Perhaps 40 per cent of the pregnancies end in spontaneous or induced abortions, but annually, more than 600,000 teenagers give birth. This accounts for approximately 20 per cent of all births. The outcomes of teenage pregnancies are shown in Figure 3–4. Note that only 27.6 per cent of outcomes represented

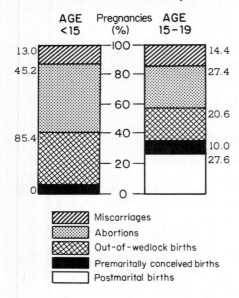

OUTCOME OF PREGNANCIES
TO TEENAGE FEMALES, 1974

Figure 3-4 (Reprinted with permission from 11 Million Teenagers: What Can Be Done About the Epidemic of Adolescent Pregnancies in the United States, a publication of The Alan Guttmacher Institute.)

Miscarriages
Abortions
Out-of-wedlock births
Premaritally conceived births
Postmarital births

births conceived after marriage, and even this group must be regarded with reservation, since teenage marriages are 2 to 3 times more vulnerable to dissolution than are marriages between older partners. Those marriages performed after conception are even less stable; 60 per cent of teenage couples married during the pregnancy will have separated or divorced before the child is 6 years old.

Socially, the risks of early pregnancy are great. Teenage mothers are more likely not to finish school, to remain unemployed or underemployed, and to live in poverty throughout their lives than women who become mothers later on. Young mothers will bear a third as many infants in their lifetimes as women who begin their families later. Physically, of course, these young women who have not completed their own growth are at increased risk for their own health and survival. Toxemia and anemia are especially prevalent. Their infants are at risk; prematurity, low birth weight, and some birth defects are more common in infants born to young teenage mothers.

Yet, births to teenage mothers have declined less rapidly since World War II than have births to other age groups, especially those to mothers 35 years of age and older. Relative to other groups, the proportion of live births to teenage mothers has actually increased over this period, and the proportion of births to unwed mothers even more. (See Figure 3-5). In part, this increase reflects more liberal sexual practices; it also reflects a lack of family planning and abortion services to teenagers.

Many women of all ages seek and obtain abortions. For each 1000 live births to unwed mothers, currently more than 1600 abortions are

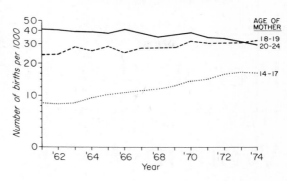

OUT-OF-WEDLOCK BIRTHS PER
1,000 UNMARRIED FEMALES

Figure 3–5 (Reprinted from 11 Million Teenagers: What Can Be Done About the Epidemic of Adolescent Pregnancies in the United States, a publication of The Alan Guttmacher Institute.)

performed. About a third of abortion patients are teenagers, about a third are women 20 to 24 years of age, and about a third are women older than that. Approximately three quarters of the abortions are for unmarried women. Overall, more than a million abortions are performed yearly in the United States (1,115,000 in 1976).

The health professional should, then, be prepared to counsel prospective parents not only about questions related clearly to medical concerns — genetic risks, fertility problems, contraception, abortion, and other health conditions — but also about the psychosocial consequences of their actions. Sometimes it is difficult for prospective parents to conceptualize the commitments which are, or should be, the birthright of their children. This is especially true in a society which requires a long period of educational preparation for adult life and offers so little in the way of natural support systems.

REFERENCES

Furstenberg, F. F., Jr.: Unplanned Parenthood: Social Consequences of Teenage Child-bearing. Riverside, N. J., Free Press, 1977.

Lee, K., Tseng, P., Eidelman, E. I., Kandall, S. R., and Gartner, L. M.: Determinants of neonatal mortality. Am. J. Dis. Child., *130*:842, 1976.

Nelson, W. E., Vaughan, V. C., and McKay, R. J.: Textbook of Pediatrics. 9th ed. Philadelphia, W. B. Saunders Co., 1969, p. 1.

Niswander, K. R., and Gordon M.: The Collaborative Study of the National Institute of Neurological Diseases and Stroke; The Women and Their Pregnancies. Philadelphia, W. B. Saunders Co., 1972.

Report of the Presidential Commission on Population Growth and the American Future. Washington, D.C., U. S. Government Printing Office, 1972.

The Alan Guttmacher Institute: 11 Million Teenagers: What Can be Done about the Epidemic of Adolescent Pregnancies in the United States. New York, The Alan Guttmacher Institute, 1976.

Wegman, M. E.: Annual summary of vital statistics — 1974. Pediatrics, *56*:960, 1975.

4

Prenatal Life and the Pregnant Woman

DAVID W. SMITH

MORTON A. STENCHEVER

The average duration of human pregnancy, counting from the first day of the last menstrual period, is about 280 days, or 40 weeks. Since the interval between the onset of menstruation and ovulation averages approximately 13 days, the mean duration of actual pregnancy, counting from the day of conception, is closer to 267 days. Prolongation of pregnancy by as much as 2 to 3 weeks beyond the expected date of confinement is common (8 to 12 per cent) and generally not abnormal. A small number of infants in prolonged pregnancy develop dysmaturity, so called "postmaturity syndrome."

PRENATAL LIFE

DAVID W. SMITH

The normal development is set forth from conception till 7 months in Figures 4–1 through 4–16.

The genetic endowment that guides the morphogenesis and function of an individual is contained within the fertilized ova, the zygote.

After the first few cell divisions, differentiation begins to take place, presumably through activation or inactivation of particular genes, allowing cells to assume diverse roles. The entire process is programmed in a timely and sequential order, with little allowance for error, especially in early morphogenesis. The following are a few of the phenomena which are critical in morphogenesis: migration of cells; aggregation of like cells; controlled mitotic rate; controlled cell death; inducive interaction between variant tissues; and high energy requirement during the most active period of differentiation for a particular tissue.

LIFE SITUATION

Physical

Figures 4–1 through 4–15 show the progression from fertilization to the 7-month fetal stage of development. The relative rates of linear and weight growth are shown in Figure 4–16. The Negro fetus, which normally matures faster and has a shorter gestational period, is slightly heavier than the Caucasian fetus until about 35 weeks of gestation; thereafter the Caucasian fetus grows more rapidly. Hence, at full-term birth the Caucasian baby is usually larger than the Negro baby, though not more mature.

Text continued on page 47

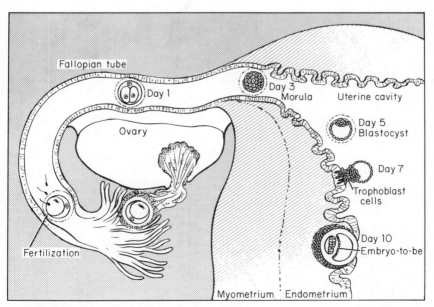

Figure 4–1 Normal progression during the **first 10 days,** from fertilization in the Fallopian tube to implantation in the uterus.

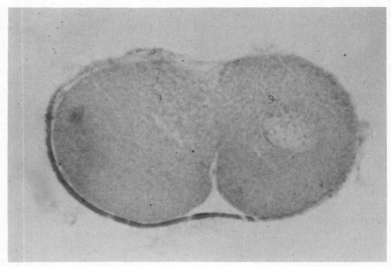

Figure 4–2 Two cell stages, within zona pellucida. The early divisions are reliant on the maternal cytoplasm of the ova for nutrition, and occur without enlargement of the ovum. (From the Department of Embryology, Carnegie Institute of Washington, Baltimore, Md.)

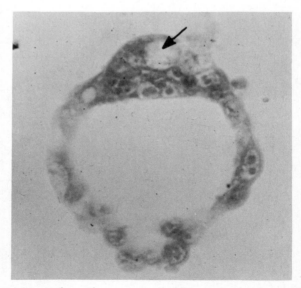

Figure 4–3 4 to 5 days. Blastocyst stage. Differentiation has begun. The embryonic cell mass shows the first indication toward an amniotic space (arrow). At this stage there are about 108 cells, of which 8 will become endoderm and ectoderm, the initiation of the embryo-to-be. (From the Department of Embryology. Carnegie Institute of Washington, Baltimore, Md.)

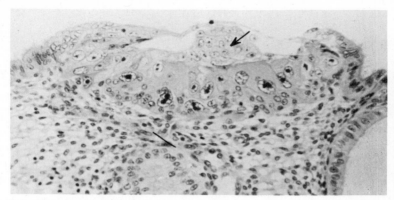

Figure 4–4   7 days. The major part of the conceptus, the cytotrophoblast, has invaded the endometrium, and the embryo-to-be (arrow) is differentiating into two diverse cell layers, the ectoderm and the endoderm. The invading syncytiotrophoblast cells must now produce chorionic gonadotropin, thus maintaining the corpus luteum of the ovary and maintaining the pregnancy. The presence of this hormone in the mother's urine is one early test of pregnancy. (From the Department of Embryology, Carnegie Institute of Washington, Baltimore, Md.)

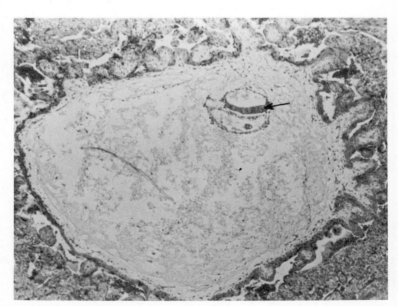

Figure 4–5   14 to 16 days. The thicker ectoderm (arrow) has its continuous amniotic sac, whereas the underlying endoderm has its yolk sac. Major changes will now begin to take place. Nutrition is by diffusion at this stage of development. The chorionic villi of the placenta are now forming. As the embryo bulges forth into the uterine cavity the chorion will become denuded in that area. (From Gian Töndury, M.D., Anatomishes Institute, University of Zürich.)

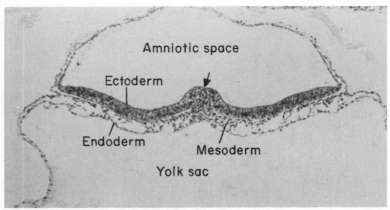

Figure 4–6   17 to 18 days. The embryo is now a flat disc, shown here in transverse section. Mesoblast cells migrate from the ectoderm through Hensen's node (the hillock marked by the arrow) and the primitive streak to specific locations between the ectoderm and endoderm, there constituting the highly versatile mesoderm. The formation of most organ tissues results from an interaction between mesoderm and adjacent ectoderm or endoderm. Anterior to Hensen's node the notochord develops, providing axial support and influencing subsequent development such as that of the overlying neural plate. (From Gian Töndury, M.D., University of Zürich.)

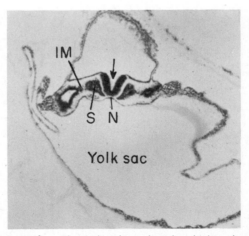

Figure 4–7   21 to 23 days. The midaxial ectoderm has thickened and formed the neural groove (arrow), partially influenced by the underlying notochord (N). This groove will fuse dorsally to form the neural tube. Lateral to it the mesoblast has now segmented into somites (S), intermediary mesoderm (IM), and somatopleura and splanchnopleura as intervening stages toward further differentiation. Vascular channels are developing *in situ* from mesoderm; blood cells are being produced in the yolk sac wall; and the early heart is beating. Henceforth development is extremely rapid with major changes each day. The next 3 to 4 weeks are the era of major organogenesis during which incomplete or faulty development may leave the individual with residual malformation. (From Gian Töndury, M.D., University of Zürich.)

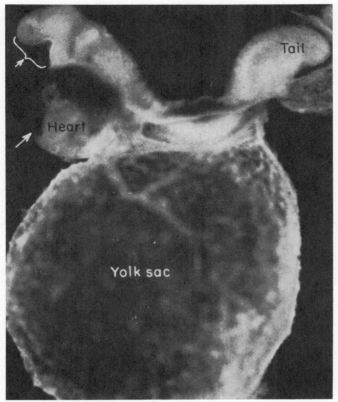

Figure 4–8   24 days. The forepart of the embryo is growing rapidly, especially the anterior neural plate. The lateral portions are growing downward while the head and tail are curling downward also in their growth. Soon the body wall will be fused and the embryo will be in a C-shaped position. The cardiac tube (lower arrow) under the developing face (upper arrow) is now functional. The yolk sac will now rapidly regress.

Physiological*

General.   The early fetus is approximately 94 per cent water, and by full term is 69 per cent water. Weight gain is accelerated during the last eight weeks of fetal life by the accumulation of adipose tissue.

Fetal blood has a low oxygen tension (30 mm Hg), partly because of the admixture of arterial and venous blood in the intervillous space of the placenta. The fetus does well by virtue of having a high level of fetal type hemoglobin relative to oxygen-carrying capacity and because he can better utilize anaerobic metabolism for his energy needs. Thus, the fetus and the newborn may be able to withstand periods of

*See also the Perinatal section of Chapter 5, especially for cardiovascular and pulmonary development and function.

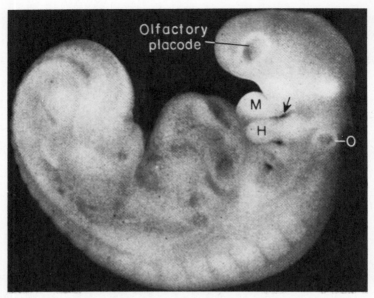

Figure 4–9   26 days. The olfactory placode has begun to invaginate to form the nasal pit, Between it and the mandibular process is the area of the future mouth, where the bucco-pharyngeal membrane, with no intervening mesoderm, is breaking down. Within the recess of the mandibular (M) and hyoid (H) processes the future external auditory canal will develop (arrow), and dorsal to it the otic placode (O) is invaginating to form the inner ear. The relatively huge heart must pump blood to the developing placenta as well as to the embryo proper. Fore-gut outpouchings and evaginations will now begin to form various glands and the lung and liver primordia. Foregut and hindgut are now clearly delineated from the yolk sac. The somites, which will differentiate into myotomes (musculature), dermatomes (subcutaneous tissue), and sclerotomes (vertebrae), are evident on into the tail, which will gradually regress. (From Gian Töndury, M.D., University of Zürich.)

hypoxemia more successfully than can mature persons. The early en-ergy needs are predominantly met by glucose through entrance of pyruvate into the energy-generating cycle. The young embryo also uses the pentose shunt pathway, which allows production of pentose necessary for RNA and DNA synthesis, to a greater extent than the mature person. Later in fetal life, protein and fat become part of the energy resource, with increasing generation of high-energy ATP.

Placenta.   This organ, fetal in origin, serves as liver, lung, and kidney for the fetus. It is responsible for fetal nutrition and homeo-stasis. In addition, it provides a large number of protein and steroid hormones and enzymes such as chorionic gonadotropin, estrogen, progesterone, alkaline phosphatase, diamine oxidase, and others. Pro-gesterone appears to be one of the poorly understood factors involved in preventing uterine contractions and may affect the duration of ges-tation. Prostaglandins also may be important in the maintenance of the uterine homeostasis. If the fetus is dying, the first measurable hor-monal change may be a decrease in maternal urinary estriol excretion. Precursors of this steroid are produced by the fetal adrenal, modified by the fetal liver, metabolized in the placenta, and then excreted into the maternal urine.

The developing placenta is relatively large in early fetal life; by 15 weeks the fetus proper has equaled the placenta in weight, and thereafter surpasses it in size. New cells are added in the placenta until about 32 weeks; thereafter the growth rate is less rapid, and degenerative aging changes are sometimes evident by birth. At birth the placenta weighs about 460 gm (14 per cent of fetal weight). If the pregnancy goes beyond about 40 gestational weeks, the placenta may no longer be an adequate resource; postmature babies may show indications of undernutrition.

The vascular villous bed of the placenta has a surface area of about 160 square feet. Substances with a molecular weight of less than a few hundred, such as most anesthetic gases and drugs, pass through by direct or "facilitated" diffusion. Caution must therefore be exercised in both the nature and dosage of agents administered to the pregnant woman. Lipid solubility, protein binding, and other factors affect placental transfer. The diffusing gradient favors a slightly higher fetal level of many amino acids, water-soluble vitamins, calcium, phosphorus, magnesium, potassium, and inorganic iodide ions.

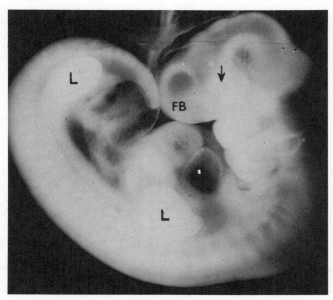

Figure 4–10   30 days. The brain is rapidly growing, and its early cleavage into future bilateral cerebral hemispheres is evident in the telencephalic outpouching of the forebrain (FB). To the right of this is the developing eye, with the cleft optic cup (arrow) and the early invagination of the future lens from surface ectoderm. From the somatopleura the limb swellings (L) have developed. The loose mesenchyme of the limb bud, interacting with the thickened ectodermal cells at its tip, carries all the potential for the full development of the limb. The liver is now functional and will be a source of blood cells. The mesonephric ducts, formed in the mesonephric ridges, communicate to the cloaca, which is beginning to become septated, and the yolk sac is regressing. (From Gian Töndury, M.D., University of Zürich.)

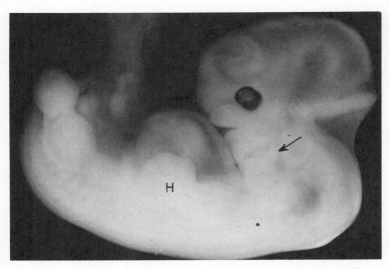

Figure 4–11   36 days. The retina is now pigmented, still incompletely closed at its inferior medial margin. Closure of the lip is nearly complete. The hillocks of His are forming the early external ear (arrow) from the adjacent borders of the mandibular and hyoid swellings. The hand plate (H) has formed with condensation of mesenchyme into the five finger rays. The lower limb lags behind the upper limb in its development. The ventricular septum is partitioning the heart. The ureteral bud from the mesonephric duct has induced a kidney from the mesonephric ridge, which is also forming gonad and adrenal. Cloacal septation is nearly complete; the infraumbilical mesenchyme has filled in all the cloacal membrane except the urogenital area; and the genital tubercles are fused, whereas the labioscrotal swellings are unfused. The gut is elongating, and a loop of it may be seen projecting out into the body stalk. (From Gian Töndury, M.D., University of Zürich.)

The transfer of iron seems to be unidirectional to the fetus. There is selective transfer of a few large proteins, such as maternal immunoglobulin G (IgG), which increasingly crosses to the fetus after four to five months, providing passive immune protection against certain infectious agents during the first few postnatal months. No maternal anterior pituitary hormones and little maternal thyroxin cross the placental barrier; hence the fetus is generally self-reliant in terms of its endocrine function. As an "auxiliary liver" the placenta synthesizes albumin and alpha and beta globulins, degrades certain molecules, stores glycogen, and makes fructose.

Minor placental leaks may occur during pregnancy, allowing a few blood cells to exchange, but the most common time for this to occur is during placental separation following delivery, when a significant fetal-maternal transfusion may occur. This is the critical time for the Rh-negative mother, the time when she may become sensitized by the Rh-positive fetal red blood cells. The period during labor and delivery is also a time when serious fetal, as well as maternal, blood loss can occur secondary to rupture of fetal vessels in the membranes or to premature separation of part of the placenta. A large reservoir of blood exists in the placenta at the time of birth and the blood

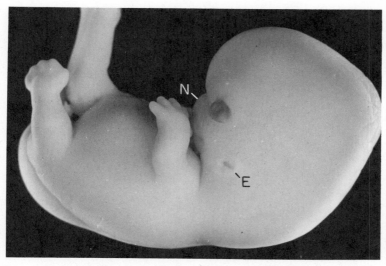

Figure 4–12　41 days. The nose (N) is relatively flat, and the external ear (E) is gradually shifting in relative position as it continues to grow and develop. A neck area is now evident, the anterior body wall has formed, and the thorax and abdomen are separated by the transverse septum (diaphragm). The fingers are now partially separated, and the elbow is evident. The major period of cardiac morphogenesis and septation is complete. The urogenital membrane has now broken down, yielding a urethral opening. The phallus and lateral labioscrotal folds are the same for both sexes at this age. (From Gian Töndury, M.D., University of Zürich.)

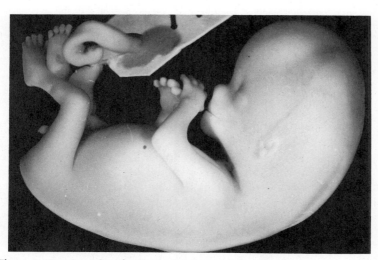

Figure 4–13　10 week male. The eyelids have developed and fused, not to reopen until four or five months. Muscles are developed and functional; normal morphogenesis of joints is dependent on movement; and primary ossification is occurring in the centers of developing bones. Ossification begins at 7 weeks in the clavicle and by birth all the primary centers are ossified with only the secondary centers at the knee being ossified by that time.

In the male the testicle has produced testosterone and masculinized the external genitalia with enlargement of the genital tubercle, fusion of the labioscrotal folds into a scrotum, and closure of the labia minora folds to form a penile urethra; these structures are unchanged in the female. (From Gian Töndury, M.D., University of Zürich.)

Figure 4–14   3¹/₂ month male. The fetus is settling down for the latter two-thirds of prenatal life. The morphogenesis of the lung, largely solid at this point in development, will not have progressed to the capacity for aerobic exchange for another three to four months. The skin is increasing in thickness, and its accessory structures are differentiating. The deciduous teeth are now developing from the interaction between invaginating ectoderm, which will form the enamel, and adjacent mesenchyme, which will form the dentin and pulp. The permanent dentition begins mineralizing at birth and is complete by about 15 years.

The fetus is active in its aquatic environment, but it is not until 4 to 5 months that the mother usually discerns the movement. Thereafter, it is seldom that a day passes without activity being noted. The amniotic fluid is being swallowed and continually replaced, predominantly by urination. It is now possible to insert a needle into the amniotic space and withdraw 5 to 10 ml of fluid (amniocentesis) for studies of the fluid or fetal cells contained therein.

During the next few months the major addition of neuronal cells within the brain continues.

volume of the newborn can be greatly influenced by "early" versus "late" clamping of the umbilical cord.

Circulation. By several weeks of age, diffusion is no longer an adequate means of supplying nutrition to the conceptus, and a circulatory system develops. The pulsatile tubelike heart folds upon itself with rotation, septation, and valvular development contributing to its final form. Vascular channels generally form *in situ,* and these coalesce and change in accordance with the tissue within which they develop. The work and size of the early heart are relatively great since it must also supply the placenta, yolk sac, and membranes.

The red blood cells which are initially nucleated are first produced in the yolk sac and then in the liver and spleen. From 7 to 8 weeks onward they are increasingly developed in the bone marrow. Under a stress such as the hemolysis of Rh incompatibility (erythroblastosis fetalis), red blood cells may continue to be produced in the liver and spleen in addition to the marrow in late fetal life. Thus the baby with erythroblastosis fetalis may be born with a large liver and spleen. Leukocytes are produced from about 40 days of age onward.

Hemostasis. Maturation of the clotting components into an effective hemostatic mechanism continues throughout gestation and in part during early infancy. Extensive hemorrhage occurs in most early abortuses, in which all hemostatic components are poorly developed. Premature infants have imperfect platelets, fragile vessels, and low levels of several clotting factors, and hemorrhage is relatively common. In full-term babies, only platelet function and certain clotting factors (principally the vitamin K factors) are incompletely developed, and bleeding is rare.

Immune System. Early lymphocyte stem cells derive apparently from the thymus. Early in fetal life the stem cells appear to differentiate into two populations. One group, termed T-cells, are thymus-dependent and reside primarily in the bone marrow; they are associated with delayed or cellular immunity. This cellular immune system begins its development by 8 fetal weeks and is largely complete by 15 weeks. The other, termed B-cells, populate the lymph nodes and spleen, and differentiate further into the normal antibody-producing (immunoglobulin) cell line, including plasma cells. This antibody im-

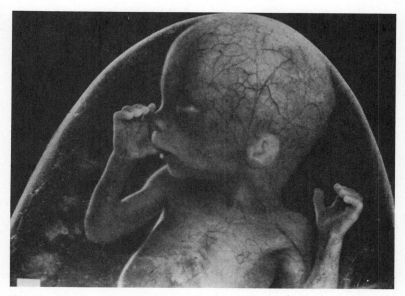

Figure 4–15 28 week fetus. At about this stage the lung has matured to the extent of usually allowing for some aerobic exchange, but it is a very hazardous time to be born. The major cause of death from this period of development till adulthood is prematurity, being born too soon. The major reason for death in the premature is respiratory insufficiency.

Adipose tissue now develops and the fetus will normally double in weight during the next 2 months and be mildly obese at full term birth. Testicular descent into the scrotum occurs at about this time in development. The lung becomes increasingly capable of aerobic oxygen exchange in late fetal life.

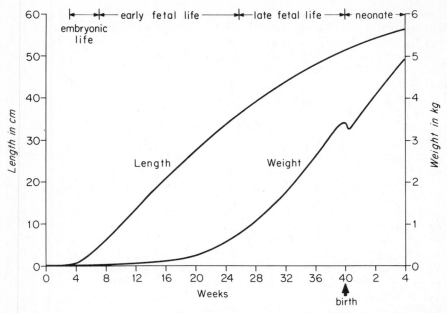

Figure 4–16 The most rapid linear growth is during midfetal life, whereas the most rapid advancement in weight is in late fetal life.

mune system first shows responsiveness at 11 weeks, but is not fully developed until after birth. The responsiveness of the immune system to antigenic stimulus is rarely challenged during fetal life. Indeed, one of the unique phenomena surrounding pregnancy is the unresponsiveness of the mother or infant to the foreign antigens unique to the other. The absence of the rejection of what is to all intents and purposes a prolonged homograft remains an unsolved mystery. Nevertheless, there is good evidence that the fetus, though it has perhaps a limited immune capacity, is capable of response. The humoral response may be partially modified by the transfer of maternal IgG to the fetus, beginning at about 16 weeks. Maternal IgA and IgM do not cross to the fetus; hence the detection of elevated IgM in the newborn baby is usually evidence of fetal infectious disease having been present. Ironically, though the fetus may produce an immune response to a viral agent such as rubella, the response is usually not adequate to rid the fetus of the infective agent. Furthermore, the early activation of the fetal immune system may actually impair normal immune development.

The embryo and the early fetus have an active macrophage defense system and lack the usual tissue injury response involving the polymorphonuclear cell inflammatory reaction and fibrosis. This difference helps to explain the absence of fibrous scars at sites damaged in early development; instead, the damaged part may be reduced in size or missing.

Renal System. At about 31 days an outbudding from the meso-nephric duct induces the metanephros to begin the formation of the kidney in the mesonephric ridge. This outbudding progressively ar-borizes to become the calyceal system, with collecting ducts which an-astomose with the tubules and their glomeruli of metanephric origin, which continue to form until about 35 weeks. Renal tubular function is present from 8 weeks, and some water reabsorption from 11 to 12 weeks. However, the distal tubules are short and, hence, concentrating ability is limited. There is also limited ability to acidify the urine.

Amniotic Cavity. The amount of amniotic fluid increases from about 50 ml at 12 weeks to 400 ml at 20 weeks. The source of early amniotic fluid is unknown. After 20 weeks' gestation, fetal urine as-sumes an increasing role and late in pregnancy is the predominant source of amniotic fluid. There is a dynamic fluid exchange such that in a matter of several hours the fluid is totally replaced. Removal of amniotic fluid is accomplished mainly through fetal swallowing plus absorption through the fetal lung, skin, cord, and amnion. After 35 weeks the fetus progressively fills out the uterine cavity and the rela-tive amount of amniotic fluid decreases as a consequence.

From 14 menstrual weeks onward it is possible to insert a needle through the lower abdominal wall and uterus of a pregnant woman and obtain 5 to 10 ml of amniotic fluid. This is presently done at the parents' request when there is a known high risk of having a child with a serious disorder detectable in early development. For example, chromosome studies of cultured amnion cells from amniotic fluid can be done to exclude a fetal chromosomal abnormality. Studies can also be done to exclude most cases of anencephaly or meningomyelocele. In these disorders there is oozing of serum or spinal fluid into the amniotic space. This contributes a fetal protein (alpha-fetoprotein) to the amniotic fluid at higher concentration than would normally be present. Enzyme studies can be performed to exclude, for example, a homozygous fetus with Tay-Sachs disease, when parents are carriers of the mutant gene for this autosomal recessive disorder. Sex can be determined in the fetus of a woman who is a known carrier for an X-linked recessive disorder such as hemophilia, in which case the male fetus would have a 50 per cent risk of being affected. Having ob-tained the definitive information, the parents can then elect to termi-nate an undesirable pregnancy prior to fetal extrauterine viability.

Intestine. Swallowing and peristalsis occur early, but there is usually no passage of the thick, dark intestinal accumulation called meconium until after birth. Earlier passage resulting in meconium staining of amniotic fluid may indicate that the fetus has, at some time, experienced distress. Trypsin is present from 16 weeks, and amylase at birth.

Brain and Behavioral Components. The neural groove closes, in-creasing numbers of neurones migrate out from the basilar layer, the anterior neural tube develops into the brain, and axone processes move out while those within the brain and spinal cord form networks. Myelinization of certain axones begins at 4 to 5 months and generally coincides with functional capacity. Fetal motor activity has been noted from 8 weeks, though the mother does not generally feel fetal movement until about 17 weeks. Any period of prolonged inactivity after 4 to 5 months should give rise to concern about a fetal problem. Functional activity proceeds from cephalad to caudad, and stereotyped reflexes are combined and superseded by increasingly complex patterns as brain centers begin to coordinate the activity. Thus, initially, jerky activity becomes more smooth and sustained.

Cerebellar development is relatively late. This is the presumed reason why the 7 to 8 month old premature baby is relatively hypotonic, with irregular jerky movements, whereas the full-term baby is mildly hypertonic, and only slightly jerky in its movements.

FETAL PROBLEMS

Mortality and Morbidity. The highest mortality is in the earliest stages of development when serious errors in morphogenesis often do not allow continued development. The studies of Hertig *et al.* indicated that only about 50 per cent of fertilized ova survive to become a recognized pregnancy. Following recognition of the pregnancy, the spontaneous abortion rate is reported as being from 10 to 25 per cent. Most of these occur in the first 5 to 8 weeks of pregnancy. The reasons for this high early mortality are not clearly delineated, but at least one major cause is chromosomal abnormalities, discussed later in this section. The lower limit of birth weight for viability of a premature is 500 to 700 gm. Some of the problems which lead to fetal morbidity and death in the later stages of fetal life are presented below.

Prematurity. Prematurity means being born 2 or more weeks before term: before 38 menstrual weeks or 36 conceptual weeks. Prematurity, with its attendant problems of early adaptation to the extrauterine environment, is the number one cause of death in early infancy. The main reason for death is respiratory insufficiency secondary to immaturity of the lung, which will be discussed in the next chapter. The premature baby is also more likely to have intraventricular hemorrhage, sepsis, hypoglycemia, hypothermia, acidosis, hyperbilirubinemia, and/or periods of malnutrition. These can be lethal or leave permanent residua, especially in terms of brain development and function. An attempt should be made to determine the cause of prematurity, which can be maternal or fetal in origin. Some of the causes are set forth in Tables 4–1 and 4–2.

Prenatal Growth Deficiency. A clear distinction should be made between the premature baby and the one with prenatal growth deficiency. About one-third of babies weighing less than 2500 grams at birth represent the latter situation and are *not* premature.

Prenatal growth deficiency is a rather gross sign which may be the consequence of one of a number of genetic or environmentally determined causes, some of which are presented below or in the tables. It is important to appreciate that the baby with prenatal growth deficiency, though usually more mature than the premature baby of compara-

TABLE 4–1 SOCIOLOGIC SITUATIONS WHICH MAY RELATE TO A FETAL PROBLEM

Sociologic	Potential Fetal Problem
Lower socioeconomic status	Prematurity
Older woman, first pregnancy	Prematurity
Older maternal age	Chromosome Abnormality
Incestuous union	Mental deficiency (presumed autosomal recessive)

ble weight, is more liable to develop problems of neonatal adaptation such as hypoglycemia or hypocalcemia within the first few days after birth than is a normally grown infant of comparable gestational age.

Placental Problems. Placental insufficiency can result in secondary fetal malnutrition. A low uterine placement of the placenta (placenta praevia) can result in premature separation or even laceration of the placenta as the cervix begins to dilate in late pregnancy. This can result in serious maternal blood loss and, on occasion, fetal bleeding; it is also one cause of premature delivery.

Infectious Problems. The early fetus is generally an excellent cultural medium for many viral agents. Once a viral agent is acquired through maternal viremia, or via the vaginal route (rarely), it tends to cause chronic, widespread fetal disease. In early fetal life there may be no inflammatory response and no fibrosis. Hence, the residua may simply be missing cells and incomplete development. Serious disease may occur in tissues which are not altered by the same viral agent in the mature person. A notable example is the rubella agent (German

TABLE 4–2 MATERNAL METABOLIC OR DISEASE PROBLEMS

Maternal	Potential Fetal Problem
Diabetes mellitus	Obesity, respiratory insufficiency, neonatal hypoglycemia, malformation (6%)
Hypertension	Prematurity
Toxemia of pregnancy	Prematurity, growth deficiency, respiratory insufficiency at birth
Hyperthyroidism	Transient thyrotoxicosis
Untreated phenylpyruvic oligophrenia	Microcephaly, mental deficiency
Cardiac disorder, especially cyanotic	Growth deficiency, prematurity
Incompetent cervix	Prematurity

measles), which, for unknown reasons, must usually be acquired during the first 12 to 16 weeks to cause fetal disease. Such viral agents may give rise to a fetal immunoglobulin M (IgM) antibody response, but this is usually insufficient to rid the fetus of the viral agent. The IgM response can be utilized at birth as a nonspecific indicator of prenatal infectious disease, since IgM does not cross in significant amounts from the mother and is provoked only by an antigenic stimulus to the fetus.

Table 4–3 lists some of the fetal pathogenic infectious agents and their potentially damaging effects, *if* the fetus survives the insult.

Rupture of the membranes before the onset of labor places the fetus at risk for both premature labor and infection. If it occurs at or near term, about 90 per cent of women will go into labor during the next 24 hours. If labor does not ensue, then serious thought should be given to induction of labor. Spontaneous labor occurs less frequently if the fetus is premature, but induction of labor is not indicated. As the interval between rupture of membranes and delivery increases, so does the risk of amnionitis. Should infection occur, treatment consists of antibiotics and prompt delivery (vaginally or by cesarean section). There is no place for prophylactic antibiotics to prevent amnionitis.

Chemical and Drug Problems.   During the period of rapid growth and differentiation, the embryo and fetus may be more susceptible to

TABLE 4–3   FETAL INFECTIOUS DISEASE

Maternal Infection	Potential Fetal Disease
Rubella during first trimester	Deafness, heart defect, cataract, mental deficiency, chorioretinitis, growth deficiency
Syphilis*	Deafness, mental deficiency, osteitis, chondylomata
Toxoplasmosis*	Hydrocephalus, microcephaly, chorioretinitis, mental deficiency
Cytomegalic inclusion disease	Microcephaly, hydrocephalus, deafness, chorioretinitis, mental deficiency, hepatitis
Herpes simplex (usually via vaginal route)	Meningoencephalitis
Coxsackie B	Myocarditis
Serum hepatitis	Hepatitis
Vaccinia	Severe generalized vaccinia
Bacterial sepsis	Sepsis

*From *primary* maternal infection. Secondary infections seldom lead to parasitemia.

TABLE 4–4 CHEMICAL AND PHYSICAL AGENTS

Maternal	Potential Effect on Fetus
Ethyl alcohol, moderate intake	Mild growth deficiency
Ethyl alcohol, heavy intake	Growth and mental deficiency, small eyes, short nose, heart defect
Cigarette smoking, heavy	Mild growth deficiency
Hydantoins (Dilantin) (anticonvulsive)	Mild growth and mental deficiency, wide-set eyes, short nose, small nails
Trimethadione (Tridione) (anticonvulsive)	Growth and mental deficiency, upslanting eyebrows, ear defect, heart defect
Warfarin (Coumadin) (anticoagulant)	Growth and mental deficiency, small nose, skeletal dysplasia
Tetracyclines (antibiotic)	Discoloration and hypoplasia of enamel in developing teeth
Heroin	Growth deficiency, postnatal withdrawal signs
Iodides, Propylthiouracil	Goiter, due to block in thyroid hormone synthesis
Rare	
Aminopterine	Growth deficiency, small nose, skeletal dysplasia
Methyl mercury	Mental deficiency
Androgenic steroids	Masculinization of the external genitalia in the female
Unknown Frequency	
Hyperthermia (high fever) in first 4–5 months	Problems of brain development and function

the toxic effect of a chemical agent than is the mature mother, as was dramatically indicated by the thalidomide disaster. Table 4–4 lists some of the *known* presently available agents which cause a problem for the fetus. Most of these agents cause growth deficiency with diminished cell number. The deficiency usually affects weight, length, and head circumference (brain size). There is usually no major "catch up" growth after birth and hence the residua tend to be permanent. The most serious residuum is mental deficiency.

Nutritional Problems.   Though the parasitic embryo and fetus will generally thrive at the expense of a mildly malnourished mother, development may be compromised in a seriously malnourished mother. Of special concern in this regard is the mid- to late-fetal period, during which time there is a major addition of neurones within the fetal brain. It is now recommended that the woman gain about 20 to 30 pounds during a pregnancy, depending upon her weight prior to the pregnancy. Little or no salt restriction is necessary.

Twinning.   About one in 80 pregnancies consists of twins, with about 30 per cent being monozygotic (identical twins), nature's most perfect and most frequent malformation. Twins grow at the usual rate until 32 weeks, to a combined weight of about 4000 gm, and thereafter tend to grow at a slower rate. The rate of growth is often unequal, especially for monozygotic twins, who at times have a placental vascular communication and therefore suffer from unequal exchange. Twins are likely to be relatively undernourished at birth and are more prone to prematurity and problems of neonatal adaptation.

Immunologic Problems. If the fetus is Rh-positive and the mother Rh-negative, the fetal red cells can sensitize the mother to produce anti-Rh-positive antibodies. The maternal antibodies can cross the placenta and result in hemolytic destruction of fetal Rh-positive red blood cells during that pregnancy or subsequent pregnancies, giving rise to the disorder known as erythroblastosis fetalis. The most likely time for a mother to receive a significant dose of fetal red blood cells is at delivery. As the placenta separates, the mother often receives a small transfusion of fetal blood into her circulation. If she is Rh-negative and the baby Rh-positive, these fetal red cells can stimulate a permanent maternal antibody response. These fetal red blood cells can be rapidly destroyed before they cause sensitization by giving the mother high titer anti-Rh antibody (Rhogam), which thereby prevents her from being sensitized. Thus, every Rh-negative woman who delivers an Rh-positive offspring should be given the hyperimmune gamma globulin within 72 hours of the delivery.

This prevention of Rh sensitization has now made ABO blood group incompatibility the more common incompatibility problem. The situation of maternal O, fetal A or B is the most frequent circumstance encountered. Since the type O mother already has anti-A or anti-B agglutinins from early life, this cannot be prevented in the manner of the above-mentioned Rh sensitization. Furthermore, the *first* pregnancy is a potential for ABO incompatibility problems, whereas this rarely occurs for Rh incompatibility unless the Rh-negative mother has been previously sensitized by an Rh-positive transfusion. The major risk of ABO incompatibility is unconjugated indirect hyperbilirubinemia in the perinatal period, secondary to the hemolysis.

Sociologic Situations and Fetal Problems. Table 4–1 lists a few of the fetal problems which can be related to a maternal sociologic situation. Of these, the most important is the increased frequency of prematurity in women of lower socioeconomic status. The reasons for this are not clearly understood, though relatively poor nutrition, crowding, and poor general maternal health and care are considered to be factors. Allowance for early termination of unwanted pregnancies has been associated with a rather striking decrease in prematurity and early infant mortality.

Maternal Metabolic or Disease Problems. Table 4–2 lists a few of the maternal disorders which can have an adverse effect on the fetus. It should be appreciated that the cause of maternal toxemia of pregnancy is unknown. One hypothesis is that it may derive from the fetal placenta.

Common Deformation Problems. It is important to make a distinction between malformation problems due to intrinsic problems in the development of a tissue and *deformation* problems that are secondary to external molding forces. Deformations are found in about 3 per cent of babies. As the fetus fills out the uterine cavity it comes to be contained as shown in Figure 4–17. Constraint of the growing, pliable fetal parts can easily give rise to deformation, which is more likely to occur in the first fetus to distend out the uterus and the abdominal musculature of the mother. It is also more likely if there are twins, or if there is a deficiency of amniotic fluid, which normally limits the molding impact of the uterus on the fetus. If the fetus becomes "caught" in an unusual position in late fetal life, he or she is likely to show some effects of the situation by birth. For example, the late fetus in breech position (buttocks down) tends to have elongated head molding and the legs tend to be flexed up into the abdomen. This latter position tends to dislocate the hips. In some series as many as 50 per cent of hip dislocations occurred in babies who were in breech presentation, despite the fact that this position occurs in only 3.5 per cent of term pregnancies. Dislocation of the hip is one of the most

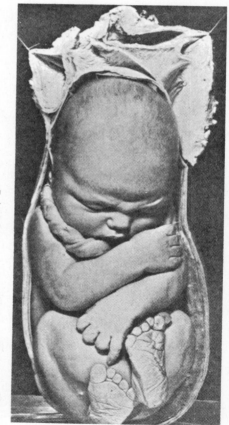

Figure 4–17 Near-term fetus in position to be born. This emphasizes the uterine constraint in late fetal life. (From Peter Dunn, M.D., Southmead Hospital, Bristol, England.)

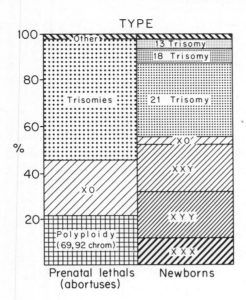

Figure 4–18 Types of chromosomal abnormalities in early life.

critical deformities to detect at birth since early conservative management gives excellent results. Deformations include compressive restraint on head, neck, trunk, and limbs. Shortly after birth it is usually easy to place the baby in the aberrant compressed position which had been present in utero and thereby appreciate how the deformations came to exist. This is the so-called "position of comfort" for the baby, since it had been the enforced position in late fetal life. Once released from uterine constraint, the prognosis for reconstitution toward normal form is excellent, though in some instances of dislocation of the hip and club foot, the temporary use of molding measures such as casting into the more usual form may be desirable.

Common Malformation Problems. Present evidence in the human implies that polygenic inheritance, interacting with as yet unrecognized environmental factors, is the major mode in the causation of most of the more common single localized defects in morphogenesis. Examples include otherwise normal individuals with cleft lip, cleft palate, cardiac defects (most of them), pyloric stenosis, meningomyelocele, or anencephaly. Taken together, these defects make up over half of the 2 per cent of babies born with a recognized malformation problem. For normal parents who have one child with such a defect, the recurrence risk for the same type of anomaly is 3 to 5 per cent for their next offspring. The risk for the offspring of an affected parent who marries a normal individual is of the same magnitude, 3 to 5 per cent. As yet we do not know of any environmental alteration which would reduce the liability for any one of these more common single localized defects in morphogenesis.

Chromosomal Abnormality Problems. Faulty chromosomal distribution leading to genetic imbalance occurs in at least 4 per cent of recognized pregnancies. For most of these this is a lethal situation, as indicated by the fact that 60 per cent of early spontaneous abortions are due to a chromosomal abnormality. About one in 200 babies born has a chromosomal abnormality and some of these, such as 18 trisomy and 13 trisomy, tend to be sublethal,with most infants dying in the early postnatal period. Figure 4–18 summarizes the types of chromosomal abnormalities found in early life.

Other Malformation Problems. There are many individually rare malformation problems which account for about a third of the babies born with a problem in morphogenesis. These include patterns of malformation due to single mutant genes, to an environmental agent, or to an unknown cause.

THE PREGNANT WOMAN

MORTON A. STENCHEVER

LIFE SITUATION

Diagnosis of Pregnancy

Realization that a child has been conceived may be one of the most critical emotional experiences occurring in a woman's life. If the pregnancy is wanted and planned for, the response may be one of great joy and happiness. If the pregnancy is unplanned and unwanted, shock, fear, and anguish may be the manifestations. Regardless of the emotional response, an accurate diagnosis of pregnancy is important for all women.

Presumptive evidence of pregnancy centers around symptoms and signs that are known to be related to pregnancy. These bits of information involve a history of unprotected intercourse, a missed menstrual period, and such well known symptoms as nausea, vomiting, tiredness, increased vaginal discharge, a feeling of bloatedness, increased breast size, and increased frequency of urination. Physical findings which may hint at pregnancy may be a bluish discoloration of the vaginal mucosa and cervix (Chadwick sign), a softening of the lower uterine segment and cervix (Hegar sign), and possibly an enlargement of the uterus. Other physical signs relating to pregnancy may include increased skin pigmentation, a darkening of the linea alba to form the linea nigra as shown in Figure 4–19, abdominal and breast striae, and a mask-like change about the face (chloasma).

The specific diagnosis of pregnancy involves the biochemical or radioimmunoassay test for human chorionic gonadotropin (HCG). In 1927 Aschheim and Zondek described the presence of HCG in the urine of pregnant women and utilized this to produce biological changes in 21 to 28 day old mice that were injected with the urine. In recent years, immunologic methods for detecting HCG in blood or urine using hemagglutination-inhibition and complement fixation

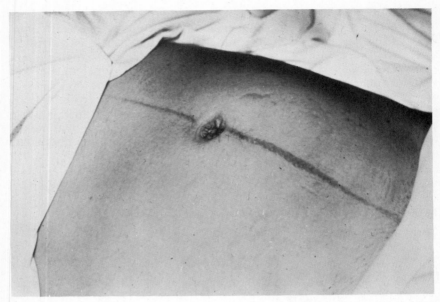

Figure 4–19 The linea nigra is a predominent brownish pigmentation over the midline of the abdomen and umbilicus.

techniques have made it possible to detect pregnancy early, cheaply, and without the need for maintaining colonies of animals. These immunologic tests, as were their biological counterparts, are sensitive at approximately 40 days past the last menstrual period. Earlier pregnancy detection, as early as 8 days postovulation, may be detected by radioimmunoassay for HCG or for the beta subunit of HCG.

Emotional Changes

The pregnant woman's emotional state is determined by a number of external factors. Primary, of course, is her preparation for the pregnancy and the realities of the life situation with which she must cope. (See Chapter 3.) The teenager to whom the pregnancy is an unwelcome shock, the young married woman who feels ready and eager to become a mother, the "emancipated" woman with a self-determined life style, the marginally infertile woman whose efforts to become pregnant have been prolonged, and the already exhausted mother of several young children all respond quite individually to the experience. Each woman's emotional response is also affected by her nonpregnant emotional makeup, her overall physical condition, her views of herself as a woman and a potentially successful or unsuccessful mother, her fears about the delivery, and so on.

Most pregnant women exhibit some lability of emotions so that feelings stimulated by circumstances may be somewhat more intense than usual. Some of the lability probably stems directly from hormonal changes, postural strains, energy requirements, and other facets of the pregnancy. Anxiety to one degree or another is a frequent finding in pregnancy and relates to the patient's concern for her general health and for that of the baby. Too, many women whose self-image is built in large part on a youthful and attractive figure are dismayed by their clumsiness and ungainly proportions. Mood changes, such as temporary mental depression, unprovoked crying spells, and irritability, occur not infrequently. Mental and physical exhaustion, and irresistible sleepiness are common, especially during the first and third trimesters; the woman accustomed to a full day of activities may find herself weak, tearful, and unable to "bounce back" with a short rest, as she is accustomed to doing. The health care specialist can help the woman understand her condition by making information available. While many pregnant women have considerable apprehension over the circumstances of pregnancy, labor, and delivery, a number of these can be alleviated by appropriate early preparation.

Changes in appetite and food preferences are very common. Coffee and cigarettes are likely to become distasteful. Many pregnant women experience unusual dietary cravings. In their extreme, these are described as *pica,* and may be influenced to one degree or another by the socioeconomic state and ethnic background of the patient. Other factors may also play a role. For example, patients with iron deficiency anemia will frequently crave ice, and other dietary deprivations have led to the desire for starch, dirt, and other unusual items. Nausea alone or with vomiting is frequently encountered during early pregnancy. The exact cause is unknown but the symptoms usually respond to appropriate therapy, almost invariably disappearing after the first trimester.

During the middle trimester, on the other hand, many women feel and look exceptionally fit and happy. During this period, physiological functioning seems well integrated. Particularly for those who have welcomed the pregnancy, the middle months are characterized by clear complexion, good color, heightened self-awareness, and for some women, a discovery of special meaning in a feminine role. During this time, the pregnancy becomes obvious to casual observers and the mother also begins to detect definite fetal movements ("quickening"), which increase in frequency and vigor.

The pregnant patient's sexual response may be quite labile. Some patients note an increase in sexual desire, particularly early in the pregnancy, and this has been thought to be related to the engorgement of the pelvic organs which occurs with pregnancy. Later, as the abdomen enlarges and coitus becomes more uncomfortable, sexual desire may decrease. There seems to be a protective element in the outlook of pregnant women; hence, those who fear that intercourse might injure the fetus may have a drop in libido. As with nonpregnant patients, however, sexual response is quite individual and varies from patient to patient and couple to couple.

During the third trimester, fatigue and mild depression often reappear. Weight gain, mild edema, progressive lordosis, increasing frequency of urination, and difficulty in finding a comfortable sleeping position all add to a growing discomfort and a feeling of unattractiveness. It is important to recognize that many mothers at this stage incompletely relate their physical state to an awareness of a separate small person growing in their bodies. They feel ungainly, and despite their conscious recognition of the fetus, their body image is only of themselves. As the expected delivery date nears, the earlier fears connected with labor often tend to diminish.

All the emotional responses of pregnancy can be markedly affected by the woman's living conditions and the support she feels from those important to her. Women who continue to work at taxing jobs and/or to care for a houseful of young children may experience excessive fatigue, poor nutrition, and depression. Those who are able to share the experience with a supportive partner are likely to fare better. Prenatal classes in self-care, delivery, and child care may be especially valuable with a first pregnancy. In any event, the many physical and emotional changes of pregnancy may be worrisome, and the patient deserves reassurance that the changes are a normal and expected part of her pregnancy.

Maternal Physiology and Anatomic Changes in Pregnancy

Although pregnancy is a "natural state," it does not take place without extremely significant physical and physiological changes in the mother. The most striking changes involve the reproductive organs themselves, but the effects that allow for the accommodation of the pregnancy are noticeable in almost every organ system of the body. In addition, disease states or conditions that the mother has prior to pregnancy may be affected by the pregnancy. Likewise, some of these conditions may adversely affect the pregnancy itself.

Duration of Pregnancy. The average duration of a pregnancy is reported to be 280 days or 40 weeks. As with any other biological system, there is variation. Part of the variation has to do with the starting point from which the calculation is made. Traditionally, the 280 day period is calculated from the first day of the last menstrual period (LMP). This generally is based on the fact that the patient has a 28 day menstrual cycle. If she does not, she may well ovulate earlier or later than the 14th day, thereby apparently decreasing or increasing the length of the pregnancy. Naegel's rule states that the expected date of confinement (EDC) may be calculated by counting back three months and adding 7 days to the first day of the LMP. Other circumstances may make it difficult to estimate the actual EDC. One such circumstance occurs when a woman conceives just after stopping oral contraceptives, because there is great irregularity from woman to woman with respect to first ovulation. Another problem patient might be the nursing mother who conceives before she has had a menstrual period. Obstetricians then need to use other means of estimating the length of gestation. These include the size of the uterus, onset of maternal perception of fetal movement (quickening), time of the first noticeable heart beat, and more recently, ultrasonographic measurement of fetal head size. Each and every one of these methods allows for error and the physician must be ever wary of this possibility.

Reproductive Organ Changes. As with all organs of the body, there is an increased vascularity and hyperemia in the vulva and vagina. This is accompanied by a general softening as connective tissue becomes more pliable. These changes are necessary so that the vagina may expand to allow the passage of the baby during labor and delivery. The pH of the vagina drops as *Lactobacillus acidophilus* produces lactic acid from glycogen normally stored in the vaginal epithelium. This increased acidity of the vagina probably helps to keep the vagina free of pathogens during pregnancy.

The cervix softens, becomes more engorged, and is generally closed by a mucus plug secreted by the mucus-secreting glands of the cervix. This plug generally seals the opening of the uterus until the time for labor approaches. In the primigravida (first pregnancy) the cervix frequently remains closed until labor begins, whereas in multiparas the cervix often appears to be somewhat dilated several weeks before labor. The uterus itself increases from 7 cm to 35 cm in length and from 500 to 1000 times in volume. The total content of the uterus at term averages about 5 liters, but may be as much as 10 liters or more. Whereas the pre-pregnant uterus averages about 60 grams in weight, the term uterus weighs about 1100 grams. Uterine enlargement occurs because of stretching and hypertrophy of preexisting muscle cells. Few or no new muscle cells are probably added. Each individual muscle cell enlarges greatly. There is an increase in connective tissue and elastic tissue, and the vascular supply to the uterus is greatly hypertrophied. There is also hypertrophy of the nerve supply to the uterus during pregnancy. Early in pregnancy the effects of estrogen and progesterone give rise to the hypertrophy of the uterus, whereas later in pregnancy the hypertrophy is due to the pressure from the expanding intrauterine contents.

Uterine growth correlates well with the period of gestation. Figure 4–20 represents the size of the uterus at various weeks of gestation. Knowing these positions helps the physician to estimate how far the pregnancy has progressed. These are, however, only averages, and great variations may be seen. The uterus rises out of the pelvis and expands to a maximum height at about 36 weeks of gestation. At this point it is located roughly at the level of the xyphoid process at the lower end of the sternum. However, as the fetus settles into the pelvis and enlargement of the head takes place, the uterus apparently diminishes in size so that it is actually lower at term than it is at 36 weeks.

The major change in the ovaries is the cessation of ovulation and the maintenance of the corpus luteum of pregnancy under the stimulus of chorionic gonadotropin from the fetal placenta. The corpus luteum is particularly large and prominent during the first three months of gestation when the progesterone it produces is responsible for the maintenance of the pregnancy. Later, the role of maintaining the pregnancy is taken over more directly by the placental hormones and the ovaries

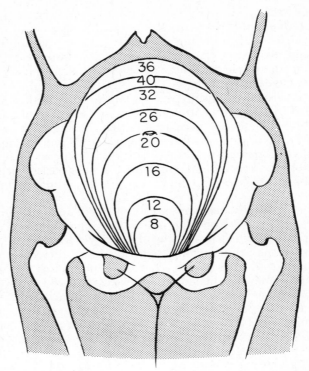

Figure 4–20 A schematic representation of the enlarging uterus at monthly intervals throughout pregnancy. By the fifth month of pregnancy the top of the uterine fundus normally reaches the umbilicus.

become less significant. The fallopian tubes change little during pregnancy, although the tubal mucosa is flattened compared with the nonpregnant condition.

The breasts enlarge, primarily by hypertrophy of the duct and alveolar system. There is also an increased vascularity in the breasts which may be noted by observing the vessels just beneath the skin. The nipples frequently enlarge and become more pigmented, as shown in Figure 4–21. Modified sweat glands along the areola of the nipples become prominent in pregnancy. As with the breasts, skin striae may be seen on the abdomen, as shown in Figure 4–22.

Metabolic Changes and Nutrition. The average gravid patient gains 25 pounds. On the average, 20 or 21 pounds are accounted for by the increase in reproductive organ size and the contents of the uterus. The remaining 4 to 5 pounds cannot be accounted for directly.

The average pregnant patient increases her total water content by 6.5 to 7 liters. About 3.5 liters can be accounted for by the fetus and the contents of the uterus, and 3 liters can be accounted for by the increase in blood volume. The remaining fluid is generally extracellular. If there is an increase in extracellular fluid much beyond this amount, edema is common. Although the exact causes of water retention in pregnancy are unknown, some reasons for it are changes in hydrostatic and osmotic

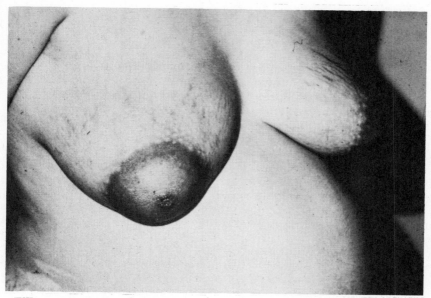

Figure 4-21 Breast enlargement and increased pigmentation of the nipple and areola are common changes of pregnancy. Striae and an accentuated venous pattern over the breasts may often be seen.

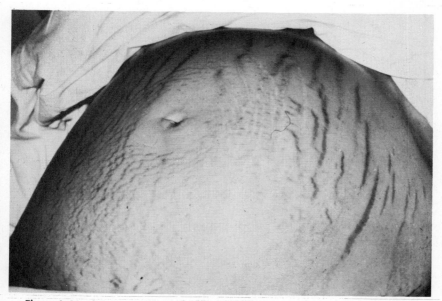

Figure 4-22 Striae gravidarum are reddish, slightly depressed streaks over the abdomen that occur in about one-half of all pregnancies.

pressure, increase in capillary permeability, and a tendency to retain sodium.

The pregnant patient exhibits an increase in total body protein of about 1000 grams, divided equally between the fetus and the patient herself. Thus, the pregnant patient requires a good deal more protein in her diet than her nonpregnant counterpart.

Carbohydrate metabolism in pregnancy is modified by two circumstances relating to insulin metabolism. Pregnancy is associated with higher levels of plasma insulin and also with more rapid destruction of insulin. Consequently its secretion during pregnancy is increased. In patients with marginal pancreatic reserve, manifestations of diabetes may first occur during pregnancy because of the stress of the change in insulin metabolism. The exact mechanism by which this change comes about is not clear. The placenta produces a hormone, chorionic somatomammotropin, which directly opposes the action of insulin and also produces an insulinase that accelerates the degradation of insulin. The direct effects of estrogen and progesterone are not clear; however, there is an obvious effect on insulin metabolism as measured by glucose tolerance tests. Glycosuria (glucose in the urine) frequently occurs during pregnancy but for the most part is due to an increased glomerular filtration without a comparable increase in reabsorption of glucose by the renal tubules.

All serum lipid levels are elevated in pregnancy, owing to changes in lipid metabolism. Changes occur in total lipids, esterified and unesterified cholesterol, phospholipids, and free fatty acids. This may be an attempt by the pregnant organism to retain an energy supply, but the exact mechanisms are unknown. Progesterone seems to play a role in fat storage.

Intravascular blood volume increases approximately 50 per cent during pregnancy owing to an increase in both plasma and red blood cells. Red blood cell mass increases only about 33 per cent, and thus a relative anemia is noted. In most cases, it is more apparent than real. Whereas normal total body iron in the adult male is about 4 grams, it is only 2 to 2.5 grams in the female. This is because total iron stores in young menstruating females are considerably smaller than in males. Roughly 500 mg of iron are required to increase the red blood cell mass in the pregnant female, and another 300 mg of iron are required for the fetus. Therefore, the average pregnant female will need to absorb approximately 800 mg of iron during her pregnancy to remain in balance. Obviously, if she already has iron deficiency anemia, her problem will be aggravated by the pregnancy. White blood cell counts (WBC) in pregnancy are quite variable but tend to be somewhat higher than in the nonpregnant state. The upper limits of the normal range in pregnancy might be considered to be 12,000 to 15,000 per ml, depending on the trimester. Most of the increase in WBC is due to an increase in neutrophils, which are frequently in the mature form.

Changes also occur in the blood coagulation mechanism. Plasma fibrinogen increases in the pregnant state to about 200 to 400 mg/100 ml. Late in pregnancy the normal range is 300 to 600 mg/100 ml. Factors VII, VIII, IX, and X are markedly increased in pregnancy, factor II is slightly increased, and factor XIII is decreased. Thus, prothrombin time and partial thromboplastin times are usually shortened slightly during pregnancy. Platelet count is generally within the normal range.

Cardiovascular Changes.   During pregnancy, several changes take place in the cardiovascular system. The diaphragm is ordinarily elevated during the later stages, and the cardiac volume tends to increase about 10 per cent. Murmurs audible over the pulmonic and apical areas are fairly common and may be due to a combination of events including torsion of the great vessels and decreased blood viscosity. Except for labor, when cardiac output increases, the change in cardiac output during pregnancy is negligible. Resting pulse rate, however, does tend to increase. Cardiac output may be affected by pressure of the uterus on the inferior vena cava, particularly during times of reflex hypotension.

Respiratory Changes.   During pregnancy the diaphragm gradually elevates. There is a decrease in functional residual capacity of the lung. However, there is no change in vital capacity, maximum breathing capacity, or lung compliance. Respiratory rate and tidal volume of the lung are both increased, as is airway conductance. Total pulmonary resistance is reduced.

Gastrointestinal Tract Changes.   Since pregnancy has a relaxing effect on smooth muscle, the entire gastrointestinal tract tends to become more sluggish. Patients are frequently bothered by regurgitation with some symptoms of "heartburn," and constipation is also often found. Mild antacids and cathartics, particularly those which work directly in the bowel without general absorption, are indicated where necessary. Gums become softened and hyperemic and may bleed when mildly traumatized. Small vascular swellings of the gum, called epulides of pregnancy, occur occasionally. These will regress after delivery. Pregnant patients often have hemorrhoids due to pressure in the pelvic area, but the symptoms frequently decrease after delivery. As with the rest of the intestinal tract, the gallbladder is quite often hypotonic and dilated, predisposing the pregnant patient to gallstones.

Urinary System Changes.   The urinary system also dilates (Figure 4–23), owing partially to pressure and partially to the relaxation of smooth muscle. This dilatation leads to stasis of urinary flow and predisposes the patient to renal stones. Renal functions are modified by pregnancy, leading to an increase in glomerular filtration and renal plasma flow, which causes most renal function studies to give extremely good results. Because of these changes, renal function tests in pregnancy must be interpreted somewhat differently. Values which would be considered normal in the nonpregnant state may be abnormal in the pregnant state. The presence of bacteria in the urine in the later stages of pregnancy is not uncommon, particularly in multiparas, where residual urine may occur. Pregnant women seem predisposed to lower urinary tract infections.

Musculoskeletal Changes.   In late pregnancy there is a general relaxation of all of the ligaments of the body, particularly those involving the pelvic bones and back. In addition, the enlarging uterus moves the patient's center of gravity farther backward. This frequently leads to a progressive lordosis, as shown in Figure 4–24. Pregnant patients often complain of backache and of pains in the pubic symphysis area due to increased mobility there.

Skin Changes.   In addition to the increased pigmentation noted previously, pregnant women frequently show increases in vascular spiders and palmar erythema. These findings are probably secondary to increased estrogen levels.

Endocrine Changes.   During pregnancy the pituitary gland becomes somewhat enlarged. Maternally produced growth hormone output is decreased, whereas fetally produced placental chorionic somatotropin levels are very high. The thyroid gland is often slightly enlarged, as a result of hyperplasia of glandular tissue and increased vascularity. Basal metabolic rate (BMR) increases 25 per cent or more during pregnancy, but this is accounted for by the fetus, with its increasing body surface and

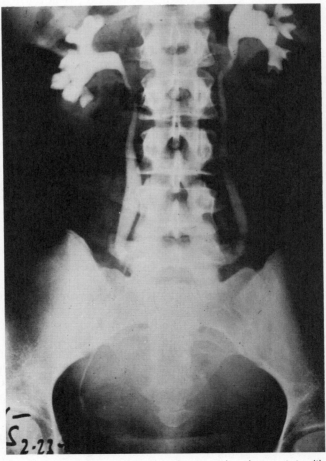

Figure 4–23 An intravenous pyelogram depicting the characteristic dilation of the ureter and renal pelvis, along with an increased tortuosity of the ureter that normally occurs during pregnancy.

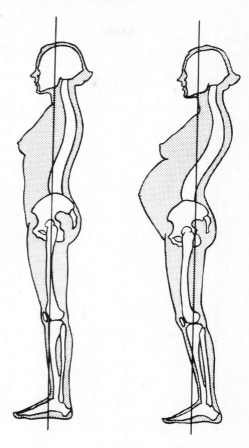

Figure 4–24 The progressive lordosis of the spine during pregnancy produces characteristic changes in gait and posture and may result in backache.

need for oxygen. Under the influence of estrogen, the serum protein bound iodine (PBI) and butinol extractable iodine (BEI) rise rapidly. Unbound serum thyroxin and absolute iodine uptake by the thyroid gland are not changed by pregnancy, but red blood cell triiodothyronine uptake is decreased.

Circulating cortisol from the adrenals rises rapidly, but most of it is protein bound in the form of transcortin, again secondary to the influence of estrogen. Non-bound hormone is slightly elevated during pregnancy. Aldosterone secretion is increased, as are renin, renin substrate, and angiotensin.

ANTEPARTUM CARE AND RISK FACTORS IN PREGNANCY

Good antepartum care is essential to insuring the health and well-being of the mother and child. Theoretically, the first antepartum visit best occurs before a fetus is conceived. This gives the physician the opportunity to review the patient's medical status and to carry out whatever medical and lifestyle counseling might be appropriate. If not before conception, the first antepartum visit should occur as early in the pregnancy as possible and should include, after verification of the pregnancy, a complete history and physical examination. This includes, along with general and medical considerations, a detailed history of previous reproductive performance. Appropriate laboratory tests for the first antepartum visit include urinalysis, hematocrit, serologic test for syphilis, culture of the cervix for gonorrhea, serum rubella titer, blood type and Rh, and an indirect Coomb's test to screen for atypical antibody. The patient should then be advised about diet, supplementary vitamins and minerals (should the physician wish to recommend these), and appropriate health habits such as rest, work activities, sexual activity, hygiene, and other factors. In a low risk patient, monthly return visits throughout the first 7 months of pregnancy are generally adequate. Patients are frequently seen every 2 weeks in the 8th month and weekly thereafter until delivery. Agenda for each antepartum visit includes the patient's blood pressure, urinalysis for protein and sugar, and an examination of the growing uterus and of the fetus, as it becomes large enough. The patient should also be questioned with respect to her health during the preceding month and quizzed for any danger signals such as bleeding, pain, presence or absence of fetal movements, and so on. The physician generally records the findings in graphic fashion so that they follow the pregnancy from month to month. In addition, special tests may be ordered, such as Rh titers or hematocrits, when appropriate.

In the latter stages of pregnancy the physician frequently makes pelvic examinations to re-estimate pelvic size and to inspect the cervix for signs of ripeness.

The following factors alert the physician to potential problems with the current pregnancy:

Maternal age (under 18 or over 35)
Parity (primigravida or greater than para IV)
Previous obstetrical history abnormalities
Previous medical problems
Previous isoimmunization
Height of less than 5 feet 2 inches
Obesity
Exposure to drugs of any kind (prescription or otherwise)
Untoward exposure to irradiation
Low socioeconomic status

In addition, risk factors during the pregnancy may change the management of the patient as they occur. These include untoward illnesses, exposure to drugs or chemicals, exposure to radiation, vaginal bleeding, and severe emotional difficulties.

COMMON DISORDERS OF PREGNANCY

Any medical or surgical condition which occurs in a nonpregnant patient can occur in pregnancy as well. In some cases the diagnosis is more difficult because of the anatomic and physiological changes of pregnancy. For instance, acute appendicitis may be masked in its earlier stages because of the tendency toward mild leukocytosis seen in the pregnant woman, the normal occurrence of a variety of gastrointestinal symptoms, and the anatomic displacement of the appendix to the upper abdomen in later pregnancy. The physiological changes in pregnancy may also mimic pathologic signs and symptoms where there are none. As an example, mucous membrane engorgement involving the nasopharynx may resemble upper respiratory infection or allergic rhinitis. Likewise, gastrointestinal instability and hyperacidity may be mistaken for symptoms of peptic ulcer or cholecystitis.

There are a number of conditions that occur commonly as a direct result of pregnancy. Some of these are discussed below.

Spontaneous Abortion. This condition, defined as the termination of pregnancy before 20 weeks' gestation, occurs in about 10 to 20 per cent of all pregnancies. It is frequently referred to as *miscarriage*. Most abortions occur in the first trimester, and indeed, in the first 8 weeks of gestation. Only about 1 per cent of second trimester pregnancies end in spontaneous abortion. The term *threatened abortion* is given to a pregnancy that is associated with vaginal bleeding and/or cramping without dilatation of the cervix. If the cervix is dilated the term *inevitable abortion* is applied. If part of the products of conception have passed, the designation *incomplete abortion* is appropriate. When all the products of conception are expelled spontaneously the term *complete abortion* is applicable. *Missed abortion* refers to fetal death without expulsion, usually for two or more weeks' duration. When the products of conception are not completely expelled and infection occurs, the term applied is *septic abortion*. If the pregnancy is surgically terminated it is referred to as an *induced abortion*.

Spontaneous abortion occurs for a variety of reasons, but most are secondary to fetal genetic defects. Among first trimester abortions, 50 to 70 per cent of fetuses have chromosomal anomalies. Infection, hormonal anomalies, anatomic defects, and serious maternal illnesses, as well as other unknown factors, are probably responsible for the remainder.

Ectopic Pregnancy. This term refers to a pregnancy that is outside the uterine cavity. While it most often occurs in the fallopian tubes, the conditon may also exist in the ovary, the perineal cavity, the cervix, or in a blind horn of an anomalous uterus. Rupture with hemorrhage is the likely course of such a condition, and the patient's life is often threatened. Therapy is surgical. Etiologic factors include previous pelvic infection, anatomic defects, hormonal dysfunction, and unknown causes. A patient who has had a previous ectopic pregnancy is ten times more likely to have one than a patient who has never had such a problem.

Premature Labor. This condition is defined as labor occurring before 36 weeks' gestation, or with an infant of less than 2500 grams birth weight. Etiologic circumstances include maternal illness, anatomic defects of the uterus or cervix, incompetent cervical os, fetal disease, and a large, poorly understood group of problems that can best be described as socioeconomic in nature. Premature labor is responsible for a major portion of the perinatal mortality rate in most centers. While there are agents that may be of value in slowing uterine activity in presumed premature labor, there is really no known agent that can dependably and effectively stop labor once it has been initiated. Bedrest and sedation seems to be as good as any other therapeutic regimen presently available.

Third Trimester Bleeding.   This condition is defined as bleeding after the 26th week of gestation. There are two major causes that can have a substantial effect on the management and outcome of a pregnancy: placenta previa and abruptio placentae. Other causes for bleeding are often found, but these are the most serious.

PLACENTA PREVIA.   This condition occurs when the placenta implants in the lower uterine segment and partially or totally covers the internal os of the cervix. In later stages of pregnancy when the lower uterine segment begins to thin out and be taken up into the body of the uterus, portions of the placenta will separate, opening vascular sinuses and causing bleeding. It is almost always painless bleeding, and is usually not associated with labor. Because of the location of the placenta and the possibility of its being dislodged and thereby causing severe hemorrhage, pelvic examination is never done when there is third trimester bleeding unless the physician is prepared to do an immediate cesarean section. About 90 per cent of all patients with placenta previa will stop bleeding after an initial bleed. The diagnosis can then be ascertained using ultrasonographic diagnostic procedures, and the mother can be managed with modified bedrest and pelvic precautions (no coitus, vaginal examinations, or douches). Subsequent bleeding increases the risk of fetal asphyxia and brain damage, and the physician may need to intercede with a cesarean section delivery in order to control maternal hemorrhage. Placenta previa is seen more commonly in multiparas and in women who have previously had placenta previa. There is a higher incidence of congenital anomalies in babies whose mothers have this condition, which may be secondary to the poorer circulation at the implantation site.

ABRUPTIO PLACENTAE.   This is probably the most serious condition associated with third trimester bleeding. Pathologically, the placenta partially or completely separates from the wall of the uterus. Bleeding occurs in the area of the separation and a clot will form. If an excessive portion of the placenta separates, fetal compromise and/or death may occur. The patient complains of pain and the uterus becomes irritable. Labor may occur. Complications such as toxemia of pregnancy, renal shutdown, and disseminated intravascular coagulopathy involving a decrease in platelet count and fibrinogen may ensue. The condition is life-threatening to the mother and baby, and must be managed by rapid delivery. The route of delivery will depend upon the clinical circumstances of the individual case.

Toxemia of Pregnancy.   This condition, which is often referred to as *pregnancy induced hypertension,* occurs principally in primigravidas, although it may be seen in other pregnancies associated with increased placental size, such as multiple gestation, diabetes mellitus, and Rh isoimmunization. Common symptoms are hypertension, albuminuria, and excessive rapid weight gain. Central nervous system hyperactivity may also occur and may be manifested by hyperreflexia in milder conditions (*preeclampsia*) or convulsions in more severe conditions (*eclampsia*). Etiology of the disease is as yet unknown but it is protean in nature, affecting all organ systems to some degree. It is progressive, can be life-threatening, and is treated completely only by delivery of the baby. Treatment objectives involve controlling maternal problems until fetal maturity can be proven. If the maternal condition deteriorates, however, delivery must be carried out.

Pregnancy induced hypertension may occur in conjunction with other conditions such as essential hypertension, chronic renal disease, and lupus erythematosus. This is often more serious, with poor prognostic implications for mother and child. In such instances it is not limited to primigravidas.

Urinary Tract Infection. Because of urinary stasis and increased bacteriuria in pregnancy, urinary infection is quite common. Causative organisms are often the same as those seen in the nonpregnant patient with urinary tract infection, but the patient may be relatively asymptomatic. Fevers of unknown origin in pregnancy mandate a urinary tract evaluation, as do unexplained abdominal and back pain. Dysuria is a frequent symptom, and when it is present, the urinary tract should be investigated. Urinary tract infection, especially pyelitis, may cause high fever, severe systemic reactions, and premature labor.

REFERENCES

Prenatal Life

Assali, N. S. (Ed.): Biology of Gestation. Vol. II. The Fetus and Neonate. New York, Academic Press, 1968.

Dawes, G. S.: Foetal and Neonatal Physiology. Chicago, Year Book Publishers, Inc., 1968.

Dunn, P. M.: Congenital postural deformities. In Smith, D. W.: Introduction to Clinical Pediatrics. 2nd ed. Philadelphia, W. B. Saunders Company, 1977.

Hertig, A. T., Rock, J., and Adams, E. C.: A description of 34 human ova within the first 17 days of development. Amer. J. Anat. 98:435, 1956.

Langman, J.: Medical Embryology. 3rd ed. Baltimore, Williams and Wilkins Company, 1975.

Moore, K.: The Developing Human: Clinically Oriented Embryology. Philadelphia, W. B. Saunders Co., 1973.

Niswander, K. R., and Gordon, M.: The Collaborative Study of the National Institute of Neurological Diseases and Stroke: The Women and Their Pregnancies. Philadelphia, W. B. Saunders Company, 1972.

Shepard, T. H.: Catalog of Teratogenic Agents. 2nd ed. Baltimore, Johns Hopkins University Press, 1976.

Singer, J. E., Westphal, M., and Niswander, K.: Relationship of weight gain during pregnancy to birth weight and infant growth and development in the first year. Obstet. Gynecol., 31:417, 1968.

Smith, D. W.: Recognizable Patterns of Human Malformation. 2nd ed. Philadelphia, W. B. Saunders Company, 1976.

Stiehm, E. R.: Fetal defense mechanism. Am. J. Dis. Child., 129:438, 1975.

Villee, D. B.: Development of endocrine function in the human placenta and fetus. N. Engl. J. Med., 281:473, 533, 1969.

The Pregnant Woman

Hellman, L., and Pritchard, J.: William's Obstetrics. 15th ed. New York, Appleton-Century-Crofts, Inc., 1976.

Ruch, T., and Patton, H. (Eds.): Physiology and Biophysics of Digestion, Metabolism, Endocrine Function and Reproduction. Philadelphia, W. B. Saunders Company, 1973.

5

Perinatal Life for Mother and Baby

LABOR AND DELIVERY

MORTON A. STENCHEVER

Labor can be defined as uterine contractions which effect progressive dilatation of the cervix and lead to the delivery of the fetus. The circumstances that initiate labor are as yet unknown, but it is likely that labor is begun by an interaction between the mother, the fetus, and the placenta. While this usually occurs 280 days after the first day of the last menstrual period, great variations do occur. Terms like premature labor (labor prior to 36 weeks' gestation or leading to an infant of less than 2500 g), term birth, and postmaturity (labor after 42 weeks' gestation) are quite relative. They are difficult to interpret, since dates are not always accurately judged and fetal weight is quite variable.

Several major factors influence the conduct of normal labor. They are the patient's general physical condition and emotional health, the size of the fetus, the presentation of the fetus, the quality and type of uterine contractions, the condition of the cervix, uterine anatomy and volume, and the architecture of the bony pelvis.

PHYSICAL CONDITION AND EMOTIONAL HEALTH. The patient's general physical condition and emotional health are of great importance, since they directly affect the function of the uterus and the conduct of labor. In a severely ill, dehydrated, debilitated patient, the contraction pattern may be quite ineffective. Likewise, an emotionally upset patient may have her labor adversely affected by the inappropriate action of the sympathetic and parasympathetic nervous systems. It is the aim of good antepartum care to allow the patient to enter labor in good general health with a minimum of fear and anxiety.

FETAL SIZE. Another extremely important factor is the size of the fetus. Small fetuses may possibly deliver through smaller pelves, whereas large ones may not. The importance of this aspect is seen when multiparous women who have delivered average sized babies previously, develop cephalopelvic disproportion with subsequently larger children, necessitating cesarean section delivery.

PRESENTATION OF THE FETUS. If the baby presents a well flexed vertex (head) to the pelvis, the general diameter entering the pelvis is smaller than if a poorly flexed head is presented, such as that seen in a brow presentation or (in the extreme) with a face presentation. Thus, a well flexed head may deliver through a given pelvis when a brow presentation may not. In like manner, a breech (buttocks) presentation may pose special problems for the normal delivery of the patient. Those which present as frank breeches (with the breech itself as the presenting part) may not affect normal labor. If the physician is satisfied that the head will pass through the pelvis (based on clinical or x-ray pelvimetry and an estimation of head size), then vaginal delivery may be reasonable. But, if the patient presents as a footling breech, giving a poor dilating wedge to the cervix and allowing for an incomplete development of the lower uterine segment, difficulties in delivering the larger parts of the baby, including the head, may arise. In addition, infants whose presenting parts do not fill up the lower uterine segment develop cord complications more readily, leading to asphyxia (oxygen deprivation). For these reasons, all breeches other than frank breeches are considered serious enough at this time to warrant cesarean section delivery. Likewise, transverse lies (e.g., babies who present a shoulder or an arm) will have an extremely difficult time maneuvering the birth canal and are always delivered by cesarean section.

UTERINE CONTRACTIONS. The quality and type of uterine contractions are very important. The contraction normally begins in the upper part or fundus of the uterus and is transmitted in wavelike fashion down to the lower uterine segment. The net result is a thickening and shortening of muscle fibers in the uterine fundus, and a thinning and drawing up of the lower uterine segment and cervix. In this manner the presenting part is pushed down into the pelvis and the cervix dilated. Although the agent or event that initiates labor is unknown, the chemical agent which apparently causes the uterine muscle fibers to contract is a member of the prostaglandin family. This system is probably activated by the posterior pituitary gland hormone, oxytocin. Because the uterus is composed of smooth muscle and is continually being dilated by the ever growing fetus, the uterus can be observed to be contracting almost continuously throughout pregnancy. However, before labor is initiated, these contractions are mild, irregular, and uncoordinated, and do not in and of themselves effect the uterine changes which lead to delivery. When labor begins under normal circumstances, the contractions are coordinated, rhythmic, and stronger. Thus, active labor will be manifested by contractions occurring every 2 to 5 minutes with a strength that makes it difficult to impress the uterus with the fingers. During most of labor, they register a pressure of 40 to 60 mm Hg while at the time of expulsion of the fetus, the contractions may become as strong as 70 to 90 mm Hg. When milder tonus persists, the uterus is said to be hypotonic, and when stronger contractions occur the uterus is said to be hypertonic. The uterus may be made hypertonic iatrogenically by the overenthusiastic use of an oxytocic substance. Hypotonus rarely leads to normal delivery simply because the expulsive force does not develop. Hypertonus may lead to dilatation of the cervix and delivery, but probably will impair utero-placental blood flow and cause the fetus to become hypoxic.

CONDITION OF THE CERVIX.   Early in pregnancy the cervix is frequently thick, firm, and closed. As pregnancy continues, however, the cervix tends to soften as connective tissue softens, and to begin to thin out (efface) as the lower uterine segment begins to be taken up. In the primigravida it is unusual for the cervix to be dilated before labor occurs. However, in the multiparous patient it is common to find some cervical dilatation. If the cervix is softened, effaced, and somewhat dilated before labor begins, the amount of effort needed to finish dilating the cervix and expel the fetus is far less than if the cervix needs to be "ripened" during the labor process itself. This finding is particularly important in deciding upon elective induction of labor. If the cervix is indeed "ripe" then induction is usually easy to initiate and the time until delivery is quite short. If the cervix is "unripe" it may be impossible to initiate labor, or if labor is initiated, the process is usually prolonged significantly.

UTERINE ANATOMY AND VOLUME.   In overdistended uteri, such as those with polyhydramnios (increased amount of amniotic fluid) or with twins, labor contractions are often weak as the uterus attempts to push against the overdistended sac. Likewise, in abnormal uteri (those with septa, double horns and so on), dysfunctional uterine activity is quite common and abnormal labor patterns occur.

THE ARCHITECTURE OF THE BONY PELVIS.   There are four basic pelvic types that refer to the shape and general characteristics of the pelvis. In general, the most common type is the *gynecoid* pelvis, which when viewed through the inlet appears round or slightly ellipsoid, as shown in Figure 5–1. The transverse diameter of the inlet is somewhat longer than the anteroposterior dimension, making most of the inlet area usable space for the fetal head. The pubic arch is wide, sidewalls are parallel, and the sacrum has a good curve and is far enough posterior to allow the vertex to easily transverse the birth canal. The ischial spines are not prominent and the sacrospinus ligament is at least 2.5 finger breadths in length. In addition, the outlet of a gynecoid pelvis is usually quite large.

The *android* pelvis, in contrast, is probably the most difficult pelvis for a normal passage of the fetus. When viewed through the inlet, it is heartshaped. The sacral promontory is forward. The sidewalls of the pelvis converge towards the outlet. The ischial spines are prominent and the sacrospinus ligaments are shortened. The sacrum does not have a good curve and is frequently inclined forward into the birth canal. The pubic arch is narrowed. The usable space within the android pelvis is greatly reduced and this is the most common pelvis type found in cephalopelvic disproportion.

The third pelvic type is the *anthropoid* type. This pelvis, when viewed through the inlet, has an oval appearance with a long anteroposterior diameter and a shorter transverse diameter. In general, the sidewalls may be straight or slightly convergent, and the ischial spines are frequently prominent. The pubic arch is often narrow. Whereas

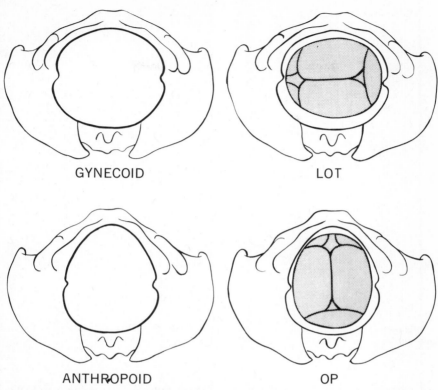

GYNECOID · LOT

ANTHROPOID · OP

Figure 5–1 The position of the fetal vertex is determined to a large degree by the configuration of the maternal pelvis. The anterior-posterior diameter of the fetal vertex orients itself to the largest pelvic diameter. In the normal gynecoid pelvis the vertex descends in the occiput transverse position as shown. If the pelvis is anthropoid, with a large anterior-posterior diameter, the fetal vertex engages and descends most commonly in the occiput anterior or occiput posterior position.

the fetal head will frequently engage in a transverse position in the gynecoid pelvis, it almost always engages in the anteroposterior position in the anthropoid pelvis.

The fourth type of pelvis is the *platypelloid* or *flat* pelvis. This, too, is an oval pelvis but with the long diameter in the transverse. It is the least common of all pelvic types. The fetus frequently engages in the transverse diameter.

Mixtures of pelves do occur and it is not infrequent to find pelves which do not follow pure patterns. Regardless of shape, overall pelvic size and the length of the various diameters are the most important factors. A large pelvis, no matter what shape, will probably accommodate a fetus, whereas a small one most likely will not.

The Labor Curve. Progress in labor can be followed by using a modified Friedman curve (Fig. 5–2), which plots cervical dilatation against time. The early portion of the curve is known as the *latent*

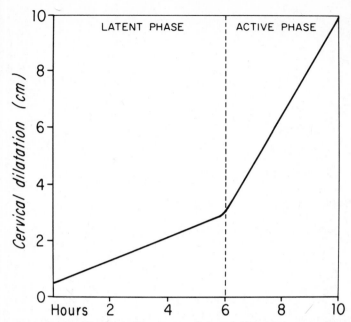

Figure 5–2 Modified Friedman labor curve of cervical dilatation in cm and time in hours, showing the two major phases of the first stage of labor—latent and active.

phase. During this phase the cervix effaces (thins out), but very little dilatation is noted. The uterine contractions may be mild and even somewhat irregular. They may, however, be perceived by the patient as painful. The physician attempts not to interfere during this labor stage, since heavy sedation, regional anesthesia, and rupture of the membranes frequently prolong this phase rather than shorten it.

Once active dilatation occurs, the patient is said to be in the *accelerated* phase of the *first stage* of labor. During this phase a primigravida will average 1.2 cm of cervical dilation per hour and a multipara, 1.5 cm per hour. However, large variations do occur and more rapid dilatation is not uncommon. When 10 cm (full dilatation) is achieved, the first stage of labor is ended and the *second stage* begins. During the second stage the presenting part descends completely through the birth canal and is delivered. With the delivery of the baby, the second stage ends and the third stage begins. The *third stage* of labor is the stage devoted to the delivery of the placenta, and is completed when the placenta is delivered into the vagina.

During labor, certain nomenclature is used to describe the position of the presenting part in the pelvis. Two general circumstances are taken into consideration. The first is the level to which the presenting part has descended. This is known as the *station*. Station 0 is achieved when the most forward portion of the presenting part reaches the level of the ischial spines. This level is designated the *mid-pelvis*. Positions of the presenting part above the ischial spines are referred to as minus stations, with minus 1 being 1 cm above the ischial spine, minus 2, 2 cm above, and so on. Positions below the spine are plus stations, with plus 1 being 1 cm below, plus 2 being 2 cm below, and so forth. In the case of vertex delivery, when the most forward portion of the vertex reaches station 0, the biparietal diameter of the fetal head is generally through the inlet of the pelvis and is said to be engaged (Figs. 5–3 and 5–4). Thus, when the presenting part is above station 0, engagement has not been achieved. Multiparas will frequently enter labor with the presenting part high or even floating out of the pelvis. For a multipara, this is not an ominous sign, but for a primigravida, entering labor with a floating part is considered serious evidence for potential cephalopelvic disproportion.

The other type of nomenclature that describes the position of the presenting part uses a specific fetal landmark in relation to the rest of the pelvis, as illustrated in Figures 5–5 and 5–1. In the case of a ver-

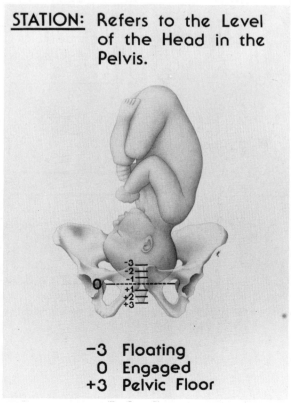

STATION: Refers to the Level of the Head in the Pelvis.

-3 Floating
0 Engaged
+3 Pelvic Floor

Figure 5–3 Graphic illustration of station of vertex.

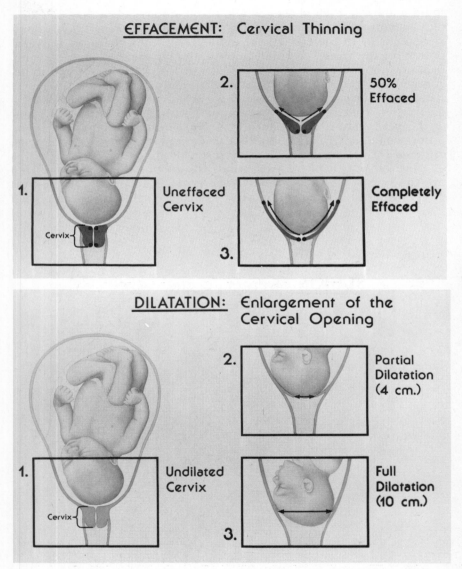

Figure 5–4   Graphic illustration of cervical effacement and dilatation.

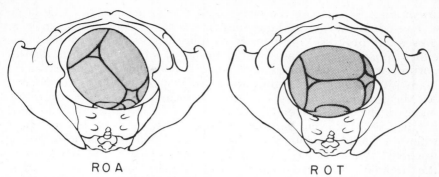

Figure 5–5 The relationship between the fetal occiput and the maternal pelyis. ROT— occiput right transverse—fetal occiput is on the mother's right side and the sagittal suture in a horizontal position. ROA—occiput right anterior—the fetal occiput is on the mother's right side and the sagittal suture is directed obliquely.

tex presentation, the occiput is the landmark and is described in relation to the right and left sides of the mother's pelvis. Thus, right occiput anterior (ROA) means that the occiput is in the right side of the maternal pelvis and anterior to a midline drawn across the pelvis. (The mother's ventral surface is considered anterior and her dorsal surface, posterior.) The various possibilities are right occiput anterior (ROA), occiput anterior (OA), left occiput anterior (LOA), left occiput transverse (LOT), right occiput transverse (ROT), right occiput posterior (ROP), left occiput posterior (LOP), and occiput posterior (OP). Similar nomenclature is applied in the case of breech presentation, where the tip of the sacrum is the landmark and S replaces O in the description. In the case of a face presentation, the chin is the landmark and M (mentum) replaces the O.

In modern obstetrical units the progress of labor is scrutinized closely by the individual attending the patient. In many instances electronic surveillance is used as well, to determine evidence of fetal distress. Close medical supervision of the course of labor is essential if the outcome is to be the best possible for the mother and child.

COMMON PROBLEMS OF LABOR AND DELIVERY

Poor Progress in a Vertex Presentation.　If progress in labor slows or stops, it is important for the physician to investigate the situation rapidly. Problems may relate to any or all of the factors previously described. Heavy sedation or regional anesthesia may slow uterine contractions, thereby slowing the progress of dilatation of the cervix and descent of the fetus.

The lie of the fetus in the pelvis may slow the progress if the pelvis is small or nongynecoid. The commonest problem position is the posterior presentation, where a wider diameter of fetal skull is attempting to negotiate the birth canal. If the fetal head size is large compared to the pelvic dimensions. *cephalopelvic disproportion* may be present. If progress is not made in spite of good labor contractions, either spontaneous or augmented by oxytocin, cephalopelvic disproportion is likely and cesarean section delivery may be necessary. Many physicians favor vertification by x-ray pelvimetry measurements, but the present trend is to avoid this because it does not contribute much to the management decision, and it is advisable to avoid fetal irradiation whenever possible. Forceps delivery may be necessary when the mother cannot aid in the delivery by abdominal muscle contraction, or in relative cephalopelvic disproportion problems where the attendant feels that vaginal forceps delivery can be safely undertaken.

Breech Presentation. Since perinatal morbidity and mortality have been demonstrated to be higher in breech presentations delivered vaginally than in comparable vertex presentations, most obstetricians have recently reevaluated how to manage breech presentations. Many such occur in premature infants and this fact must be considered in evaluating the course of management. With recent improvements in the care of even very small prematures in newborn intensive care units, it is apparent that for the best possible outcome, these infants require a more aggressive management program. Small prematures are at risk because of the relatively large head size which may allow delivery of the breech through an incompletely dilated cervix, but lead to head entrapment. In addition, these infants are more easily damaged by manipulative procedures. Term breeches with buttocks presentations (frank breech) can be managed vaginally if there is good progress in labor and no apparent fetal distress or suspected cephalopelvic disproportion. Should any complication arise, cesarean section is mandatory. Footling breeches are best managed by cesarean section because of the problem of fetal asphyxia (approximately 25 per cent) due to umbilical cord prolapse or other cord complications, and because of the possibility of head entrapment.

Transverse Lie. This presentation involves a baby lying transversely in the uterus. Often labor has begun, a shoulder or an arm is usually presenting, and cord prolapse is very common. Normal birth is virtually impossible and cesarean section delivery is the treatment of choice.

Multiple Gestation. Traditionally, twins have been delivered vaginally and have been associated with a 2- or 3-fold increase in perinatal mortality for twin A, and up to 15 per cent mortality in twin B. Many of these problems stem from abnormal presentations of one or both twins. Similar difficulties have been encountered in multiple gestations of higher number. In addition, prematurity is common in multiple gestation, adding to the chance of compromise. Current management philosophies view abnormal presentation (i.e., footling breech or transverse lie in twin A or unstable lie in twin B) as an indication for cesarean section delivery. Other combinations of presentations are managed in much the same way as breech presentations. Cesarean section is applied in the case of cephalopelvic disproportion, poor progress, or fetal distress.

Previous Cesarean Section. Two schools of thought exist with respect to the management of a patient who has had a previous cesarean section delivery. One position is "once a cesarean section, always a cesarean section." The other school advocates attempting vaginal delivery with careful monitoring of the mother and fetus during labor. The risk of rupturing a previous lower uterine segment incision following an uncomplicated cesarean section is less than 1 per cent. The risk of rupture of a fundal incision (classical) is as high as 3 to 5 per cent. These risks must be balanced against the risk of subsequent abdominal surgery in an additional cesarean section. If vaginal delivery is attempted, most physicians exclude patients with proven cephalopelvic disproportion or uterine anomalies, as well as those who have previously suffered severe postoperative complications. The physician provides careful observation of mother and fetus, has blood available, and sees that the operating room is ready for instant surgery. After delivery, the uterine scar should be palpated carefully transvaginally. The use of oxytoxin should be avoided and regional anesthesia is probably not indicated, as it may mask abdominal pain that can imply uterine rupture. When all of these precautions are exercised, many women will be able to safely deliver vaginally.

THE PERINATE

RICHARD P. WENNBERG

DAVID E. WOODRUM

W. ALAN HODSON

JANET H. MURPHY

There is no age in life when adaptive requirements are so compressed in time and so critical to continued survival as the period surrounding birth. This precarious transition from fetus to infant extends beyond the moment of delivery and is often referred to as "perinatal adaptation."

During the nine months of fetal life, the human lives in an aquatic environment and in a parasitic relationship with the mother. The placenta plays a vital role in growth, metabolic homeostasis, gas exchange and excretory function; it shares or totally usurps the vital regulatory functions of nearly every major organ in the body, including the gut, kidney, liver, neuroendocrinologic systems, and lung. At birth, these placental functions are abruptly interdicted, and many body organs must suddenly assume for the first time the peculiar postnatal functions for which they are genetically programmed.

During the 28-day neonatal period, approximately one in 100 liveborn humans will die, and perhaps one in 25 will suffer difficulties such as perinatal asphyxia or have a congenital defect which will adversely affect the future lives of both infant and family. The risks of birth are high and are in large part related to a failure to meet the physiologic and biochemical adaptive requirements of the perinate.

LIFE SITUATION

Psychosocial

NANCY ROBINSON

The "normal" setting for perinate and mother during the first few days of life is the hospital. In this environment, the initial interaction between parents and baby is often disrupted in favor of efficient institutional routine. This tendency can be thoroughly detrimental to parent-infant bonding, the establishment of the enduring and irrational parent-child relationship which is essential to healthy child development. (It is often commented that only parents would do for their children what no one could pay them enough to do for someone else's children.) Research has shown the value of handing mothers their unclothed infants immediately after delivery (providing an opportunity for cuddling in the first few hours of life), and housing the neonate in the mother's room. According to indices such as breast-feeding, mutual gazing, and expressed maternal attitudes, the benefits of such practices have been detected months later. It is clear that within the limits of the mother's and neonate's physical state, mutual exposure and maternal caretaking is to be encouraged. While the evidence is less clear for fathers, there are indications which also favor early paternal exposure, such as contact during the first hour of life and protracted visiting with the baby in the mother's room.

Upon returning home, when the neonate is normally 2 to 5 days old, the parents must assume total responsibility for the care of the baby. In our society, many parents have had little or no exposure to newborns and feel anxious and overwhelmed by responsibility for the fragile new life. If the baby cries more than they expect, they may take this as a sign confirming their inadequacy as parents, or may even feel that their baby "doesn't like" them. Support may be provided by prenatal education, help from other family members, and friends, but new parents (especially primiparous mothers) are likely to seek what at first may appear to be excessive telephone contact with their infant's physician. Health professionals may do a great deal to reassure parents and strengthen their ability to provide confident, calm, and sensitive caretaking.

During the neonatal period, the infant's rhythms of breathing, sleeping, feeding, elimination, and wakefulness emerge. The parents discover how to anticipate needs, interpret signals, and modify the baby's behavior. They may, however, need help in responding to temperamental differences, and with "tricks of the trade," such as swaddling to calm a jumpy baby or stimulation to rouse an habitually sleepy one.

The newborn characteristically sleeps about 16 hours, with the longest period of uninterrupted sleep being (on the average), a little over four hours. Approximately half of the sleep however, is active sleep, characterized by rapid eye movements, total relaxation of postural muscles, irregular breathing, frequent small movements, sucking, and even smiling. Quiet sleep, on the other hand, is synchronized, characterized by a slow and regular pulse, lack of conjugate eye movements, lack of body movement, regular breathing, and partial relaxation of postural muscles. By the age of three months, quiet sleep constitutes approximately two thirds of the infant's total sleep. Many infants at first show little differentiation of night and day, but within six weeks are usually sleeping for longer periods at night and have longer periods of wakefulness during the day. This adaptation is, needless to say, most welcome to parents.

Breastfeeding confers advantages during the first year by transmitting certain maternal antibodies, reducing the likelihood of constipation and other digestive disorders, and increasing mother-infant closeness. Some mothers find it inconvenient; other reject it for cosmetic reasons. Encouragement and information from the obstetrician, pediatrician, and nursing staff may help a mother establish a strong suckling response in the neonate, an adequate milk supply, and confidence in her ability to nurture the infant. Even mothers who return to work after the neonatal period can continue to suckle their infants for some feedings.

Newborns are surprisingly capable and responsive organisms. During the first hour of life, especially if not medicated during labor and delivery, the justborn may be unusually alert, turn toward faces, track moving objects, and be generally more capable and responsive than he or she will be again for days or even weeks. (This may be the reason it is so effective to expose parents and infants shortly after birth; the alert baby looks at the parents and "hooks" or "wins them over".) Even after this initial heightened state has passed, neonates can find the breast (the "rooting response" or reflex when touched on the cheek), and can withdraw from a pinprick, turn toward light, respond to odors, and even detect visual patterns. They prefer sugar-water to plain, and visual patterns with more black and white contrast to those with less contrast. They have such poor motor control and exhibit so many random movements that it is hard indeed to see that in the first few days, if properly positioned, they can (somewhat unreliably) reach toward objects, turn toward sounds, and even move in a responsive rhythm to adult speech. Although learning tends to be temporary, neonates can be taught to turn their heads to one side or the other at a signal (tone) in order to obtain a suck of sugar water, and can also learn to reverse the response. Infants as young as three weeks can sometimes imitate adult movements with their mouths, even though they cannot see themselves and presumably can only dimly "know" that their own mouth movements match the visual image of the adult as shown in Figure 5–6. Parents may or may not be able to elicit these responses from their neonates; conditions need to be just right.

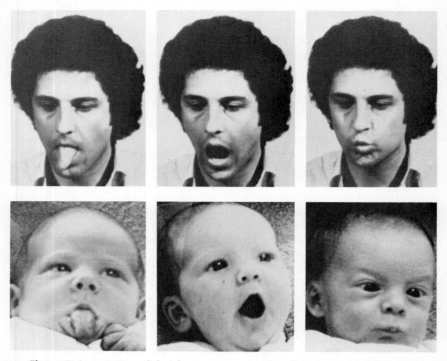

Figure 5–6   Imitation of facial movements can be elicited surprisingly early. From Meltzoff, A. N., and Moore, M. K.: Imitation of facial and manual gestures by human neonates. *Science, 198*:75, 1977. Copyright 1977 by the American Association for the Advancement of Science.

Cardiopulmonary Adaptation

The most critical adaptive requirement at birth is the delivery of oxygen to tissue and the elimination of carbon dioxide. Several major changes in the cardiopulmonary system must occur in the first minutes of life in order to ensure intact survival.

Late Fetal Circulation.   During fetal life blood flows through four channels which normally close after birth: the umbilical arteries and vein, the ductus venosus in the liver, the foramen ovale lying in the atrial cardiac septum, and the ductus arteriosis connecting the pulmonary artery with the descending aorta as shown in Figure 5–7. Following oxygenation in the placenta, blood flows into the fetus via the umbilical vein. Approximately 50 per cent of the umbilical venous blood enters the liver, perfuses the hepatic parenchyma, and is collected in the hepatic venous system before entering the inferior vena cava (IVC). The remaining 50 per cent of umbilical venous flow is shunted, via the ductus venosus, through the liver into the IVC, where it mixes with blood returning from the lower body. Because of the anatomical juxtaposition of the IVC and the foramen ovale, most of the well-

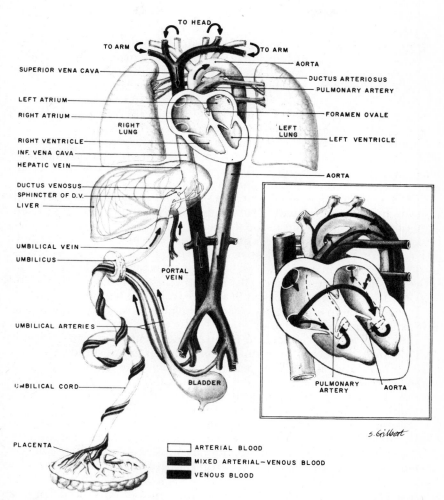

Figure 5–7 Fetal circulation. Arrows indicate course of blood. Oxygen saturation is highest in the umbilical vein and progressively lower in the vessels to the head and neck, the aorta, and, finally, the inferior vena cava below the liver, which has the most desaturated blood. The insert illustrates the course and distribution of blood in the fetal heart and large vessels more clearly. Note that the oxygenated placental blood entering the heart via the inferior vena cava flows preferentially to the left ventricle and head. (From Bonica, J. H.: *Principles and Practice of Obstetric Analgesia and Anesthesiology.* Philadelphia, F. A. Davis Co., 1967; adapted from Ross Clinical Aid No. 1, Fetal Circulation, Ross Laboratories, Columbus, Ohio 43216. Reproduced with permission.)

oxygenated blood from the IVC passes directly into the left atrium. This blood enters the left ventricle and subsequently perfuses the coronary arteries, the upper body and the head, via vessels originating from the arch of the aorta. Thus, the coronary and cephalic vessels are perfused with the most oxygenated blood.

Venous blood returning to the heart from the upper body via the superior vena cava (SVC) flows preferentially into the right atrium, the right ventricle, and then into the pulmonary artery. Only 10 per cent of this blood perfuses the fetal lungs, while the other 90 per cent bypasses the lungs by flowing through the ductus arteriosus into the descending aorta. Roughly 50 per cent of the blood flow through the descending aorta perfuses the lower body, and the other 50 per cent passes directly to the placenta where it is reoxygenated.

Lung: Fetal Development and Perinatal Adaptation. The state of maturation of the lung which determines its ability for gas exchange is the major factor in the successful transition to extrauterine life. Well-developed terminal air saccules are not present until about the time of birth (38 gestational weeks). The lung appears glandular initially and has a high glycogen content. The bronchial generations are completed by about 16 weeks of gestational age, and the terminal air saccules appear at about 24 weeks. Cuboidal epithelial cells begin to flatten, and capillary plexuses develop near the potential air surface. Structural differentiation would allow limited gas exchange at about 24 to 25 weeks. Type II epithelial cells, rich in cytoplasmic osmiophilic inclusions, form after 25 weeks and appear to be the source of "surfactant," a lipoprotein substance providing surface tension stability in the terminal air saccules.

The lung *in utero* is filled to about 40 per cent of its capacity with fluid distincly different in composition from amniotic fluid. It is secreted at a rate of about 3 ml per kilogram per hour with some being swallowed and some mixed with amniotic fluid. The phospholipid content (surfactant) increases in the lung over the last three months of gestation, and the ratio of lecithin to sphingomyelin concentrations in the amniotic fluid is an index of lung maturation. In those situations where an early termination of pregnancy may be indicated, sampling of amniotic fluid permits an antenatal assessment of the risk of development of respiratory distress syndrome with hyaline membrane disease.

Intermittent shallow, rapid respiratory movements occurring *in utero* are probably related to fetal electrocortical activity which varies with fetal sleep states. The onset of regular rhythmic respiration at birth is most likely due to asphyxial changes in the blood gases which stimulate peripheral and central chemoreceptors. Other nonspecific changes such as a decrease in environmental temperature and an increase in tactile, proprioceptor, visual and auditory stimuli may help to stimulate the first breath. With the first breaths, air replaces the fluid in the lungs, and the partial pressure arterial of oxygen (PaO_2) rises, followed by closure of the fetal cardiovascular shunts. The increase in PaO_2 stimulates closure of the ductus arteriosus and constriction of the umbilical arteries. Increased blood flow through the lungs increases the left atrial pressure in the heart, effecting closure of the foramen ovale. The ductus arteriosus is functionally closed within 3 to 4 hours of birth.

Nutritional Adaptation

Fetal growth accelerates dramatically early in the third trimester. With a normal placenta and a healthy mother, the fetus will double its weight in the last six weeks of gestation. A part of this late growth is manifested as an increase in glycogen and lipid stores which will assure nutrition for the newly born infant prior to the establishment of adequate oral intake. In the full-term infant, these glycogen stores may be depleted by 24 hours of age. The prematurely born infant has little or no nutritional reserve and is vulnerable to nutritional deficiency since adequate oral intake may take some time to establish.

Homeostatic mechanisms modulating the blood level of nutrients prior to birth are shared by mother, placenta and fetus. The fetus receives a relatively constant influx of nutrients and maintains a blood glucose level at 70 to 80 per cent of maternal values. Following birth, the infant's blood glucose concentration falls, stabilizing between four and six hours of age at 45 to 60 mg per 100 ml. Homeostatic mechanisms for regulating blood glucose normally adapt rapidly to the postnatal environment, although several days or weeks are required before gluconeogenic and other regulatory mechanisms reach maximum potential. If an infant is very premature, or if he has had placental insufficiency with resulting decrease in glycogen stores, he may develop hypoglycemia within the first days of life, if not supplied with an exogenous source of glucose.

It is therefore important to establish and maintain an adequate nutritional intake soon after birth. Sucking and swallowing reflexes, important in accomplishing oral intake, are well integrated by 32 to 33 weeks of gestation. Most digestive enzymes are present in both premature and mature infants, and lactase, required for digesting the principal sugar in milk, is found in greater abundance in newborns than in adults.

The perinate will normally lose about 5 per cent of its birth weight during the first two to three postnatal days, largely due to an adjustment in total body water. With adequate nutrition (about 120 cal/kg/day), the infant will then gain 20 to 25 grams a day during the first four postnatal months.

Temperature Regulation

The deep body temperature of the newborn commonly falls 1 to 2 degrees centigrade during the first few minutes after birth. A number of factors are responsible for this rapid heat loss at birth: evaporation of amniotic fluid from the skin, a relatively high skin to room temperature gradient at birth, and a relatively high ratio of surface area to mass in the newborn. The premature is even more susceptible to cooling in the first moments after birth.

It is uncertain whether the thermal stress at birth is advantageous or deleterious. While cooling may serve as a stimulant for the ·initiation of breathing, marked heat loss is associated with an increased infant mortality. There is also evidence that postnatal cooling inhibits recovery from metabolic acidosis and potentiates hypoglycemia.

Both full-term and premature infants respond to a cold environment by peripheral vasoconstriction and by increasing heat production. Heat is produced by increasing the metabolic rate rather than by shivering. Not only cooling, but also overheating of the newborn influences resting metabolic rate. A naked full-term newborn infant has a minimum oxygen consumption at rest when placed in an environment of about 32° C, the "neutral thermal environment." If an infant is premature, has respiratory distress, or is otherwise ill it is important to minimize oxygen requirements for thermogenesis by preventing heat loss in the delivery room and by placing the infant in a neutral thermal environment. In the delivery room, heat loss may be minimized by rapidly drying the infant following birth and by placing him under a radiant heat source.

Host Defense to Infectious Disease

Infections occur more often in the neonatal period than at any other age. Although cellular immunity is apparently normal, the newborn's serum is deficient in opsonic factors which potentiate phagocytosis of foreign antigens such as bacteria. The newborn appears to have a deficient inflammatory response and localizes infections poorly. Since the newborn normally has had little previous antigen exposure, passive immunity is limited to a large supply of maternal immunoglobulin G (IgG), which selectively crosses the placenta. Maternal IgM and IgA do not readily cross the placenta, and exist in low concentration in the newborn infant.

As a result of these numerous handicaps, the newborn, and especially the prematurely born infant, is susceptible to infections by organisms for which circulating IgM, opsonization, and efficient tissue localizations are essential defense mechanisms. These organisms include most gram negative bacilli, group B beta-hemolytic streptococci and staphylococcus aureus.

Renal Adaptation

The fetal kidney produces urine, which contributes significantly to the amniotic fluid volume. However, the usual renal functions of removing waste products and maintaining acid-base, electrolyte, and blood volume homeostasis are accomplished for the most part by the

TABLE 5–1 COMPARATIVE RENAL FUNCTION IN
NEWBORN, INFANT, AND ADULT

	Kidney Weight (gms)	Glomerular Filtration Rate (ml/min/1.73M²)	Maximum Tubular Excretory Capacity TMPAH (mg/min/1.73M²)	Concentrating Capacity (m osm/l)	Acidifying Capacity	
					pH	H+ excretion (mEq/min/1.73M²)
Newborn	22	45	16	600–1100	6.0± .3	16–40
6 month old	40	115	60	800–1200	4.8±.2	65–200
Adult	300	125	80	800–1500	4.8± .2	65–200

placenta. Thus, a fetus with bilateral renal agenesis (absent kidneys) may survive until shortly after birth.

The principles of renal function are identical in the perinate and adult, although the newborn kidney does not achieve maximum function until one to three months of age (Table 5–1). The glomerular filtration rate in both premature and full-term infants is about 45 ml/min/1.73 m², compared with 125 ml/min/1.73 m² in adults. Renal tubular transport is diminished at birth; the newly born has a lower transport maximum for bicarbonate and para-amino hippuric acid (PAH), cannot excrete a sodium load as efficiently as an adult, and has a limited capacity to excrete ammonia in response to an acid load.

The newborn is also limited in his ability to concentrate or dilute urine. The adult kidney will excrete urine varying in concentration from 50 to 1500 mOsm per liter, depending upon the amount of water intake, in order to preserve a serum solute concentration of 300 mOsm per liter. Many newborns can concentrate their urine only to 600 to 700 mOsm per liter under conditions of water deprivation. This may be related in part to the low urea load to the kidney of newborns, which results in a diminished urea concentration in the medulla of the kidney and, therefore, a low total solute concentration in the urine.

The limitations in renal function have great clinical relevance in regard to fluid and electrolyte therapy and feeding, acid-base balance in a sick infant, and the administration of drugs such as kanamycin and penicillin, which depend upon renal tubular excretion for elimination.

Hepatic Detoxification

Most drugs and toxic endogenous substances are either excreted unchanged through the kidneys (*e.g.*, penicillin) or modified by the liver to facilitate excretion by the kidney (*e.g.*, chloramphenicol) or hepato-biliary system. Most hepatic detoxifying enzymes have very low activity *in utero*. Substances normally catabolized by the liver cross the placenta and are detoxified and excreted by the maternal liver.

One such detoxifying enzyme, glucuronyl transferase, conjugates bilirubin, a breakdown product of heme, with glucuronic acid. Conjugation transforms the lipid-soluble bilirubin into a water-soluble bilirubin diglucuronide, which can then be excreted via the biliary tract into the gut.

The nine-month fetus produces 20 to 30 mg of bilirubin each day, but most of this crosses the placenta and is excreted by the maternal liver. Following birth, the perinate is confronted with an accumulation of unconjugated bilirubin until the hepatic conjugating and excreting mechanisms become adequate. The serum bilirubin concentration in most term infants continues to rise until about the third day, then gradually decreases to a normal adult value of less than 1 mg per 100 ml. In normal infants, bilirubin concentration will usually not exceed 11 to 12 mg per 100 ml, and in most cases will remain much lower. This degree of bilirubinemia, acquired through the normal adaptive processes, is referred to as "physiologic jaundice of the newborn." If the infant produces more bilirubin than usual, as in the case of hemolytic disease caused by maternal antibodies destroying fetal red cells (Rh or ABO incompatibility), considerable amounts of bilirubin may accumulate in the serum.

Unconjugated bilirubin is toxic to cellular systems and if allowed to reach high concentrations may cause irreversible brain damage (kernicterus), resulting in mental retardation, athetoid cerebral palsy, deafness, or death. Kernicterus usually occurs only when the bilirubin concentration exceeds 20 to 24 mg per 100 ml. At this concentration of bilirubin, loci on serum albumin which bind bilirubin tightly become saturated, potentiating transfer of bilirubin into tissues. When the bilirubin concentrations reach dangerous levels, they may be lowered by an exchange transfusion which replaces the jaundiced blood with fresh donor blood.

Hematologic Adaptation

The production of red cells is controlled largely through a humoral factor, erythropoietin. Levels of erythropoietin increase in the normal fetus with increasing gestational age, leading to a high level in cord blood at term. The red cell mass in the newborn is relatively high (about 17 gm of hemoglobin per 100 ml) and the reticulocyte count is also high (2 to 6 per cent at birth). From the second day through the first six to eight weeks of life, erythropoietin is normally not measurable in either blood or urine. During this time, red cell production does not keep pace with body growth and red cell destruction, and by two to three months of age hemoglobin concentration will drop to about 11 gm per 100 ml, the so-called physiologic anemia of infancy.

At birth, about 80 per cent of hemoglobin is in the form of fetal hemoglobin (Hgb-F), with only about 20 per cent adult type hemoglobin (Hgb-A). By four to five months of postnatal age, normal adult values of Hgb-A are found. The mechanism regulating the change from Hgb-F to Hgb-A is unknown. Hgb-F has a higher oxygen affinity than Hgb-A, resulting in a left shift of the oxygen-Hgb association curve. This shift might facilitate oxygen transfer across the placenta from mother to fetus, but at the same time might inhibit oxygen unloading to tissue. Thus, it is uncertain whether Hgb-F conveys any physiologic advantage to the fetus with regard to oxygen delivery.

Neurologic Adaptation

During the latter half of pregnancy there is a rapid proliferation of brain cells. Proliferation (increased DNA content) decreases after birth and reaches adult levels by about five months of age. In contrast, brain RNA, protein, and weight (reflecting cell size) increase linearly from mid-gestation through the first year of life. Myelin lipids (cerebroside and sulfatide) exist in low concentrations at birth, and by the first year of life reach only about 20 per cent of adult content.

Other than its role in sustaining and regulating vital functions such as temperature and breathing, the nervous system has few recognized adaptive requirements in the perinatal period. Functionally, the human brain is very immature at birth, and the newborn's movements are guided largely by primitive reflexes with relatively little cortical control. In fact, an infant can be born without a cerebral cortex (hydranencephaly) and behave almost like a normal newborn. In contrast to most species, the human infant requires several weeks before he effectively finds his way to the breast, months before he will be able to ambulate, and years before he can protect himself from adverse climates (by clothing himself) and other life-threatening situations. Consequently, the human is born into a situation of prolonged maternal dependency that is unique among animal species. His successful adaptation to the first years and his preparation to face future adaptive crises are therefore inextricably linked to skillful mothering and an appropriate adaptive response to his birth by his parents.

COMMON PROBLEMS OF THE PERINATAL PERIOD

Behavioral

NANCY ROBINSON

Irregularity and Asynchronies. Term babies differ considerably in their maturity and in the ease with which they settle into a pattern. Usually parents can help infants to establish a regular rhythm by a "modulated self demand" schedule in which the infant is fed when hungry but either water is given or some other means of distraction is tried before feeding if crying occurs in less than three hours. Within the first 10 days of life, one can show that babies fed on a 4 hour schedule have adapted to that schedule in terms of waking, restlessness, and crying, while babies fed on a 3 hour schedule have adapted to that. Sometimes, however, parents and infants are unsuccessful in establishing adapted rhythms. Irregularity in feeding and wakefulness may stem from physiological immaturity, temperamental factors in the newborn, or occasionally from undernutrition (more likely in the early days of breastfeeding, when frequent feedings stimulate greater milk production), as well as from anxious handling by parents. The interaction of anxious parenting and fussy baby may lead to a particularly negative first few weeks, when pediatric advice may be less effective than modeling by an experienced relative or public health nurse.

Colic. Colic is a malady of unknown origin which appears generally about 2 weeks of age and disappears spontaneously by 3 or 4 months. It is generally defined as intense, noisy crying which persists more than 3 hours a day, 5 or more days a week. Babies often draw up their legs and give behavioral evidence of abdominal pain. Crying generally is worst in late afternoon and early evening, and peaks between 6 and 8 weeks of age, gradually tapering off after that. It does not, contrary to old wives' tales, appear more often in first babies or males, although there is some tendency for colic to run in families, i.e., for infants with a previously colicky sibling to have colic. The condition cannot be considered abnormal, since it appears in 15 to 20 per cent of infants, and since it does not affect growth parameters or other developmental indices. Although it has been thought that anxious mothers caring for infants who are physiologically prone to colic provided the necessary interaction, mothers who seem anxious during pregnancy show no greater tendency to produce colicky offspring than nonanxious mothers. Rather, the physician dealing with an anxious parent of such an infant may be seeing an *ex post facto* condition, as colic is highly stressing to parents and may well interfere with the positive adaptation which normally occurs within the first few weeks of life.

Depression. Depression may occur in either parent after the birth of a baby. Financial pressures and competition with an "intruder" for a wife's attention may trigger paternal depression. More frequently, it is the mother whose depression reaches clinical levels. It is a "normal" condition for women to experience occasional crying jags and transient blues in the neonatal period, probably as a combination of physiological changes, fatigue, and feelings of inadequacy in the new role. Occasionally, more severe and persistent postpartum depression appears. Here there may be more basic conflicts about role changes, unrealistically high standards, and quite possibly, biochemical predisposition to depression. The alert physician will monitor such episodes carefully and advise the parents to give a higher priority to their own needs. If the problems do not resolve quickly, a referral to an appropriate mental health professional should be made promptly, and relief care for the infant arranged.

Prematurity. Prematurity constitutes an abnormal condition for the initiation of the parent-child relationship, as well as a biologically abnormal condition. Even so, present evidence indicates that with good neonatal care, prematurity per se usually does not lead to developmental deficit. Indeed, groups of prematurely born infants who have been followed over substantial periods of time do not tend to show overall developmental lags, although those who are small for gestational age and/or of very low birth weight constitute special high risk groups in which spastic diplegia, mental retardation, and other developmental handicaps are more common. Development can be compromised by a number of adverse conditions in the perinatal period, but premature birth (at normal birthweight for gestational age), even with the addition of hyaline membrane disease, is not by itself sufficient reason for long range concern.

Longitudinal studies do, however, tend to show that premature infants born to low income families tend to be at a disadvantage compared with term infants. One suspects that families who have difficulty coping with their life situation may not be well tuned to the infants' needs, nor able to compensate for minor developmental anomalies. Since prematurity rates are substantially higher in low income families, this is a population of special concern. Prematurity is frequently the outcome of physical and/or psychosocial stress, and should be considered a physical symptom of compromised maternal health status, a stressed marriage, or single parenthood. Special services, such as those of a homemaker or public health nurse, are often appropriate. The staff of the neonatal nursery may be advised to provide support and to make an extra effort with young and/or low income parents to establish initial parenting skills.

There is also a growing body of evidence to suggest that even in socioeconomically more advantaged families, normal parent-child interaction may be at risk. Not only is the early "bonding" likely to be disturbed by the separation and artificiality necessitated by procedures enabling the newborn to survive, but also the premature baby arrives unexpectedly and looks totally unlike the newborn that the parents may have been biologically and psychologically "primed" to accept. Further, the premature tends to be socially rather unresponsive, a lag in sociability which persists for at least six or eight months in attenuated form. Investigations have shown that in response, parents seem to try harder to elicit a response, thereby risking overstimulating the infant and "turning off" the very responsiveness they desire. Careful guidance, advising parents to "slow down" and to take their cues from the infant, may help to bring parents and premature into better synchrony.

Asphyxia and Fetal Monitoring

Fetal asphyxia is an important contributor to infant mortality and a major cause of mental retardation and cerebral palsy. Fetal asphyxia may result from any of the following: insufficient uterine blood flow (maternal hypotension, tonically contracted uterus); interference with placental gas exchange (premature separation of the placenta, placental scarring); and umbilical cord compression (cord wrapped around neck of fetus, knot in the umbilical cord, prolapse of cord through cervix).

Recent electronic advances in continuous monitoring of fetal heart rate and uterine activity have improved our ability to detect fetal asphyxia during labor. The fetal heart rate may be monitored continuously, indirectly by means of transabdominal ultrasound, or directly by attaching an electrode to the presenting part of the fetus through the cervix. Uterine contractions can be monitored externally by use of an abdominal transducer (tocodynamometer), or internally by means of an intrauterine pressure catheter inserted through the cervix and attached to a pressure transducer. Mild asphyxia may cause an increase in the baseline fetal heart rate or loss of its normal beat to beat irregularity, and moderate to severe asphyxia may result in pronounced deceleration of the heart rate in association with uterine contractions. The pattern of deceleration of the heart rate in relation to the uterine contraction provides some clues as to the cause of fetal asphyxia. Uterine contractions serve as a recurring stress to the fetus by reducing the placental intervillous blood flow or, if placental exchange is already compromised, there is compression of the umbilical cord. Periodic uterine contractions can cause transient fetal asphyxia which can become severe. Fetal heart rate patterns are broadly classified into the following three types based on the time relationships between the heart rate deceleration and the uterine contractions: early decelerations, late decelerations and variable decelerations (Fig. 5–8).

Early decelerations appear to be a normal vagal reflex slowing of the heart rate, occurring simultaneously with uterine contractions. They are attributed to fetal head compression and are ordinarily not related to fetal distress. Late decelerations are a slowing of the heart rate, occurring after the onset of the uterine contraction, that persist beyond the contraction. They are abnormal and are frequently caused by insufiicient placental oxygen — so called "uteroplacental insufficiency." Variable decelerations are variable in onset, shape, and duration and are usually caused by umbilical cord compression. Variable decelerations are the most common fetal heart rate pattern associated with the clinical diagnosis of fetal distress. By recognizing the causes of acute fetal distress, initial obstetrical management can be directed at correcting the underlying pathophysiology, *e.g.,* changing maternal position to reduce cord compression, treating maternal hypotension, or reducing uterine hypertonus to correct uteroplacental insufficiency. If these measures are unsuccessful within a reasonable period of time, delivery is indicated to prevent permanent and severe damage to the infant.

Occasionally, fetal heart rate monitoring may give ambiguous or incomplete information about the status of the fetus during labor. Therefore, fetal capillary blood sampling can be utilized to evaluate the acid-base status of the fetus. This can be an invaluable technique providing vital adjunctive information. This, combined with continuous fetal heart rate monitoring, provides complete information about fetal condition. Normally, fetal capillary blood pH tends to decline

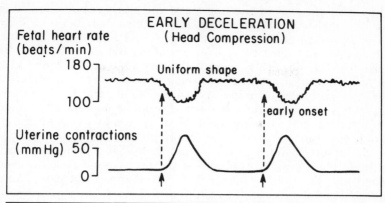

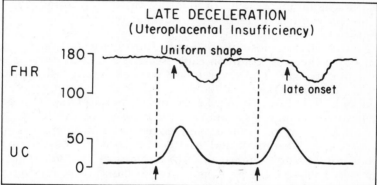

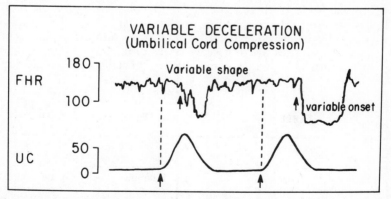

Figure 5–8 Three major types of fetal heart rate deceleration patterns. *a.* Early deceleration—thought to be due to fetal head compression and not normally related to fetal asphyxia. This pattern is uniform in shape and has its onset at approximately the same time as the uterine contraction. *b.* Late deceleration—thought to be due to decreased placental blood flow during contractions—acute uteroplacental insufficiency and is an indication of acute fetal distress. This pattern is usually uniform in shape but has its onset late in the contraction of the uterus and persists beyond the completion of the contraction. *c.* Variable deceleration—thought to be due to umbilical cord compression; is the most common pattern associated with clinically diagnosed fetal distress. The pattern is variable in shape, time of onset and duration.

slightly near the end of the first stage and during the second stage of labor. Normal fetal pH should be above 7.25. A pH between 7.20 and 7.25 is equivocal and bears repeating. A pH less than 7.20 indicates fetal acidosis and must be repeated, while a pH of 7.15 or less shows severe acidosis, requiring prompt delivery of the compromised baby. The technique has several disadvantages in that it requires meticulous technique, is time consuming and cumbersome, and does not give instantaneous information. One must also obtain simultaneous maternal acid-base data, and sampling must be done serially to establish a trend. A single random sample may be meaningless.

Meconium staining of the amniotic fluid is another sign of fetal asphyxia. The intestinal contents of the fetus contain a dark greenish mucoid material called "meconium." Meconium is not passed into the amniotic fluid except under conditions of stress such as cerebral hypoxia. Recognition of signs of fetal asphyxia may sometimes make possible prevention of fetal brain damage or death, by appropriate obstetrical intervention.

Fetal asphyxia most often occurs during the terminal stages of labor and is the most common cause of severe central nervous system depression at birth. The severely asphyxiated infant will appear flaccid and cyanotic. There may be a period of no respiratory effort followed by a period of gasping. Lesser degrees of asphyxia may be associated with irregular respirations, mild slowing of the heart rate (to about 100 per min), cyanosis and occasional movements of the extremities. It is customary and useful to record the condition of the newborn at 1 minute and again at 5 minutes of age, using an Apgar score (see Table 5–2). The Apgar score is based on a maximum of 2 points assigned to each of five parameters: heart rate, respiratory effort, muscle tone, reflex irritability and color. A score of 2 or less indicates severe asphyxia; 3 to 5, moderate asphyxia; and 6 to 7, mild asphyxia. The healthy newborn rarely has a 1 minute Apgar score of 10 as the extremities are not completely pink. Low Apgar scores are correlated with a high infant mortality, especially at lower gestational

TABLE 5–2   APGAR EVALUATION METHOD

Sign	0	1	2
Heart rate	Absent	< 100/min.	> 100/min.
Respiratory effort	Absent	Weak cry Hypoventilation	Good strong cry
Muscle tone	Limp	Some flexion of extremities	Well flexed
Reflex irritability (response to stimulation of feet)	No response	Some motion	Cry
Color	Blue; pale	Body pink, extremities blue	Completely pink

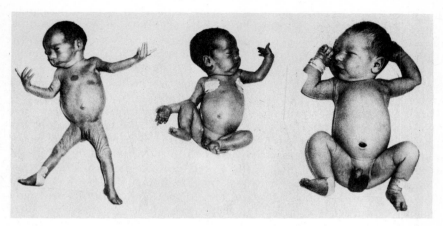

Figure 5–9 Infants (left to right) were born at 28 weeks, 33 weeks, and 40 weeks of gestation. Note the increase in subcutaneous tissue mass and flexion tone with increasing gestational age.

ages. Infants with Apgar scores of 2 or less, and weighing less than 2000 grams, have a mortality rate approaching 80 per cent.

The treatment of asphyxia is directed at rapid oxygenation of the baby. The airway should be cleared of secretions, amniotic fluid or blood, and followed immediately by oxygen administration. If spontaneous respirations are absent, a resuscitation bag and face mask should be used. If the lungs have never been aerated, high inflationary forces may be needed to initiate ventilation; a spontaneously breathing newborn may generate 50 to 80 cm H_2O negative transthoracic pressure with the first breath. Care must be taken to ventilate with an appropriate air volume in order to avoid tissue injury. The full-term infant has a total lung capacity of 300 ml and a tidal volume of only 25 ml. In a severely depressed infant, alkali (sodium bicarbonate) should be administered via the umbilical vein to buffer noncarbonic acids which have accumulated subsequent to anaerobic metabolism. Cardiac massage is necessary if the heart rate falls below 50 per minute. The importance of immediate recognition and treatment of neonatal asphyxia cannot be overemphasized. The appropriate management requires a person in attendance who has knowledge and skills pertaining to the specific problems in the newborn and who can provide undivided attention to the baby.

Prematurity

Figure 5–9 shows a comparison of two prematurely born babies to a full term baby. An infant is considered premature when born prior to the thirty-seventh week of gestation. Formerly infants with a birth weight of less than 2500 grams (5½ pounds) were considered to be premature. Recognition of intrauterine growth deficiency resulting in low birth weight infants born later than the thirty-seventh week of gestation has led to the abandonment of birth weight as a satisfactory index of maturation. The term "low birth weight," therefore, includes normal and undergrown premature infants as well as undergrown full-term infants (see Appendix for normal standards).

The incidence of prematurity in the United States is about 7.5 per cent, but varies from a high of 16 per cent in low socioeconomic areas to about 3 per cent in middle and upper income communities. There is no apparent racial predilection. Populations with very low neonatal and prenatal death rates, such as the Scandinavian countries, have a very low prematurity rate. Since neonatal morbidity and mortality are related to prematurity, one of the most important solutions to lowering infant mortality is the prevention of prematurity. Unfortunately, the causes of premature labor are poorly understood. Many maternal situations, such as young unwed mothers, multiple pregnancy, maternal infection, and cervical incompetence, are associated with a higher incidence of prematurity.

The problems of the premature are in large part related to unreadiness for both immediate and late adaptation to extrauterine life. Frequent problems of the premature include: hyaline membrane disease; asphyxia; periodic apnea; inadequate nutrition; jaundice; poor temperature regulation; infections; hypoglycemia; and anemia. Of these problems, hyaline membrane disease is by far the most common cause of death.

Hyaline Membrane Disease

Hyaline membrane disease (idiopathic respiratory distress syndrome) affects approximately 75,000 infants each year in the United States, of whom 12,000 to 15,000 will die. The disease occurs in 15 per cent of all premature infants in inverse proportion to gestational age (see Table 5–3). Although there is insufficient supportive evi-

TABLE 5–3 INCIDENCE AND MORTALITY OF HYALINE MEMBRANE DISEASE (HMD) RELATED TO GESTATIONAL AGE

Gestation	Incidence of HMD	Mortality in Affected
40 weeks	0.05%	5%
36 weeks	0.7%	5%
34 weeks	20%	10%
32 weeks	40%	15%
28 weeks	66%	95%

dence, factors such as antepartum bleeding or delivery by caesarian section, in addition to prematurity, may increase the susceptibility to the disease.

Characteristically, the infant will show signs of respiratory distress in the delivery accompanied by tachypnea, expiratory grunting and retractions of the chest wall. The disease progresses in severity for 48 to 72 hours, during which time the respiratory rate may increase to 120 per minute, accompanied by severe xyphoid, subcostal and intracostal retractions, nasal flaring, and cyanosis. Recovery, if it occurs, requires several days, the duration varying with the severity of the disease.

The chest radiograph reveals a characteristic reticulogranular pattern with an air bronchogram, due to the focal collapsed areas of the lung contrasted with overexpanded airspaces.

PATHOPHYSIOLOGY. At autopsy the lungs are airless, appear liverlike and do not float in water. On histologic section there is a "Swiss cheese" pattern with overexpanded bronchioles and alveolar ducts and patchy areas of atelectasis. The dilated terminal air spaces are lined with membranes which contain plasma proteins. These membranes are not present early in the disease and are thought to be a result of either altered surface forces in the lung or capillary endothelial damage or both. The membranes are not a necessary component of the disease, hence many have preferred to rename the disease "idiopathic respiratory distress syndrome."

The extensive alveolar collapse severely restricts oxygen transfer to the blood. Pulmonary arterial blood courses through atelectatic lung without oxygenation, causing a right to left shunting of the blood. Therefore, hypoxia is the major pathophysiologic event. Metabolic acidosis due to the anaerobic metabolism of hypoxia tissue may ensue.

The focal atelectasis causes a decrease in lung compliance, hence, the chest wall retractions, tachypnea and nasal flaring. The expiratory grunt is probably an attempt to prevent alveoli from collapsing.

ETIOLOGY. The precise etiology is not understood. Pulmonary immaturity seems to be the most important factor. Studies on maturation of the lung indicate that surfactant, the proteolipid substance responsible for lowering surface tension, and thus preventing collapse at end expiration, is not present until about the twenty-eighth week of gestation. The type II alveolar epithelial cells, responsible for surfactant production, are either absent or lacking in the cytoplasmic osmiophilic inclusions which manufacture or store surface active phospholipids. By 34 to 38 weeks there is usually a sufficient alveolar lining layer to prevent hyaline membrane disease. Other developmental features of the fetal lung such as structural maturation of terminal air spaces may be important.

TREATMENT. The treatment of hyaline membrane disease is primarily supportive, in attempts to maintain physiologic homeostasis. Sometimes ventilatory support is necessary to provide an adequate arterial oxygen and carbon dioxide tension. The ambient temperature and the temperature of inspired gases is carefully controlled and monitored to keep the infant within his zone of thermal neutrality, thus maintaining minimal oxygen consumption. Acid-base and fluid balance are maintained with intravascular infusions of 10 per cent glucose in water, and $NaHCO_3$, sodium and potassium are added when indicated. The application of a positive end-expiratory pressure appears to be beneficial in preventing alveolar collapse and improving pulmonary oxygen exchange.

The long term outlook for survival from hyaline membrane disease is favorable and lends strong support to continued efforts at vigorous management in the neonatal period.

REFERENCES

Labor and Delivery

Friedman, E. A.: *Labor: Clinical Evaluation and Management.* New York, Appleton-Century-Crofts, Inc., 1967.

Pritchard, J. A., and McDonald, P. C.: *Williams Obstetrics,* 15th ed. New York, Appleton-Century-Crofts, Inc., 1976.

Perinate

Avery, M. E.: The Lung and its Disorders in the Newborn Infant. 2nd ed. Philadelphia, W. B. Saunders Company, 1968.

Cornblath, M., and Schwartz, R.: Disorders of Carbohydrate Metabolism in Infancy. 2nd ed. Philadelphia, W. B. Saunders Company, 1976.

Dawes, G. S.: Foetal and Neonatal Physiology. Chicago, Year Book Medical Publishers, 1968

Klaus, M. H., and Kennell, J. H.: Maternal-Infant Bonding. St. Louis, C. V. Mosby Company, 1976.

Maisels, M. J.: Bilirubin, Pediat. Clin. N. Amer., *19*:447–501, 1972.

Nelson, N. M.: On the etiology of hyaline membrane disease. Pediat. Clin. N. Amer., *17*:943–965, 1970.

Oski, F., and Naiman, J. L.: Hematologic Problems in the Newborn. 2nd ed. Philadelphia, W. B. Saunders Company, 1972.

Schwartz, J. L., and Schwartz, L. H.: Vulnerable Infants: A Psychosocial Dilemma. New York, McGraw-Hill, 1977.

Stave, U. (Ed.): Physiology of the Perinatal Period. 2 vols. New York, Appleton-Century-Crofts Division Meredith Corp., 1970.

6

Infancy — The First Two Years

CLIFFORD J. SELLS

Infancy encompasses a time period during which the baby demonstrates dramatic changes in physical growth, in physiological maturation, and in psychosocial development. During this period, the infant progresses from an almost totally dependent organism with a rather limited range of behaviors, to an individual with increasing control over his own body environment. By 2 years of age, the child will be exhibiting progressively greater independence, while at the same time becoming highly imitative, and increasingly aware of and responsive to others.

LIFE SITUATION
Physical Changes

Although there are a number of parameters that reflect physical growth of infants and young children, the most useful measures in a clinical evaluation of young children are length or height, weight, and head circumference.

The average normal term infant is approximately 50 cm (20 in) in length at birth and weighs approximately 3.4 kg (7½ lb). Most full term infants will regain their birthweight by 10 days of age, will have doubled their birthweight by 4 to 6 months, and tripled their birthweight by 1 year of age. By age 2, the average child will have quadrupled his birthweight. At maturity, weight will have increased approximately twentyfold.

Normal infants will generally increase their length by approximately 50 per cent during the first year of life. During the second year, the average child will increase his length by an additional 25 per cent of the birth length. As a rule of thumb, stature will increase approximately 3½ times from birth to maturity.

The length of the full term newborn infant correlates well with the height of the mother, but does not correlate well with mean parental height. Eventual height, however, correlates best with midparental height. Although birth length appears to correlate best with maternal size, following birth, genetic background exerts its influence with linear growth gravitating within 1 to 2 years toward the percentile of midparental height. Smaller mothers tend to have smaller babies with higher morbidity and mortality rates, who remain smaller and generally do not perform as well as babies born to larger women. Larger full term babies, on the other hand, have lower morbidity and mortality rates.

For practical purposes, occipital frontal circumference or head circumference reflects brain size. Hence, head growth can be used as a gauge of brain growth. Deviations from the norm raise concern about the developing brain and its surrounding structures. At birth, the average head circumference is approximately 35 cm (13½ in). The vast majority of brain growth occurs during the first 2 years of life, with 90 per cent of brain growth occurring by age 2. The anterior fontanelle (soft spot) is generally open at birth, but closes between 9 and 18 months. The posterior fontanelle generally closes before 4 months of age, but may be closed at birth.

Many disorders that affect linear growth also affect brain growth. Thus, diminished linear growth may herald early abnormal brain development. Linear growth and weight gain are rather sensitive indicators of general health and well-being. Linear growth is more heritable and is a better indicator of chronic problems, while weight may be a better indicator of acute problems. Single measurements, whether of length, weight, or head circumference, although useful, are less valuable than serial measurements. Growth patterns, as determined by serial measurements, provide the clinician with considerably more information than any single measurement. During infancy, when growth is occurring at a rapid pace, serial measurements and their interpretation, using charts and graphs standardized for age and sex, are imperative for proper monitoring of a child's growth.

Most infants are born without teeth, although occasionally teeth are present at birth. The first teeth, the lower central incisors, usually erupt between 5 and 9 months of age, followed by the eruption of the upper central incisors and the lower lateral incisors. By age 2, the infant may have all 20 of his deciduous teeth. During infancy, calcification of most of the permanent dentition also begins.

Physiologic Changes

Although less dramatic than during the immediate postnatal period, certain physiological changes do occur during infancy. Infants are not little adults. The infant, for example, may be more sensitive than the adult to the pharmacologic effects of drugs. This increased sensitivity may relate to a number of factors including host differences in absorption, distribution, metabolism, or excretion. Variations in the clinical manifestations of disease produced by a specific agent is another example where infants may differ from adults. Usually there is a direct relationship to age: the younger the child, the greater the differences.

Gastrointestinal Tract. The gastrointestinal tract of the newborn infant is relatively immature. Food that will be tolerated later may not be well tolerated during the first few months of life. Unaltered cow's milk, for example, if used in infants' formula, requires heating to alter the curd to aid in infant digestion. There is some evidence to suggest that exposure to certain foods in early infancy may contribute to future allergies in susceptible individuals due to the absorption of certain large protein molecules through the immature gut.

Urinary Tract. In early infancy, normal kidney function is significantly different from that of the adult. The renal reserve capacity is considerably smaller than the capacity of an adult. Changes in renal function during the first several weeks of life are of considerable magnitude, hence, values of significant functions vary widely. The early immaturity of the kidney, resulting in the inability to handle a solute load, necessitates the modification of cow's milk in infant formula. By the end of the first year, however, the kidneys generally reach full functional capacity.

Immunologic System. The immune system of the newborn infant is capable of responding to antigenic stimuli and is conditioned by the growing child. The newborn infant normally produces little or no immune globulin, but does receive some maternal immune globulins across the placenta. Soon after birth, the infant begins to respond to various antigenic stimuli (bacterial flora, microbial and parasitic infection, and administered vaccines) with the production of various immunoglobulins and progressive lymphoid tissue hyperplasia. At the same time, maternally derived immunoglobulins and their associated passive immunity is gradually decreasing (Fig. 6–1). The duration of the passive immunity depends upon the maternal antibody level and the specific infection involved. This protection from maternally derived antibodies may persist for 6 to 12 months or more, and consequently may interfere with active immunization. Because of maternal antibody interference, current immunization practices include delaying measles immunization until the infant is 15 months old.

Central Nervous System Changes. Despite the rather striking physiologic changes occurring in a number of systems during infancy, the neurophysiological changes in the CNS are the most dramatic. The newborn's range of behaviors at birth is limited, but even at this age there are qualitative differences among infants with regard to levels of activity and intensity of reactions. Recently, investigators have shown very young infants to be able to imitate facial gestures. Neurophysiological maturation during infancy proceeds rapidly in a sequential manner. The infant demonstrates numerous reflexes present at or shortly after birth which persist for varying periods of time (Table

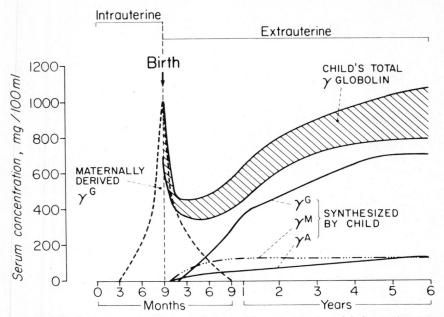

Figure 6–1   Average normal concentrations of the major immunoglobulins in the serum during fetal life and in the first few years of infancy and childhood. From Vaughan, V. C., and McKay, R. J.: Nelson Textbook of Pediatrics, 10th ed. W. B. Saunders Company, Philadelphia, 1975.

6–1). The absence of certain reflexes or their persistence beyond the time when they usually disappear may indicate central nervous system dysfunction.

The eye, as well as the brain, achieves a maximum postnatal growth rate during the first year and continues on at a rapid, but slowing pace until the third year, when anatomic maturity of the eye is reached. Visual maturity, however, is not reached until the sixth year. At birth, the eye is three quarters of adult size. Visual acuity may be about 20/150 at birth, improve to 20/40 by age 2, and to 20/20 by age 4. Although not functional at birth, the tear glands begin to function by 2 weeks of age. Formal visual acuity testing is generally not possible before the age of 3. Prior to age 3 however, visual acuity can be at least partially evaluated by observing the responses of the child to a small toy or similar object of intent.

Audiologic screening of infants can generally be carried out at 6 to 12 months of age by a skilled technician. Current behavioral techniques and a new technique called Brain Stem Evoked Potential allow the audiologist to ascertain auditory responses even in the newborn infant. Although more subtle hearing impairment may be overlooked in infants, current available techniques allow for the audiologist to ascertain in the first few months of life whether an infant has adequate hearing for speech and language development.

Psychosocial

NANCY ROBINSON

During infancy, one sees the emergence of sensorimotor skills, cognitive skills, close attachment to family members, and — that most human of all behaviors — verbal communication. During no subsequent phase of life is there such a rapid emergence of complex skills and individual differences.

Motor Skills. The two most prominent motor abilities to emerge during infancy are walking, or *locomotion*, and use of the hands as tools, or *prehension*. Both are largely maturational in origin, although experience can also play a role. (See Chapter 1.) Typical ages at which motor milestones occur are shown in Figure 6–2. There are few differences among children in the order in which these milestones occur, but significant differences in the ages at which they are attained. For example, 5 per cent of normal infants are walking independently at

TABLE 6–1 AGES OF APPEARANCE AND DISAPPEARANCE OF NEUROLOGIC SIGNS PECULIAR TO INFANCY

Response	Age at Time of Appearance	Age at Time of Disappearance
Reflexes of Position and Movement		
Moro reflex	Birth	1 to 3 months
Tonic neck reflex (unsustained)*	Birth	5 to 6 months (partial up to 2 to 4 years)
Palmar grasp reflex	Birth	4 months
Babinski response	Birth	Variable +
Reflexes to Sound		
Blinking response	Birth	
Turning response	Birth	
Reflexes of Vision		
Blinking to threat	6 to 7 months	
Horizontal following	4 to 6 weeks	
Vertical following	2 to 3 months	
Postrotational nystagmus	Birth	
Food Reflexes		
Rooting response—awake	Birth	3 to 4 months
Rooting response—asleep	Birth	7 to 8 months
Sucking response	Birth	12 months
Handedness	2 to 3 years	
Spontaneous stepping	Birth	
Straight line walking	5 to 6 years	

*Arm and leg posturing can be broken by child despite continued neck stimulus.
+ Usually of no diagnostic significance until after age 2 years.
Adapted from: Children are Different, Ross Laboratories, November, 1978.

DEVELOPMENT FOR THE FIRST YEAR OF LIFE

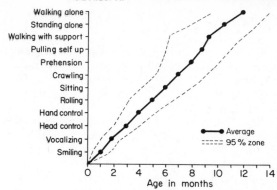

Figure 6–2 Average age for the achievements selected and zone in which 95 percent of observations fell in a group of 215 normal infants. From Children Are Different: Developmental Physiology. Johnson, T. R., and Moore, W. M., Ross Laboratories, p. 33, 1978.

age 9 months, but 5 per cent (some of them also normal) have not begun to walk even at age 16 months. Restriction of opportunity for walking (provided that personal-social stimulation is adequate) does not significantly retard emergence of the skill; casts on the legs and feet of an infant, for example, do not significantly impede locomotion once the casts have been removed. On the other hand, a highly stimulating environment can to some extent accelerate locomotor skills, though the effects of such early stimulation may be largely temporary.

Skills develop in a cephalocaudal (head to foot) direction; they also develop in a central to peripheral gradient. Thus, midline development tends to precede equivalent development in the extremities. At birth, infants exhibit a variety of oral and facial responses which are necessary for breathing and food intake. When placed in a prone position, the newborn's face will turn to the side to avoid suffocation. By 3 months, infants can raise their heads and chests with arms extended and can direct their vision, freely searching for and following moving objects. At 6 or 7 months, infants are often able to sit alone and will stand with support. By 9 months, they can cruise by holding onto furniture, or can take some steps with hands held. Independent walking occurs between 12 and 15 months; stiff running, by 18 months; and by 24 months, most infants can run well without falling. Figure 6–3 presents a mnemonic device to help recall the progression of motor skills in the first year.

Prehension also follows a predictable sequence. Very early, one may see crude movements of the hands; infants seem to throw their hands in the direction of an object, frequently sending it flying. The first voluntary grasp is in the palm, followed by progressive improvement in finger and thumb dexterity. By 12 months, small pellets and pieces of dust can, with some effort, be picked up precisely by thumb and finger (Fig. 6–4). These changes are exemplified in play with simple one inch cubes. At 1 month, infants will give little evidence of

Age	Anatomic Progression	Motor Skill

Birth
(full term)

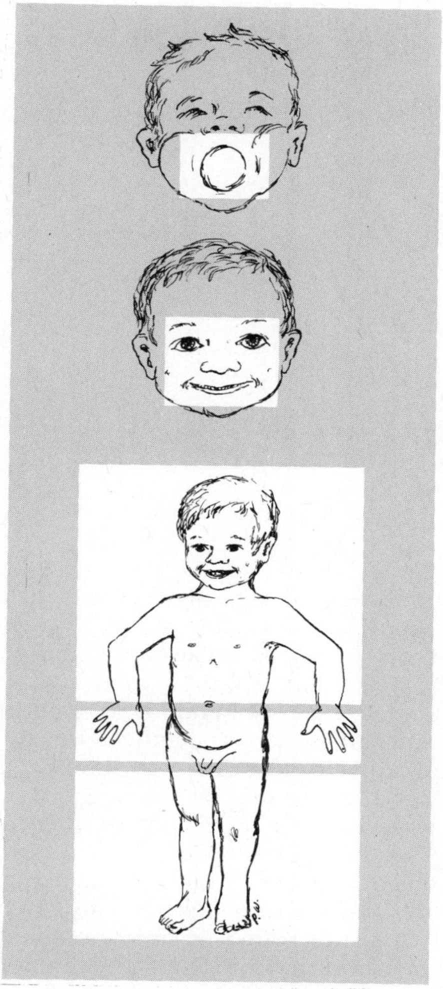

Suck, breathe, and swallow in a coordinated fashion*

3 Months

Directed vision—reaching for objects with eyes

6 Months

Sit with head erect when hips are supported; reach for objects, though grasp of them is immature

9 Months

Sit unaided indefinitely; grasp, using opposition of thumb and fingers (pincer grasp)**

12 Months

Walk unaided

---

*This motor skill can be better appreciated if compared to the necessity of passing a feeding tube into the stomach of an infant born at 28 rather than 38 weeks of gestation.

**Sitting unaided indefinitely is but one of the skills children acquire with control over movement at the hips. Creeping (moving on hands and knees), getting from a prone into a sitting position and back to prone—all of these become a part of the child's activities about this age.

Figure 6–3   Mnemonic for motor development.

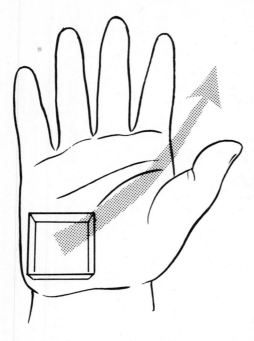

Figure 6–4   Schematization of changes in the portion of the hand used to grasp a one-inch cube during the second six months of life.

even seeing such a cube unless it is specifically "shown" in the line of vision. By 4 months, the hands become active when they see the cube and they may glance back and forth between hands and cube, occasionally making contact. By 5 or 6 months, though, an infant will have achieved directed, one handed reaching and by 6 months, will be transferring a cube with interest from one hand to the other. By 7 months, more than 1 cube at a time will be of interest, and by 9 months they may be combined by banging or touching. By 1 year, the infant may place 1 or several cubes in a container; by 13 or 14 months, stack one on top of another, having solved the problem of voluntary release. The problem of taller towers will emerge only gradually, since this task requires additional cognitive skills of compensating and balancing. By 2 years, the youngster may be able to copy a "train" made by the examiner and may discover other interesting patterns to build with a set of simple cubes.

Perceptual Development.   What does the world seem like to an infant? We know something about the sensory acuity of infants, but perception — the organization and interpretation of sensations — is not quite so easy to decipher. We no longer think, however, that an infant's perceptual world is a "blooming, buzzing confusion," as it was once described by William James. Rather, there is considerable organization built into the central nervous system. We know, for example, that infants perceive objects to remain the same size and shape even though the image on the retina changes as the object is moved nearer or farther away or is turned to reveal a different perspective. Depth perception is also present very early, at least as soon as the infant can crawl. There may even be some "built in" propensities to attend to human faces and voices. Very early, infants are aware of the relation between sights and sounds, and within the first few weeks of life are observed to turn toward sounds such as the calling of their name or the ringing of a bell.

Cognitive Development. During the first 2 years of life, there are rapid advances in what Jean Piaget, a prominent Swiss psychologist, has termed the *sensorimotor stage*. Piaget has called attention to the development of *schemas*, mental representations or ideas about the world. When something comes along that does not quite match babies' schemas, they pay close attention unless the event is so strange that it cannot be understood at all. In time, babies enlarge and refine their schemas and become less interested in minor discrepancies. By about 9 to 12 months of age, however, they begin to try to figure out *why* a discrepant event seems odd. Kagan has called this the *hypothesis stage*. For example, if year old babies are shown a mask on which human features are scrambled, they are likely to stare at it for a much longer period of time than will younger infants.

Piaget has described cognitive development during the first 2 years as "sensorimotor," because the child learns by actually doing and perceiving results. Piaget has described six substages. At first, cognitive activity is mainly composed of practicing the reflexes (such as sucking) already in the repertoire. Gradually, babies start experimenting with producing or prolonging interesting effects they happen to make as they play. They begin to anticipate results, and to find new ways of accomplishing their goals. (For example, they are able to learn to reach around a barrier to get an object when they cannot reach it directly. If a ball rolls under the couch, they will gradually learn not to follow its path, but seeing it roll, to turn and go around the couch to retrieve it.) By the end of infancy, toddlers can even think about previous, familiar events not present at the time, but they are closely tied in time and space, thought and action, to the events they are able to think about.

Communication. The earliest communication patterns are not, of course, words, but rather a complex of vocalizations, facial expressions, and body movements. The baby first communicates by crying. Parents often ask whether they should let infants "cry it out" for fear of "teaching" them to cry for what they want. Quite the opposite is true. Parents who respond promptly and sensitively to their infants' signals do not teach the infants to cry; their babies in fact tend to be happier, calmer, and more outgoing than others. While of course no parent can respond immediately to every infant signal (and indeed, in so doing, would rob the infant of the opportunity to learn self calming skills), there is certainly no reason to encourage parents to be unresponsive to crying, especially during the first half of the first year. Infants in the second year may indeed "use" crying in a manipulative fashion, or may become upset when the adult sets limits. That is a different matter which needs to be settled according to the demands of the specific situation. In the second year, infants can and should be taught that some things in the environment and some behaviors are forbidden ("no-nos") but generally speaking, the best teaching tends to occur when the parent is able to reinforce wanted behavior rather than to punish unacceptable behavior.

The most dramatic early communication aside from crying is the infant's smile, which emerges at about 6 weeks of age, with truly social smiling and chuckling occurring by about 3 months. This smile is highly reinforcing to parents, who until that time may have felt deprived of feedback from the infant. Many will say that at this age, "babies become human." The infant is then capable of participating in a social interchange, with or without vocalization. A clever adult who adapts his or her rhythm of nodding and vocalizing to that of the baby, and pauses to let the infant respond, may produce rapt attention, smiling, and vocalizing for several minutes before the infant turns away. An infant is usually unable to sustain an intense interchange for more than a few minutes before "shutting down" at least briefly. If one watches mothers playing baby games with their infants, it is clear how complex is the mutual process taking place.

Vocalizations increase during the first year. Early vowel sounds give way to syllables beginning with consonants (*ba, ma*) and to double syllables (*mama*) which adults may take to be words long before they become truly specific to a given person or object. By 8 or 9 months, the infant usually becomes attentive to his own name. One or 2 words are expected by a year of age; by age 2, most toddlers have at least 50 words, mostly nouns. Intelligibility at this age may be poor, however, and to "understand" a child the adult may literally have to know already what he or she is thinking. Advances in syntax also begin. By age 2, most children are combining 2 or 3 words in a telegraphic way which reveals simple syntax (the grammatical rules for relationships among words). For example, "Mommy shoe" may mean, "Mommy, please put on my (your) shoe," "Mommy's shoe fell off the couch," and so on. Pivotal sentences are frequent, consisting of a stem word or phrase (e.g., *more*) followed by interchangeable expressions: "More milk," "More bye-bye." Even these early "sentences" show that children are beginning to learn the rules of the language with astonishing accuracy, and many theorists believe that at least some of the rules for the "deep structure" of the language must be built into the biological substrate.

Social Development: Attachment.   The early, stable love relationship, or bonding, between parents and child has both biological and learned components. The human species, with its prolonged developmental period, could not survive unless parents became "hooked" on caring for their infants. Similarly, infant attachment has its adaptive aspects. The mother-child relationship is primary during infancy because of breastfeeding. By the age of 3 months, babies respond somewhat differently to their parents than to strangers, but it is not until perhaps 5 months that definite preferences are shown. Some infants show "stranger anxiety" which peaks at about 8 to 10 months; this is more common in babies who have had restricted experience with other adults. By a year, this stranger anxiety usually diminishes. Infants normally continue to desire their mother's presence, this *attach-*

ment reaching a peak at about age 2 and then decreasing, as the infant *detaches* from the mother and establishes peer relationships.

Infants normally use their mothers as a firm base of security as they begin to move out into the world. As long as the mother is available, the mobile infants may go and come rather freely. Should the mother leave, they may cry and fuss for her, and when she returns, the reunion is usually a joyful one for both. Such infants are said to be *securely attached*. Ordinarily, the mothers enjoy their presence as well and it is clear that attachment is a two way proposition.

COMMON PROBLEMS OF INFANCY
Behavioral

NANCY ROBINSON

Mistrust.   The period of infancy, during which so many skills and individual characteristics emerge, is assumed to be a critical period for personality development. Erik Erikson, a modern day psychoanalyst, discusses infancy as an era of initial orientation. Infants either learn to *trust* or to *mistrust* others, depending on the degree to which their needs have been met and the sensitivity of their care. One way in which a mistrust of the world might be exhibited is an *anxious attachment* to the mother, as opposed to a *secure attachment*. During the latter half of the first year, some babies begin to demonstrate an insecurity which makes itself known through whining, clinging, and fussing for the mother's attention. Anxiously attached infants are often rather passive, and they explore less and exhibit less curiosity than securely attached infants. Paradoxically, when anxiously attached infants are reunited with their mothers after an absence, at first they may show ambivalence toward or even avoidance of their mothers, as though they are responding negatively to the return of a mother they cannot count on. (Yet we should be conservative about labeling "anxious attachment" as "abnormal," since it appears in perhaps a third of infants to a mild degree.) This behavior tends to be a precursor of later problems. Such babies tend to show poorer social skills as preschoolers, less frequent smiling, and less maturity in play than those who were securely attached as infants.

"Difficult" Temperament.   As early as the first few months of life, reasonably stable temperamental differences can be detected in infants. Some infants are "easy" to care for; they are predictable, calm, and organized in their responses to familiar and unfamiliar experiences. Even under stress they tend to remain calm and adaptable, or to experience only temporary, self limited periods of distress. Other children are stolid, apathetic, and unresponsive. Still others are difficult to handle. They are likely to be restless, "skittish," fussy, and vulnerable to overstimulation. Whereas "easy" babies teach their parents how to care for them and give their parents signals which are easy to interpret, "difficult" babies may give confusing signals and may make their parents feel insecure and discouraged. Unhappy circular patterns may be set up, as disappointed and defeated parents respond less and less sensitively to their unrewarding, problematic infants. Special guidance may be called for when such patterns are detected. Parents may be able to use help in acquiring a level of skill in child care which "easy" babies would not require.

Depression.   One sometimes sees infants who have been understimulated and/or neglected, and who have an exceptionally passive and sad orientation which should be interpreted as depression. Many show growth retardation as well. One may also see profound depression in infants who have been hospitalized and deprived of the presence of their parent(s). (Such depression usually follows a brief period of intense protest after which the baby "gives up.") Such signs, if persistent, warrant prompt intervention.

Developmental Delays.   Tests of infant developmental status are notorious for their unreliability. The unreliability is, however, much more characteristic of indices of normal and superior development than of developmental delay (developmental rates roughly three quarters of average, and below). While some children will show developmental lags because of transient illness, surgery, or sensory handicaps, by the latter half of the first year performance which is significantly delayed should be some cause for concern. While dire predictions about long range development should usually be avoided, a referral for evaluation might well be in order, and/or referral to one of the growing number of infant stimulation programs capable of providing sensitive programming for infants and supportive help for parents. (One should also be aware, however, that the long range efficacy of such programs has yet to be demonstrated for truly delayed infants.) Early screening is particularly important for the detection of spastic cerebral palsy, in order that therapy may be instituted promptly.

Nutritional Disorders

Iron Deficiency Anemia.   The most common nutritional disorder in infancy is iron deficiency anemia. The normal full term infant born to a healthy mother generally has iron stores that are adequate until the infant doubles his birthweight (approximately 4 to 5 months of age). As growth proceeds with its associated increased red cell mass, the infant requires additional iron. Since neither human milk nor cow's milk contains significant amounts of iron, other dietary sources must meet the infant's requirements. Dry prepared iron fortified baby cereal, commercial formulas containing iron, or supplemental iron either alone or in a vitamin preparation introduced by 3 months of age will generally prevent this disorder.

Obesity.   Infantile obesity is being recognized increasingly as a problem in developed countries. No longer are fat babies "healthy babies." Obese babies are more likely to grow up to be obese adults than normal weight infants, as are infants born to obese parents. Infants who are overfed produce increased numbers of fat cells which persist throughout life. Experience has shown that attempts at permanent weight reduction of obese adolescents and adults almost uniformly results in failure. Thus, the prevention of obesity through parent education, appropriate infant and childhood feeding practices, and regular exercise throughout childhood and adolescence, is paramount.

Malnutrition. The brain undergoes a series of physical, chemical, and functional changes as it matures. Brain growth is most rapid in the last trimester of pregnancy, and continues at a rapid but decelerating rate throughout infancy. By age 1 year, the brain has reached two thirds of its adult size, and by 2 years it has reached approximately four fifths of adult size. It is during the time of rapid growth that the brain appears to be most vulnerable to the effects of malnutrition. Chronic maternal malnutrition as well as severe malnutrition shortly after birth may be associated with infants with smaller heads, decreased numbers of brain cells, psychomotor delays, and certain behavioral abnormalities. Although a number of factors may be involved, and although the issues are extremely complex, there is increasing evidence that severe malnutrition at the time of critical brain development may be responsible for permanent central nervous sytem impairment.

Accidents and Poisonings

Accidents remain the leading cause of morbidity and mortality in children over 1 year of age in the U.S. In fact, in the 1960's in the United States, accidents accounted for more deaths between 1 and 4 years of age than the next 8 categories of disease combined. It is estimated that for each accidental childhood death that occurs, there are 840 nonlethal serious accidents. If true, this means that approximately 1 of 5 children experiences a minimum of 1 significant accident per year.

No common childhood disorder is more closely tied to childhood development than accidents (Table 6–2). Accidents of infancy occur primarily in the home. Falls, aspiration of foreign objects, ingestions, burns, and drownings are frequent accidents that involve infants. In late infancy and early childhood, accidents involving motor vehicles become increasingly important. Not infrequently, an accident occurs because the infant makes a developmental advance for which the parent is unprepared, i.e., the first time a child rolls over and off the counter or bed, stands up and pulls over the coffeepot, or walks over and investigates the open medicine container.

The level of development and hence, the type of potential accident, determines the type of preventive measures indicated. The young infant must be protected. As the infant grows older, he can gradually learn how to avoid certain hazards. Unfortunately, some accidents will continue to happen. Currently, more than 4 million accidental poisonings occur in the United States each year, and several

TABLE 6–2 ACCIDENT PREVENTION IN INFANCY

Typical Accidents	Normal Behavior Characteristics	Precautions
	First Year	
Falls	After several months of age can squirm and roll, and later creeps and pulls self erect	Do not leave alone on tables or on any surface from which falls can occur
		Keep crib sides up
Inhalation of foreign objects	Places anything and everything in mouth	Keep small objects and harmful substances out of reach
Poisoning		
Drowning	Helpless in water	Do not leave alone in tub of water
	Second Year	
Falls	Able to roam about in erect posture	Keep screens in windows
	Goes up and down stairs	Place gate at top of stairs
Shocks	Has great curiosity	Cover unused electrical outlets; keep electric cords out of easy reach
Motor vehicles	Has great curiosity	Keep in enclosed space when outdoors and not in company of an adult
Ingestion of poisonous substances	Puts almost everything in mouth	Keep medicines, household poisons, and small sharp objects out of sight and reach
Burns	Has great curiosity	Keep handles of pots and pans on stove out of reach and containers of hot foods away from edge of table
Drowning	Helpless in water	Protect from water in tub and in pools

Adapted from: Shaffer, T. E.: Pediatric Clinics of North America, *1*:426, 1954.

times that number of "near misses" occur. With more than one half million commercial chemical compounds available for ingestion, as well as a number of other poisonous substances often readily available to infants and children, it is surprising that more deaths from poisonings do not occur. The development of a national network of poison control centers, as well as a number of other programs which allow rapid identification and treatment of specific poisons, has undoubtedly had a major impact on poisonings in this country. Better medical care, the incorporation of syrup of Ipecac in many medicine cabinets, and childproof medicine containers have all contributed to the decreasing mortality and morbidity associated with childhood poisonings in this country.

Despite popular opinion, scientific evidence suggests that immediate environmental circumstances and family situations, as well as personality patterns, are primarily responsible for childhood poisonings. Prevention, the key to childhood poisonings, rests with close parental supervision, careful monitoring of infants' immediate environments, and the gradual education of the child as development progresses.

Child Abuse

Probably no subject dealing with children is more emotionally charged than the subject of child abuse and child neglect. Since the term "battered child syndrome" was first coined more than a decade ago, the abused or neglected child has been recognized as a major medical and sociological problem. The terms "child abuse" and "neglect" include physical abuse, nutritional deprivation, sexual abuse, emotional abuse, and neglect of medical care. Although accurate statistics are unavailable, it is estimated that child abuse and neglect involves 1 per cent of all children, with approximately 650 new cases per million population occurring each year, resulting in several thousand deaths. Although child abuse may occur at any age, infants and young children are most vulnerable, with one third of cases occurring in infants less than 6 months old and an additional one third occurring in infants between 6 months and 3 years of age. Adults who abuse children come from all ethnic, educational, religious, occupational, and socioeconomic groups. Approximately 5 per cent of those who abuse children are psychotic or sociopathic, but the vast majority do not generally have serious psychopathology. Many child abusers were child abuse victims themselves as infants or had otherwise inappropriate care as children. Characteristically, as adults they feel isolated with few friends or family to provide support in times of crises.

Parents who abuse children desperately need help. Although treatment of child abuse is beyond the scope of this text, protection of a child from further abuse is of utmost importance in any treatment program. Lessening the isolation and providing support and relief to parents in times of crisis are central to any effective treatment program. All parents need help with their children and relief from their care on occasion, particularly during times of crisis. In this respect, parents of abused children are no different from other parents. Why some individuals abuse their children is unclear. There is much to be learned about child abuse, its causes, and its prevention. The problem is becoming increasingly clear; its solution is extremely complex.

Infectious Diseases

Acute Respiratory Disease. Acute respiratory disease (the common cold) in infancy, as in other stages of life, is the most common infectious disease syndrome. The newborn infant, with its maternal antibodies and limited contact, generally has few colds during the first month of life. As passive protection wanes, the infant becomes increasingly susceptible to a host of viruses in the environment. By 3 months of age, approximately 50 per cent of infants have contracted an acute respiratory disease (ARD) infection and by 6 months of age, virtually all have done so. By ages 1 to 2 years, the infant has 8 to 9 ARD infections per year. Certain anatomic and physiological aspects of infants make ARD a particular problem. Newborns and very young infants are obligatory nose breathers. Nasal obstruction therefore presents particular problems in this age group, especially when feeding. Infants also have relatively smaller, less rigid airways with large amounts of lymphoid tissue. Inflammation associated with ARD compromises airflow more readily than in older children, and thus is more likely to result in airway obstruction.

The infant's eustachian tube is shorter, straighter, and more horizontal than the adult's. ARD, with its associated inflammation and swelling, frequently causes obstruction of the eustachian tube resulting in otitis media in the infant. Otitis media, if unrecognized and untreated, can result in significant hearing impairments. In the infant less than 2 years old, one half of otitis medias are caused by two bacteria, Pneumococci and H-influenza. Because of the infant's peculiar immunologic status, H-influenza infections are more common in the 6 months to 2 year old range than in any other time of life. Although less common than otitis media, this organism can cause a host of different infections in infants including meningitis, pneumonia, septic arthritis, empyema, osteomyelitis, cellulitis, pericarditis, and bacterial endocarditis.

Bronchiolitis. During the first year of life, infants may develop, following a typical ARD infection, severe viral respiratory disease involving the lower respiratory tract and particularly the terminal bronchioles. The disease is characterized by terminal bronchioli obstruction and hyperaeration of the lungs. The acute phase may last 2 to 3 days, followed by several more days of symptoms. Treatment is symptomatic and involves rest, fluids, mist, and occasionally oxygen. Generally, bronchodilators, antibiotics, and systemic steroids are of little value. The mortality rate may approach 1 per cent. There are no known sequelae, but some infants with this disorder may be "preasthmatic."

Neoplasia

Two tumors account for the majority of malignant tumors in the first 2 years of life, the neuroblastoma and Wilms' tumor. The peak incidence of neuroblastoma occurs in the first year of life, while Wilms' tumor peaks in the second year. Neuroblastomas arise from sympathetic nervous system ganglia, often in the adrenal medulla, and frequently present as an abdominal mass. Metastases occur early and involve the skeletal system and bone marrow. Treatment usually involves surgery, radiation, and chemotherapy. Spontaneous remissions occur, however, particularly in infants under 6 months of age. With proper treatment in children under 2 years, cure rates exceed 50 per cent.

Wilms' tumor is a form of teratoma arising in the kidney. In approximately 10 per cent of cases, the tumor is bilateral. This tumor generally presents as an abdominal mass and frequently metastasizes to the lungs. With appropriate treatment that generally involves surgery, radiation, and chemotherapy, cure rates in this age group also exceed 50 per cent.

Sudden Infant Death Syndrome

Sudden Infant Death Syndrome (SIDS), also known as "crib death" or "cot death," has become an increasingly important public health problem. SIDS is defined as "the sudden and unexpected death of an infant who was either well or almost well prior to death and whose death remains unexplained after the performance of an adequate autopsy." Approximately 10,000 babies in the United States die each year with SIDS. Although numerous hypotheses have been entertained, the mechanism of SIDS is unknown. Most deaths occur in infants 2 to 4 months of age. Prematures and males are more likely to be involved, as are infants of minorities and lower socioeconomic groups.

Physicians can play a major role in helping families deal with this common, but poorly understood tragedy. By helping to procure an adequate postmortem examination and by assuring parents that they were not responsible for their infant's death, the physician can do much to allay the guilt and anxiety associated with SIDS.

Morbidity and Mortality During Infancy

In 1976, 47,800 infants were born in the United States who died before their first birthday, resulting in an infant mortality rate of 15.1. Stated another way, for every 1000 live births in the United States in 1976, 15.1 infants died before reaching age 1.

The major causes of death in the first year are related to congenital malformations, immaturity, the birth process, and infectious diseases (Fig. 6–5). Of deaths occurring in the first year of life, approximately two thirds occur in the first 28 days. Since 1970, the death rate for infants between 1 month and 1 year has remained relatively constant. The improvement in the infant mortality rate more recently has been related primarily to improving neonatal survival rates (Fig. 6–6).

Accidents are responsible for relatively few deaths during the first year of life, but after age 1 they are the leading cause of death in

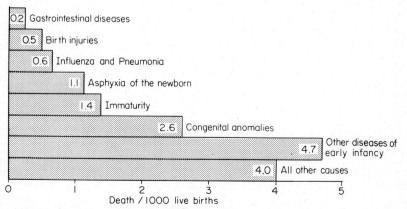

Figure 6–5   1976 Infant mortality in the United States. Based on 10 percent death sample. Data from National Center for Health Statistics.

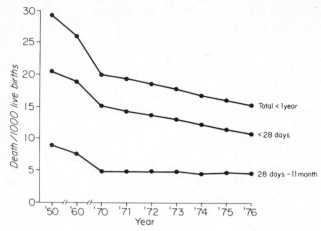

Figure 6–6 Infant mortality by age in the United States for selected years. Data from National Center for Health Statistics.

children. Between the ages of 1 and 4, nonmotor vehicle associated accidents account for two thirds of the accidental deaths. Other leading causes of death between these ages include infectious disease, congenital malformations, and malignant neoplasms.

Accurate morbidity data for infants during the first 2 years of life are difficult to obtain. Acute infectious disease of the respiratory tract, congenital malformations, GI disorders, and various types of traumatic disorders are the most common causes of morbidity in this age group.

PREVENTIVE HEALTH MEASURES
Immunizations

Any discussion of preventive health measures in children should begin with immunizations, for immunizations have been, and continue to be one of the most important preventive health practices in medicine. The impact of current immunization practices on such diseases as diphtheria, tetanus, pertussis, poliomyelitis, rubeola, rubella, smallpox, and to a lesser extent mumps, is well known. Unfortunately, these preventable diseases continue to occur in the United States (except for smallpox), frequently as a result of public apathy, a problem so often associated with preventive health measures.

Current immunization schedules vary, but generally include 3 diptheria, tetanus, and pertussis (DPT) injections, and 3 oral poliomyelitis doses in the first year; a measles, mumps, and rubella immunization at 15 months of age; and a DPT and oral poliomyelitis booster at 18 months and 4 to 5 years of age. Smallpox vaccinations are no longer recommended routinely in the United States. Immunization practices will undoubtedly continue to change as more data become available about current vaccines and as new vaccines become licensed.

Anticipatory Guidance and Parental Counseling

Probably no task in life is more important than the task of raising one's child. Yet, for the average student going through our public school systems, almost no time is devoted to this extremely important aspect of one's adult life. Society assumes if one is biologically able to have children, one is able to be an effective parent. Nothing may be further from the truth. The toll taken by accidents, child abuse and neglect, childhood emotional disorders, and behavioral disorders supports the need to increase help for parents.

Most accidents, particularly those occurring in infancy, are preventable if parents are forewarned. The parent who neglects or abuses his/her child is crying for help. Parental support and guidance begun prenatally and carried through infancy may do much to lessen this significant problem. Emotional and behavioral disorders of childhood frequently have their roots in infancy. Appropriate early parental guidance and counseling as to normalcy and as to what constitutes appropriate parent interaction with infants and children can contribute much to a healthier parent-child relationship.

Other important preventive health measures in infancy include the addition of fluoride to the infant's diet to prevent dental caries if local drinking water is deficient in fluoride, the periodic assessment of the health and development of the infant with particular attention to vision and hearing, and the provision for appropriate, adequate nutrition.

REFERENCES

American Academy of Pediatrics: Standards of Child Health Care. 3rd ed. Evanston, Illinois, American Academy of Pediatrics, 1977.
American Academy of Pediatrics: Report of the Committee on Infectious Diseases. 18th ed. Evanston, Illinois, American Academy of Pediatrics, 1977.
Bower, T. G. R.: A Primer of Infant Development. San Francisco, Freeman, 1977.
Brazelton, T. B.: Infants and Mothers. New York, Dell, 1969.
Erikson, E.: Childhood and Society. 2nd ed. New York, Norton, 1963.
Ginsburg, H., and Opper, S.: Piaget's Theory of Intellectual Development: An Introduction. Englewood Cliffs, New Jersey, Prentice-Hall, 1969.
Smith, D. W.: Growth and Its Disorders. 2nd ed. Philadelphia, W. B. Saunders Company, 1977.
Thomas, A., Chess, S., and Birch, H. G.: The origin of personality. Scientific American, 223:102, 1970.
Wegman, M. E.: Annual summary of vital statistics — 1976. Pediatrics, 60:797, 1977.

7

Childhood

VANJA A. HOLM

The following snapshots show the childhood of the daughter and son of the author (VAH) from infancy through adolescence, and thus relate to both the preceding and following chapters.

Infancy

Figure 7–1 The arrival of the first child effects a drastic change of life for the new parents, but it is also an important event for grandparents. At age 3 weeks, Ingrid already has grandpa "hooked." Note her visual regard of the adult's face.

Figure 7–2 At age 7 months, the typical black hair of the newborn has been replaced by a blond fuzz which reflects Ingrid's genetic background (Northern European). She now sits independently, though with a rounded back, and has discovered that mother is a special person. As a result, she shows "stranger anxiety".

Early Childhood

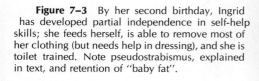

Figure 7–3 By her second birthday, Ingrid has developed partial independence in self-help skills; she feeds herself, is able to remove most of her clothing (but needs help in dressing), and she is toilet trained. Note pseudostrabismus, explained in text, and retention of "baby fat".

Figure 7–4 Baby brother Erik arrived when Ingrid was two years of age. Four months later, Ingrid still is adjusting to the change. An increase in thumb sucking and lapses in toilet training indicate her stress and are common symptoms of sibling rivalry. (Note the baby's tibial torsion.)

Figure 7–5 At age 2½, Ingrid is experimenting during water play, a favorite activity. Keeping busy and having fun helps her become used to her baby brother. (Note the stance with the protruding abdomen.)

Figure 7–6 Ingrid and Erik learn to take turns by "helping" mother when she bakes. Many household activities are fun and interesting to young children. Participation promotes learning, helps children to feel they are part of the household, and provides an opportunity to practice getting along together.

Ingrid 5, Erik 3

Figure 7–7 Being read to is another favorite activity for preschoolers. A bedtime story helps Ingrid and Erik wind down and get ready for sleep.

Figure 7–8 Special days are important in the lives of children. For many young children, Halloween is the most special of them all.

Figure 7–9 Dress-up and pretend are used by preschoolers to recreate and understand the world around them. This time the theme is set by the occasion—it is trick-or-treat time.

Ages 6 to 8

Figure 7–10 The first day of school brings another major change in Ingrid's life. (Note the tendency toward knock-knees.)

Figure 7–11 Mixed dentition begins at age 7. Ingrid swallows with a tongue thrust which tends to push the front teeth outward (note the forward position of the tongue). She still wears an identification bracelet but now also has use for a watch.

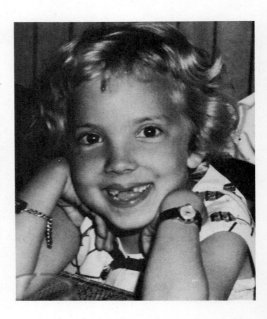

Figure 7–12 Increased independence exposes children to new hazards; Erik broke his arm at day camp. At age 7, he still retains his baby teeth, but like his sister at this age, he is ready for a watch.

Figure 7–13 Fine motor tasks are difficult for Erik and he needs to practice his printing. He does not like it, but it helps to be able to do it outside!

Ages 8 to 10

Figure 7–14 Erik loves to climb and jump; gross motor activities are easy for him and therefore fun.

Figure 7–15 The peer group is important to older elementary-school age children. They cooperate and can be creative and constructive, organizing games, building intricate structures for hiding, etc. Here Erik is making a board for a new game he and his friends are inventing.

Figure 7-16 Like so many girls her age (10), Ingrid is fascinated by horses for a brief period. She now wears braces on her teeth and never smiles around a camera.

Preadolescence to Early Adolescence

Figure 7-17 Older children profit from travel. At ages 11 and 9, respectively, Ingrid and Erik are fortunate to have an opportunity to learn about their "roots" during a trip to Scandinavia. Note that they both still are children in this picture.

Figure 7-18 Two years later, at age 13, Ingrid has suddenly grown up (note body and facial changes). Erik, age 11, is still a child. They may occasionally watch the same T.V. program, but otherwise they have little in common.

Figure 7-19 Children of the same age may show considerable variation in size. At age 11, there are advantages for 3rd percentile Erik in having a 97th percentile 11 year old buddy for safety on the playground.

Figure 7-20 Swimming is a good sport for children of all sizes and shapes (as well as handicapped ones). At age 15, Erik is a slow maturer and thus late in beginning his adolescent growth spurt. His new hair style is dictated by local fashion. (Note the increase in muscle mass, large hands, and mammary fat pads.)

Adolescence

Figure 7–21 Adolescence brings rapid physical and behavioral changes. Parents are apt to note a large appetite and a new interest in grooming, but will probably have less direct contact with their youngsters than when the children were smaller. Most adolescents develop strong special interests, like music or sports. Erik discovers that a short but agile youngster can compete in tennis. His large friend in Figure 7–19 is into football and wrestling. (Note the adult posture with both thoracic and lumbar curvature.)

Figure 7–22 Friends and peer groups continue to be important but socializing is now usually in sexually mixed groups. Erik is finally taller than Ingrid (right behind him) at age 17. At this New Year's Eve party, he is still shorter than several of the girls, however.

Figure 7–23 Adolescence is a time to find out who you are. That necessitates privacy and time to think, to read, and to dream. Here, Erik is captured in a serene interlude during otherwise tumultuous times. (Note the change in facial appearance with the growth of the mid-facial area.)

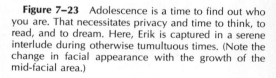

18 years — A Young Adult

Figure 7–24 Ingrid at a friend's wedding admiring the best man—her high school boyfriend. (Note that her hair now is darker and that she smiles again after years of orthodontic work.)

Figure 7–25 A few months later Ingrid has left her boyfriend and family, and is making new friends in college far away from home.

Figure 7–26. Erik is not as sure of his future plans but expects to probably end up in an occupation and with a lifestyle similar to "the old man's." He is shorter than his father, but being a late bloomer, he is still growing.

LIFE SITUATION

The years from the end of infancy to the beginning of adolescence span approximately a decade. It is a time of rapid physical, mental, and emotional growth and development. Daily changes are subtle during childhood, but appear dramatic when one compares the gestalt (total picture) of the infection prone, family dependent, imaginative preschooler (Figs. 7–6 through 7–9) to the robust, peer oriented, enterprising child of secondary school age (Figs. 7–14 through 7–16). Physical, physiological, and behavioral phenomena change with growth, and thus "normality" changes in the individual who is still developing. Hearing parents' concerns about problems in the child, professionals are tempted to reassure them, "He'll grow out of it." Before doing so, however, the professional should consider the child's state of maturation. Some childhood problems are common and temporary phenomena, some are signs of serious disorder.

Physical Development

The rates of growth in height and weight during the childhood years are undramatic compared to those in preceding and ensuing life periods, but height and weight constitute a summation of changes in many parts of the body. An appreciation of differential growth rate (Fig. 7–27) is needed to understand the variations found in physical characteristics during the childhood years. Growth of different tissues is discussed in detail in Chapter 1.

Body Proportions. One result of the variations in growth rate of different systems is a change in body proportions during childhood. The extremities grow relatively quickly compared to the trunk. The brain and the skull accomplish 70 per cent of their growth by age 2 and will reach almost adult size by age 5. Subcutaneous adipose tissue shows a relative decrease in growth rate during the early part of this period and muscle mass increases slowly but steadily. As a result, though the 2 year old appears chubby, with relatively short legs and large head (Fig. 7–5), the baby turns into a slender, lithe 5 year old (Fig. 7–10), who insidiously becomes a long legged and increasingly sturdier school age child (Fig. 7–17).

Posture. Posture also changes with growth. The rounded back of the infant who has just learned to sit (Fig. 7–2), turns into the stance characteristic of the toddler: lumbar lordosis and a protruding abdomen (Fig. 7–5). This posture is transformed as the earlier forward tilt of the pelvis is straightened and the abdominal muscles become better developed. The convex curvature of the thoracic spine finally develops during the early school years (Fig. 7–15), but full adult posture is not assumed until after the increased muscular growth during adolescence (Fig. 7–21).

Growing children should be examined periodically for the possibility of a sideways curvature of the spine (scoliosis). Figure 7–28 demonstrates how this is done. Tell the child to clasp both hands together and bend down reaching toward the floor. Visual inspection combined with a straight object, such as a ruler, will detect asymmetry of the thoracic cavity which signals the presence of scoliosis. Scoliosis detection programs in schools have shown that 10 per cent of children have this condition. These children need to be followed in order to detect the ones with progressive scoliosis, which will need bracing.

Lower Extremities. Great variations in the appearance of the lower extremities are found among children. Most of these are of no functional concern, but are a cause of worry to parents for cosmetic reasons. Some of these variations reflect normal growth; for example, toeing-out and toeing-in. The relatively top heavy 2 year old has a wide stance and the feet usually point out (Fig. 7–5) because there is a normal outward rotation of the legs at the hip. Growth and functional stresses subsequently contribute to an inward rotation of the hips (in the older child the hip allows approximately 30 degrees rotation inwards and 60 degrees rotation outwards), which results in the disappearance of the typically everted feet of early childhood. Instead, the older preschooler might be pigeontoed. This toeing-in may occur if inward rotation of the lower legs (tibial torsion), which is normal in

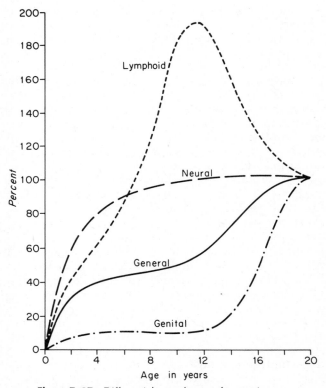

Figure 7–27   Differential growth rate of some tissues.

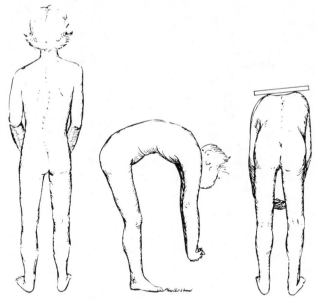

Figure 7–28 Scoliosis and how to assess it.

early infancy (Fig. 7–4), is still present. It might also occur if the legs are straight but the forefoot turns inward. A more severe form of this so called metatarsus adductus is an abnormal congenital condition which merits treatment in early infancy. Finally, toeing-in might be due to excessive inward rotation of the hip beyond the neutral position called femoral anteversion. Most instances of these conditions (tibial torsion, mild metatarsus adductus, and femoral anteversion) disappear with or without treatment. Corrective shoes or appliances, which create stress that influences the direction of growth of the bones, can be prescribed. They are needed by children who are literally falling over their own feet, to shorten the time it takes them to grow out of their toeing-in.

Other normal growth phenomena which often cause parental concern about the appearance of the legs include the presence of a fat pad in the instep of most toddlers, which makes them appear flatfooted, and a mild degree of knock knee, which is frequently present during the late preschool years (Fig. 7–10). Both conditions are usually temporary.

Face. Facial appearance shows characteristic changes during childhood. The toddler's face appears small compared to the skull, the mandible is small, the eyes appear relatively far apart, and the nasal bridge is low. As a result, the young child may appear cross eyed, demonstrating the so called pseudostrabismus (Fig. 7–3). One can detect that this phenomenon is an optical illusion by noting how a source of light reflects in a child's eyes looking at a distant object. Note that there is a light reflex at the same place (at 3 o'clock) related to the outer rim of the iris in Figure 7–3.

As the child ages, the face seems to grow out from under the skull (compare the boy's face in Figs. 7–6, 7–14, 7–20, and 7–23). This stems from the relatively rapid growth of the maxilla and the mandible. The sequential replacement of the primary teeth by the larger, more yellowish permanent teeth has an additional profound effect on the facial appearance of the school age child (Fig. 7–11). The complicated differential growth process of the facial structures frequently results in maladaptive development, not all of which is temporary. A large percentage of children ideally require professional supervision by dental specialists during this growth phase to allow for satisfactory development of the lower part of the face in terms of bite occlusion as well as for cosmetic purposes (Fig. 7–24).

Physiological Development

Physiological measurements change with age as a result of the complex interplay of growth, maturation, and aging. It is therefore common to refer to age norms when evaluating blood pressure, heart and respiratory rate, and blood count. Changes in some of these measurements are significant during childhood. For example, the differential white blood cell count changes from a larger percentage of lymphocytes in early childhood, to a greater proportion of leukocytes in the older child, and the hematocrit shows a steady increase.

When assessing certain physiological processes in childhood, it is sometimes important to correct for physical size rather than age. There are great variations in the height and weight of normal children of the same age (Fig. 7–19). Hence it is generally preferable to consider nutritional requirements and drug dosage in relation to height and weight (usually weight) rather than in terms of age. Surface area, estimated from height and weight measurements, is often used when a most exact correction for size is necessary, as for calculating intravenous fluid requirements.

Gastrointestinal and Urinary Tracts. Most body systems are functionally mature at the onset of this biologic age. The kidneys are well differentiated, and specific gravity and other urine findings are now similar to those of the adult. The toddler's gastrointestinal tract can handle most adult foods, but children's nutritional requirements change with age.

The neurophysiological pathways necessary for voluntary control of the sphincters, which regulate the elimination from these two body systems, mature in early childhood. There is considerable variability in the individual's achievement of this control. If left alone, most normal children toilet train themselves by imitation during their third year of life. The process may, however, be interfered with by psychosocial factors. To be clean and smell good still has high priority in our society, and the temptation to hurry toilet training is therefore great. Habit training can become a battle between parent and child. If the adult carries coercion to an extreme, the child may develop chronic constipation accompanied by soiling (encopresis).

Enuresis is another example of how physiological and psychosocial factors interact in children. Most children probably become physiologically "ready" to stay dry during their third year, but 10 to 15 per cent still wet their beds regularly at age 5. The incidence varies in different socioeconomic groups and there are cultural and familial variations. Enuresis is much more common in boys than girls. That some children wet their beds only after a stressful day, and that the incidence of enuresis is high in both boys and girls who are considered disturbed is additional evidence of the role psychosocial factors play in enuresis.

Another childhood problem, which is so common that it is often considered "normal," is the complaint of abdominal pain. The pains are real and probably related to the physiology of the gastrointestinal system. However, they may occur at breakfast time on school days or follow some other patterns that indicate a strong psychosocial component which needs to be further explored.

Immunologic System. The immunologic system reaches functional maturity early and allows for adequate response to challenges from infectious agents during childhood. The child builds up immunity to common pathogens upon exposure to them. The young child, therefore, easily succumbs to colds, intestinal infections, the common contagious diseases, and other infections prevalent in the community. Again, social factors may influence immunity. The first and only child often experiences frequent infections when social contacts are first broadened upon entering nursery school or kindergarten. A child with siblings a few years older often suffers these infections at an earlier age.

Circulation and Respiration. The circulatory and respiratory systems have, of course, been operating since birth, but their functions are influenced by physical size. Heart murmurs resulting from the passage of blood through normal heart valves are often heard in the growing child. Soft, so called physiological or functional murmurs of no medical consequence are present in as many as 50 per cent of children at one time or another, because of the thinness of the chest wall and the changing relations between the chest and the inner organs due to growth. The diameter of the upper respiratory tract in a young child is small compared to that of the adult. Disastrous effects from obstruction of the critical upper airway can be caused in small children by swelling from inflammation, such as that which occurs in an infection of the epiglottis, or by inhalation of even tiny foreign bodies.

Reproductive and Endocrine Systems. The reproductive and endocrine systems change little until late in childhood, when the profound changes of adolescence are heralded by an initially slow, then rapidly increasing change in endocrine functions. Of course, the endocrine system with its many interrelating hormones has profound effects during childhood as it interacts with almost all aspects of physical growth and development. Its influence is probably best appreciated when studying the "experiments of nature" afforded by the appearance of abnormal endocrinological states in childhood (see Chapter 1).

Central Nervous System and Sensory Organs. In contrast to most other systems, this neurophysiological maturation continues throughout childhood and is of far reaching importance. Sequential maturation of the central nervous system allows the growing child to perform increasingly complex tasks requiring coordination of gross and fine motor control. At 3 years of age, most children can ride a tricycle; by 7, a bike. At 4 years of age, they can cut with scissors and button their coats; by 9, most children can sew or build models. There are great individual variations in the maturation of fine and gross motor skills, which should be considered when planning for a child's participation in activities such as competitive athletics or organized music programs.

Neurophysiological changes pave the way for language, learning, and behavioral development. Observations of these processes are made by behavioral scientists studying intellectual, social, and emotional growth and development, as discussed in the next section.

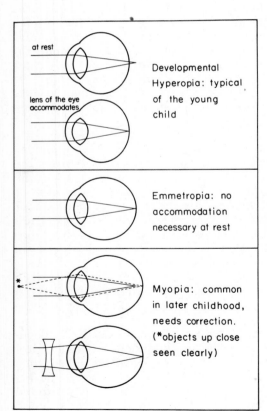

at rest

lens of the eye accommodates

Developmental Hyperopia: typical of the young child

Emmetropia: no accommodation necessary at rest

Myopia: common in later childhood, needs correction. (*objects up close seen clearly)

Figure 7–29   Changes of the eye during childhood.

Of the specialized sensory organs, the physiological changes in the eye during childhood are of most practical importance (Fig. 7–29). The young child's eye is normally hyperopic (the image of an object at a distance falls behind the retina). This condition is of no consequence, however, as children easily accommodate by increasing the power of their malleable lens to refract the light waves. In fact, most children's power of accommodation is so great that they can clearly see an object right in front of their nose. As the eye grows in length and changes during childhood, children often become emmetropic (the image of a distant object falls on the retina without accommodation). Persistence of mild hyperopia is common into adulthood. If the eye becomes too long, the child becomes myopic, i.e., the image of the distant object focuses in front of the retina and appears blurred. This situation is common, often familial, and should be corrected with glasses. It is important to appreciate that the myopic (nearsighted) child does not complain of poor vision, since such a child knows nothing else. Astigmatism, the uneven refraction of light through the different meridians of the eye, is another variation of eye growth. If marked, it needs correction, especially in the older child, as it may distort the image of letters and numbers enough to blur them and confuse the child.

Vision, as it can be measured, seems to improve up to about 5 years of age, when most normal children have a measured vision of 20/20 (Table 7–1). This apparent improvement in vision is due to behavioral and neurologic maturation, not to changes in the eye *per se.* Note that a marked discrepancy in vision between the two eyes (more than one level, e.g., vision of 20/20 in one eye and 20/40 in the other) is abnormal at any age.

Children's response to the testing of their hearing also changes with age. A satisfactory hearing screen by conventional means cannot usually be obtained until a child is 4 to 5 years old. Responses on audiologic testing of younger children have to be interpreted with a background knowledge of how children typically behave during hearing testing at different ages. Children in whom hearing problems are suspected should therefore be evaluated by specially trained audiologists. Significant hearing loss is one of the most commonly overlooked serious handicaps in young children.

TABLE 7–1   DEVELOPMENT OF VISUAL ACUITY*

Age	Visual Acuity
1	20/200
2	20/40
3	20/30
4	20/25
5	20/20

*L. B. Holt, Pediatric Ophthalmology, Philadelphia, Lea & Febiger, 1964, p. 15.

Psychosocial Development

NANCY ROBINSON

Remarkable psychosocial changes occur during childhood, as the child moves through the preschool era, when home is the major base of operations, to the school years, when the "out of home" environment and the peer group assume special importance.

One way to conceptualize the developmental tasks of this era is that proposed by Erik Erikson. You will remember that Erikson states that the major task of the first year is to establish a feeling of *trust* in the world. During the second year, when the child is first being socialized in an organized way (for example, when toilet training is instituted), a major task becomes that of preserving the child's sense of *autonomy* and self direction (the alternative being dominance by feelings of shame and doubt). For the preschooler, Erikson stresses the development of a sense of *initiative* (versus guilt). The healthy preschooler is a busy, confident, expansive, active person who enjoys doing things for the sake of doing them. By the grade school years, a sense of *industry* is needed; children learn to win approval and self acceptance by making and doing things approved in the culture, such as learning to read and cope with the world outside the home. Persistent failure at such tasks leads to a sense of inferiority, a discouragement and undervaluation of the self which complicates and solidifies the original reason for failure to succeed. Although Erikson's vantage point is that of a modern day psychoanalyst, these life tasks are meaningful from many other viewpoints of normal childhood development.

Cognitive Development. Let us return to the work of Piaget to understand some of the striking intellectual changes occurring during this period. Piaget describes the period of approximately ages 2 to 7 as the *preoperational period*. He means by this that logical operations have not yet developed. During the first part of this period (to approximately age 4), the *preconceptual* stage, one sees the first big steps toward symbolic thought, but the child does not truly reason. Concepts are developing, including language, but children make many mistakes and often their concepts do not coincide with those of adults. They may call all fruits "apple," for example, or conversely, may not recognize (as an apple) an apple of any color other than red.

During the *perceptual* or *intuitive* stage (ages 4 to 7) reason comes into play, but it is a reason based on the way things seem. The child reasons very unsystematically, proceeding only a bit at a time, and is not yet capable of grasping the "big picture" of how things work. Children may reason that if their birthday party is postponed, their birthday will not occur, or a boy might reason that if he were to put on a dress, he might change into a girl. (The latter confusion is very common.) Children at this age are egocentric in their thought and cannot see things from another's point of view. They assume that everyone sees things the same way they do. Their thinking also has a naive and magical quality. For instance, they believe that things and phenomena in the physical world are alive (e.g., wind, airplanes) or dead (e.g., trees on a calm day) according to whether they move. They have difficulty perceiving that some of their vivid experiences, such as dreams or television plays, are not real. They may also think that they can control the world through wishes and rituals. One of the most striking features of their thought is the inability to focus attention simultaneously on more than one aspect of an event. Piaget calls this the tendency to *center*. Preoperational children are thus stuck with the most compelling part of what they perceive. For example, if one of two equal balls of clay is rolled into a "weenie" shape, the child probably will think it is larger, because it is longer than it was; if one of two equal rows of pennies is bunched up, it will seem to the child to contain fewer pennies. In other words, the child does not show *conservation*; reasoning is too unsystematic for that. Similarly, the preoperational child shows *irreversibility* (what goes up does not necessarily come down; $2 + 2 = 4$ is unrelated to $4 - 2 = 2$).

By school age, however, children are on the verge of entering the stage of *concrete operations*. Suddenly, perceptions of the world become more systematic. Thinking becomes much more flexible and integrated. Conservation problems become very easy; arithmetic operations make sense. Children become interested in classifications of knowledge and are able to set up hierarchical systems which are more complex than the simple clusters of which they were previously capable. Their systems now can take two or more dimensions into account at once, with some higher order classifications able to encompass lower order ones. Still, the children are rooted in concrete experience and have difficulty with abstract concepts. They have trouble, for example, sorting out the events of history into any refined time sequence, and their concepts are still likely to be unexpectedly literal and specific. The main periods of cognitive growth are summarized in Table 7–2. Ages should not be taken too literally; they are approximations.

TABLE 7–2 PRINCIPAL PERIODS OF COGNITIVE GROWTH ACCORDING TO JEAN PIAGET

Sensorimotor Period (0 to 2 years)
    Progress through six stages, from practice of reflex activity through experimentation with producing and prolonging interesting effects and then creating new effects, to the point that some foresight and initial symbolic representation occurs. (See Chapter 6.)

Preoperational Period (2 to 7 years) Thinking tends to be naive, egocentric, animistic, and magical
    Preconceptual stage (2 to 4 years) Unsystematic thought processes; initial concepts may be inaccurate, does not "reason."
    Perceptual or intuitive stage (4 to 7 years) "Reasoning" remains prelogical, intuitive, tied to appearances. Centering and irreversibility are prominent.

Concrete Operational Period (7 to 11 years)
    Systematic thought processes emerge, including logical operations and reversibility. Classification becomes complex, but concepts are rooted in concrete experience.

Formal Operational Period (11 years onward)
    Highly logical and abstract hypotheses appear. "Reality" (concrete experience) seen as only one possibility of many. Truly scientific hypothesis testing appears. (See Chapter 8.)

Communication. The development of language during early childhood is astonishing. By school age, most aspects of adult language have been mastered, and from there on growth is a matter of refinement and expansion. By age 2 most children are combining 2 or 3 words in "telegraphic" sentences; their vocabulary may be 50 to 100 words, on the average. By age 3, vocabulary has expanded to some 1000 words and approximately 80 per cent of a child's utterances can be understood by strangers. But it may well be age 8 or so before the child pronounces all sounds in an adult fashion. By age 3, children are able to invent sentences at will to express the variety of their experiences. These sentences are formed following the rules of the language, which children absorb very rapidly. Indeed, their mistakes reveal just how strongly they do follow the rules. Although at first they may accept irregular verbs (which they learn as separate words), soon they begin to regularize them ("Daddy goed to work," "I beed a good boy"). Well into first grade, they may persist with "mouses" for "mice," and "seed" for "saw." There may eventually be some compromises such as "mices" or "wented," as though even having understood that the forms are different, they cannot quite give up the notion that basic rules always apply.

Table 7–3 describes the development of syntax. Although the ages are only approximations, note the impressive speed with which children begin to use adult forms of speech.

A child who is not exhibiting generalized developmental delay, and yet has no words by age 2, or who is not combining 2 or 3 words by age 3, should have an audiological examination followed by a careful speech and language evaluation, with prompt therapeutic intervention if it seems appropriate.

Social Development. Qualitative changes occur at the beginning of the preschool period in the parent-child relationship. As children acquire increasing mobility (and mischief making ability), they also begin to test out their powers and limitations as individuals. The "Terrible Two's" describes a typical change from a compliant and easily managed toddler to one who insists on doing everything "myself," and objects to parental suggestions as a matter of principle. Successful parents manage the environment so that it is interesting but safe, make themselves available as resources, teach as much by example as possible, and concentrate on reinforcing wanted behavior while ignoring as much of the unwanted behavior as they comfortably can. Selected limits are enforced consistently, but the parent tries to manage matters astutely enough that confrontations are minimized. When they occur, they can be handled matter of factly, the tantruming child simply being placed in his room or picked up and transported, without comment, out of the grocery store and into the car. As language develops, explanation and compromise become more possible, particularly with a child who has established some feeling of confidence and autonomy.

Many parents find age 3 to be a compliant and expansive age. At age 4, however, some tensions again appear in parent-child relationships, in part perhaps because the children are becoming highly imag-

TABLE 7–3 SIX STAGES IN CHILDREN'S SYNTACTIC DEVELOPMENT

Stage of Development	Nature of Development	Sample Utterances
1. Sentencelike word (1–2 yrs.)	The word is combined with nonverbal cues (gestures and inflections).	"Mommy." "Mommy!" "Mommy?"
2. Modification (1.5–2 yrs.)	Modifiers are joined to topic words to form declarative, question, negative, and imperative structures.	"Pretty baby." (declarative) "Where Daddy?" (question) "No play." (negative) "More milk!" (imperative)
3. Structure (2–3 yrs.)	Both a subject and predicate are included in the sentence types.	"She's a pretty baby." (declarative) "Where Daddy is?" (question) "I no can play." (negative) "I want more milk!" (imperative)
4. Operational Changes (2.5–4 yrs.)	Elements are added, embedded, and permutated within sentences.	"Read it, my book." (conjunction) "Where is Daddy?" (embedding) "I can't play." (permutation)
5. Categorization (3.5–7 yrs.)	Word classes (nouns, verbs, and prepositions) are subdivided.	"I would like *some* milk." (use of "some" with mass noun) "Take me *to* the store." (use of preposition of place)
6. Complex Structures (5–10 yrs.)	Complex structural distinctions made, as with "ask-tell" and "promise."	"Ask what time it is." "He promised to help her."

Adapted from Wood, Barbara S.: Children and Communication: Verbal and Nonverbal Language Development, pp. 129, 148, 1976. Reprinted by permission of Prentice-Hall, Inc., Englewood Cliffs, New Jersey.

inative but not yet quite able to distinguish their fantasies from reality. They are therefore likely to run into conflict with their parents' view of reality and responsibility. Around age 5, relationships may become more complex, with special closeness developing with the parent of the opposite sex. When children reach school age, the intensity of the parent-child relationships tends to diminish (the so called "latency age") as the child becomes a full fledged participant in the outside world, although of course the family remains an essential focus and support throughout childhood.

Peer relations emerge during the preschool era. Toddlers engage in *solitary play,* often acknowledging and watching other children but not really playing with them. *Parallel play* follows; preschoolers play side by side, with similar materials, but interacting minimally. By age 3 or so *cooperative play* emerges, with complementary role taking, which becomes a major avenue of learning. By school entry, stable friendships appear, with "best friends" becoming central, and the child without friends is lonely and unhappy. Parallel with these one to one friendships, groups emerge in the school and neighborhood. Whereas preschool "groups" are simply collections of individual children, informal school age groups tend to have acknowledged leaders, rules, locations, and activities of their own. Children's groups by third or fourth grade may become distinctly exclusive, defining identity as much by who is left out as by who belongs. These manuevers can be cruel and hurtful to others. Adult led groups (such as Scouts and soccer or baseball teams) can exert a positive influence.

Peer influence increases sharply during the elementary years, reaching a peak in adolescence. Conformity becomes the rule in dress, in language, and in tastes and preferences. During the school years, games take on new importance. These reflect the stages of cognitive growth we have discussed. Until about age 5, most children do not care much for games with rules; soon they begin to insist on playing games "by the rules" they first learn, and resist any revision. Then they become fascinated, along with their friends, with developing their own elaborate sets of rules, which may be detailed and arbitrary. Eventually the rules become accepted as flexible conventions to be adopted for specific purposes, with respect for fair play. By this time, children are comfortable in systematic thought processes and can see that a total mental structure, or game, will not be destroyed if one part is modified. This is indeed a significant advance.

MORTALITY AND MORBIDITY

As can be seen in Figure 7–30, the death rate (mortality) of children 1 to 4 years of age is more than twice that of children 5 to 14 years of age, 0.9 per 1000 versus 0.4 per 1000. The incidence of disease (morbidity) for ages 5 to 14 is presented in Figure 7–31. Age significant differences, when present, will be alluded to in the text in the section below on "Common Problems."

COMMON PROBLEMS

Problems of Behavior

NANCY ROBINSON

Children are expected to behave essentially as parents ask, and later, as school authorities and peers expect. The degree to which they fail to do so may range from trivial to severe, and the reasons

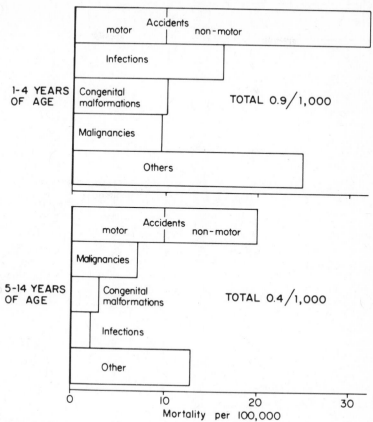

Figure 7–30 Mortality rates in early and later childhood, U.S.A., 1965. (Adapted from the Public Health Service, National Vital Statistics Division.)

may lie in constitutional factors, inappropriate learning, or both, as is usually the case. Indeed, the behavior problems common to childhood are numerous. (See Figure 7–31.) A partial list would include accident proneness, aggressiveness, destructiveness, disobedience, eating problems, encopresis, enuresis, fire setting, hyperactivity, immaturity, language delay, lying, poor peer adjustment, reading problems, school phobia, lack of school readiness, sibling rivalry, sleep problems, stealing, and thumb sucking. A variety of physical symptoms such as asthma, obesity, and chronic stomachache also may have significant behavioral components.

"Normal" Problems of the Preschool Years. There are unavoidable stress points for even the most "normal" children and families from ages 2 through 5. Early, the parents must cope with toddlers who have enormous mobility but lack judgment, who cannot anticipate dangers and must be monitored at all times to avert catastrophes. Toddlers come with no built in inhibitions, no tact or "cover up."

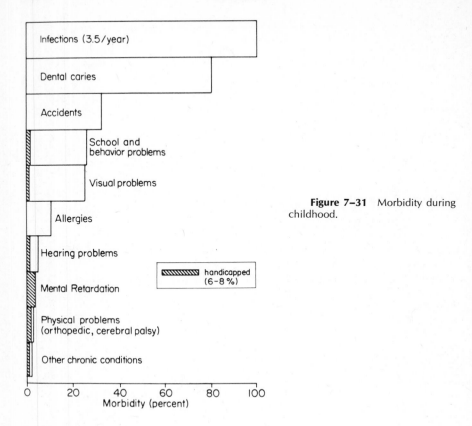

Figure 7–31   Morbidity during childhood.

Adults may be upset by behavior such as smearing of feces, property destruction, and frank statements of fact ("Grandma, why are you so fat?"). The "Terrible Twos" run head on into adult authority, and the adults find it very hard to set limits consistently, for they sympathize with the growing autonomy of the young child. Young children also have a difficult time distinguishing reality from fantasy and may be accused of "lying" to adults; the children, on the contrary, cannot take anyone else's point of view. They understand only their own immediate experience and do not reason rationally. Little wonder that the preschool years are a time of vulnerability, when it is easy for relationships with parents and peers to take an unhealthy direction.

Disobedience.   Noncompliance covers many problems of childhood in which the child does not do as adults direct. Parents typically spend a great deal of time verbally trying to make the child mind without following through on their demands. If the child is asked to mind once and does not, some logical consequence, such as spending a few moments in another room, should follow disobedience. Handling the situation this way tends to decrease the amount of noncompliance, but it is equally important that cooperative and desirable behaviors be appreciated and reinforced by the parents.

School Achievement Problems. Most children in the United States attend preschool (some three quarters of 4 year olds and virtually all 5 year olds in urban areas), but aside from problems of noncompliance and aggressiveness, most preschools are flexible enough that there is a wide range of latitude for individual differences. But upon entry into regular school, children are suddenly faced with a whole new set of demands to keep still, pay attention, and learn new skills and concepts on a predetermined schedule. Most children do cope with these demands, but those with subtle perceptual, social, or other developmental problems may not succeed in an unsympathetic school environment. By the age of 8 or 9, most children who experience school failure also suffer severe damage to their self image. Reading is by far the most frequent school task at which children of normal intelligence fail. Such children are sometimes said to be *dyslexic* (which simply means they have trouble reading) or to show *specific learning disabilities* or *language/learning disabilities.* These terms are not very precise. Such disabilities occur more often in boys, tend to run in families, and may reflect subtle developmental problems of genetic, prenatal, or perinatal origin which have not been apparent until school entry. Even when the problem is of underlying biological origin, the solution lies in teaching adapted to the child's own individual needs and at least as much focus by teacher and parents on what the child does well as on what he needs to learn. Most of these youngsters eventually learn to read, but it is important to attempt to reduce the amount of discouragement and frustration they experience before mastering this skill.

Hyperactivity. Poor attention span, inability to attend to tasks, and many forms of annoying activity are loosely referred to by the term "hyperactivity." There is great controversy surrounding appropriate therapy for the child who exhibits this problem. The constellation of symptoms has a physiological base in some children, and is sometimes associated with "soft" neurological signs; many parents of hyperactive children were themselves hyperactive during childhood. In other children, it appears to be the result of anxiety and other factors of environmental origin. Perhaps a third of preschool and young school age boys are considered "overactive" by parents and teachers, so reports of "hyperactivity" should be carefully evaluated by the professional. A number of medications, methylphenidate (Ritalin) being most prominent, have been offered as therapy for hyperactivity. Long term side effects of these drugs are not known, although sleeplessness, appetite loss, and reduced growth are known to result from some. It is advisable to monitor behavior in a double blind method (both teachers and parents unaware) to be sure that such medication actually has the desired effect (and does not reduce desirable as well as undesirable behavior), that the dosage is not excessive, and that the pay off is not simply more manageable behavior, but is, in fact, enhanced learning (an outcome which is less frequent than is often supposed). Behavioral management is also a potent tool to use at home and at school, with reduced reinforcement (e.g., teacher attention) when the child is out of seat or otherwise overactive, and attention deliberately given for desirable behavior—quite the opposite pattern to that found in most homes and classrooms.

Aggression. Learning to curb one's inclination to hurt others when frustrated or hurt oneself is a complicated process in our society. Different segments of the society handle and value aggression in different ways, and many children receive very inconsistent messages about how to behave. Even within the family messages may conflict. One may be expected both to "turn the other cheek" and to "stand up for one's rights" or those of the underdog. Aggression may be increased by (1) continued frustration of the child's needs; (2) reinforcement (especially inconsistent reinforcement) for aggressive behavior (the bully may get his way; the tantrum may succeed); and (3) aggressive models, especially neighborhood peers, parents, and possibly television.

Peer Adjustment. As we have seen, the peer group assumes enormous importance for the school age child, and rejection by peers has a significant effect. Early encouragement of positive ("prosocial") behaviors is one way to prepare a child for success in this realm. When a child encounters difficulties, there is little a parent or teacher can do by direct intervention, but it is often helpful to listen to the child's perceptions supportively, to acknowledge the pain being experienced, and to help him or her to think through causes and alternative solutions.

Sexual Development and Sex Education. Overt manifestations of abnormalities in sexual development (mainly significant gender confusion) are rare in children, but parents may misinterpret normal expressions of childhood development in this area. At about 4 years of age, when most children become aware of the physical differences between sexes, mutual visual inspection of sex organs is common. In their role playing, young children may play doctor and undress each other or even pretend to perform the sex act. Masturbation continues all through childhood. In older children, it is more common in boys and is usually done in privacy. Preadolescent children often have "crushes" on teachers and other persons of their own sex.

Sex education has not kept pace with social changes which encourage a new openness about sex in the public media. In most communities, schools and other institutions offer little support to parents in this realm. Children need to learn not only the facts, but also to gain an understanding of the highly cooperative nature of sexuality; as adolescents, they will also need information about contraceptives, venereal disease, avenues through which to seek assistance, and a serious attitude of responsibility with respect to reproduction.

The matter of sexual molestation within the family has recently come to professional and public attention, usually molestation of preadolescent and adolescent girls by male members of the family or family friends. Usually these incestuous and exploitative relationships occur in disorganized families where the mother cannot be counted on to protect or even to support the child, and the adult male feels inadequate and a failure. Sexual exploitation is frequently only a part of a general picture of child abuse. Like other forms of abuse, it is the responsibility of the professional to see to it that the child receives protection from an appropriate agency.

Chemical Agents and Trauma

In children, these two causes of mortality and morbidity are closely linked. Even though they cause symptoms by different routes and their treatment differs, the epidemiology and psychosocial implications are so similar that they can profitably be discussed together as "accidents."

Accidents. Accidents are the main cause of death during childhood. Some 15,000 children die in accidents in the United States every year; 3 times as many are permanently disabled. Three out of 10 children under 15 years of age sustain some kind of injury requiring treatment within any one year (Fig. 7–12). Five per cent of school absenteeism is caused by accidents, and 15 per cent of the visits to the physician's office are due to injuries. Forty per cent of accident related deaths at all ages in childhood are secondary to motor vehicle accidents.

ACCIDENT PREVENTION. The most effective form of accident prevention for the very young child is supervision and environmental control of potential hazards. As the child gets older, the parents' teaching and control are internalized, so that in the preadolescent child, as in the adult, accident prevention becomes largely a matter of self discipline. There is, however, always room for safety precautions. For example, putting poisonous substances in pop bottles is potentially homicidal, regardless of the age of household members. The growing child is most vulnerable to accidents when participating in newly learned activities and when exercising newly won freedom in the ever expanding world. For example, the 3 year old can play unsupervised in the backyard, but does not know which berries are poisonous. The 4 year old is able to walk to a nearby friend's house, but may run out in the street to retrieve a ball. By age 6 most children can cross even busy streets and 8 and 9 year olds bicycle around their neighborhood, both hazardous undertakings. In the expanding world of the older child, new dangers are found in the home, such as burns from cooking. Parental guidance and tactful supervision — not nagging — are needed as the child learns new skills. The modeling of safe behavior by adults is most effective in teaching accident prevention to children.

Accident prevention is also a public health matter. Laws prescribing that children's night clothes must not be manufactured from flammable material, that dangerous medicines must be sold in childproof containers, and that poisonous products must be clearly labeled as such, are examples of ways in which society can reduce hazards for children.

THE ACCIDENT PRONE CHILD. These children may be poison repeaters or may experience an excessive number of cuts and fractures. They are well known figures in emergency rooms and physicians' offices, and deserve careful professional evaluation and treatment of the psychosocial factors influencing their behavior. Maybe they are daredevils. If so, why the need to show off? Maybe they cannot be controlled in any situation. If so, how can the parents learn to be more effective disciplinarians? Maybe the children do not care about their own safety. If so, how can they be helped to feel that they are worthwhile persons?

LEAD POISONING.   Lead deserves special mention as an omnipotent and harmful chemical agent. Acute and chronic lead poisoning resulting in lead encephalopathy has been endemic in large cities in the Northeast, where peeling, old paint is ingested by young children with pica (the eating of unnatural products). Lead has been found in pottery glaze and is abundant in dirt near factories that produce batteries. Lead from car exhaust fumes is a significant part of air pollution and is present in the dust in large cities. Ingestion and inhalation of lead from these sources seldom cause overt symptoms, but has been blamed for mental retardation, learning disabilities, and hyperactivity in children. Results from studies attempting to prove such relationships have been contradictory, but because of its known toxicity to children, the campaign to remove lead in any form from the environment should continue.

Infections

Morbidity from infections of one kind or another is an almost universal occurrence. The average school age child had 3.5 episodes of infectious disease during any one year. Seventy one per cent of school absences are caused by infections and they contribute to 25 per cent of the visits to physicians' offices by young children. Not only are nonserious infections such as colds and gastrointestinal upsets more common in young children, but potentially lethal illnesses such as pneumonia and meningitis are also more frequent. As can be seen in Figure 7–30, infection is the second most frequent killer in the younger child, but ranks forth in the older child. The decrease in incidence and seriousness of infections during the childhood years is related to immunologic factors and exposure, as previously discussed, but increase in physical size also plays a role. For example, the smaller the child, the more devastating the effects of dehydration from gastroenteritis may be.

Epidemiologic Aspects.   Certain diseases common in one part of the country are unheard of in another. For the practicing health professional, it it imperative to have up to date information from local health departments regarding diseases prevalent in a community at any one time. The so called common childhood diseases constitute a group of contagious or communicable disorders of viral or bacterial origin which occur in epidemics typically affecting children. Immunizations have now all but eradicated some of the more serious of these communicable diseases such as pertussis, diphtheria, and poliomyelitis. More diligent use of measles (rubeola) immunization could wipe out this potentially serious disease. Vaccines are also available for mumps and rubella. New vaccines continue to be developed and tested. Because of immunizations (see section on preventive health practices later in this chapter), many of the previously common childhood diseases are no longer an inevitable part of growing up. However, there are some infections still common in childhood or peculiar to this age group which will be discussed.

Otitis Media. Acute middle ear infection is a common complication of upper respiratory tract infection in infancy (as previously discussed) and early childhood. It is one of the most frequent illnesses of childhood, owing both to the common occurrence of colds in this age group and to anatomic factors. The eustachian tube is short and wide in the young child, and large amounts of lymphoid tissue (adenoids) may encroach upon its orifice as the child gets older. The first stage of middle ear infection is blockage of the eustachian tube from inflamed tissue in the nasopharynx (Fig. 7–32). Secretions are trapped in the middle ear, and organisms which are present there multiply. Otitis media is accompanied by pain, fever, and if not treated, often by rupture of the ear drum and drainage. Adequate antibiotic therapy is at least partially based upon the knowledge of the most likely infective agent relative to the age of the child. About half the infections are bacterial, the most frequent bacterium being the penicillin sensitive Pneumococcus, and in the very young child, *Hemophilus influenzae,* which is not sensitive to penicillin. Adequate treatment includes nasal decongestants to keep the eustachian tubes open, and a follow up appointment to inspect the eardrum and to ensure complete resolution of the infection and drainage of the fluid from the middle ear. Inadequate treatment of acute middle ear infection might be a contributing factor to serous otitis media, a nonpainful collection of fluid in the middle ear which is common during childhood.

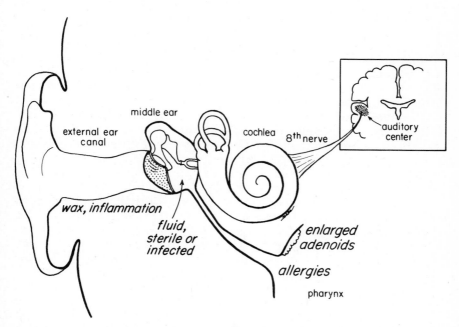

Figure 7–32 The anatomy of hearing, indicating common sources of interference with air conduction.

Another reason for vigorous treatment of acute otitis media is to prevent complications such as mastoiditis and (rarely) meningitis. Recurrent and chronic middle ear infections sometimes occur. As these may cause destruction of tissue in the middle ear and permanent hearing loss, they require intensive medical intervention. (See the section on hearing handicaps.)

Streptococcal Infections. Infections caused by Streptococcus bacteria are common in childhood during the winter and spring months in temperate climates. These infections illustrate age variability in host response to a given agent. Before 3 years of age, it is often a long, drawn out, nonspecific disease with relatively mild symptoms. After this age acute tonsillitis and pharyngitis often result from streptococcal infections with sudden onset of fever, malaise, pain on swallowing, headache, and sometimes vomiting. For poorly understood reasons, some children (about 20 per cent) show few or no symptoms with a streptococcal pharyngitis, but contribute to the spread of epidemics. In addition, streptococci cause other infections in childhood. They are etiologic agents of otitis media in older children; they also cause impetigo, a common, superficial, contagious skin infection. One of the streptococcal strains causes scarlet fever (scarlatina), which in essence is a pharyngitis accompanied by a characteristic rash. In childhood it is important to recognize diseases caused by streptococcal infections since they respond to antibiotics (the penicillins).

Two serious complications of streptococcal infections occur in susceptible older children: rheumatic fever, an important cause of lifelong crippling heart disease, and acute glomerulonephritis, a usually self limiting, but sometimes life threatening kidney disorder. Eradication of Streptococci by antibiotics appears to prevent these complications. Prophylactic treatment is used to ward off recurrences of rheumatic fever, which were previously common. For reasons that are poorly understood, the incidence of rheumatic fever has declined during the last few decades. It is still a problem in crowded, low socioeconomic populations and in some developing countries.

Urinary Tract Infections. A common childhood problem which continues to plague some individuals in adulthood is urinary tract infection. Bacterial infections of the bladder (cystitis) or the kidneys (pyelonephritis) cause symptoms which include increased frequency of urination, pain or burning when voiding, and dribbling of urine, which may be foul smelling. Pyelonephritis may cause fever, and urinary tract infection should always be suspected in children with fever of unknown origin. Sometimes urinary tract infections are asymptomatic. It is assumed to be an ascending infection. The responsible infective agents are usually from the fecal flora, and the short distance from the pubic area to the bladder (the urethra) in the female is thought to explain the fact that urinary tract infections are 3 to 4 times more common in females than in males. Recurrences are common. Congenital malformations of the urinary tract predispose some children to urinary tract infections. The physician should check for this by x-ray after the original infection has been controlled by appropriate antibiotic treatment.

Malignancies

Neoplasms rank second in the older child and fourth in the younger child as a cause of death, contributing a total of 15 per cent to mortality in childhood (Fig. 7–30). Both the site of predilection and the tumor type are unique to children, in whom most of the common adult malignancies are extremely rare. The symptomatology is also different. The onset is often acute with fever, vomiting, or hemorrhage. Childhood malignancies tend to have a short explosive course compared to the chronicity associated with these diseases in adults.

Common Childhood Malignancies. Leukemia is the most common childhood malignancy, and usually has its onset between 2 to 5 years of age, when it constitutes almost half of all the childhood malignancies. Childhood leukemias have been considered universally fatal in the past. New treatment methods now allow a progressively longer survival period than the average 8 week course of untreated leukemia. In rare instances, children go for years after treatment without recurrences; such children may be considered "cured."

Tumors of the brain are the second most frequent form of malignancy in children. Different types of brain tumors affect children, but many show particularly malignant cellular patterns and are most commonly located in the deeper part of the brain, close to areas controlling vital processes. As a result, surgical removal, with a few exceptions, is difficult and seldom curative. Recent noninvasive treatment has drastically improved the clinical outcome in some types of brain tumors.

A variety of neoplasms of bone, some benign, some malignant, occur in later childhood. The presenting complaint is usually pain, frequently blamed on trauma, which is so common in that age group. Nonspecific "growing pain" is also common in childhood. In the rare case when leg pain is due to bone tumors, x-rays usually reveal their presence. Soft tissue tumors (different forms of sarcomas) are another example of a group of tumors peculiar to childhood. Some childhood malignancies seem to be of developmental congenital origin, but the basic reasons for the distinctiveness of childhood tumors are not entirely clear.

The Effects of Malignant Disease on the Child. Even though malignancy figures high on the mortality list in childhood, it is not a major factor in morbidity. In spite of the fact that it affects a small number of children, malignancy contributes significantly to hospitalizations in childhood. It is difficult to explain the need for hospitalization and painful procedures to a child, who usually equates them with punishment. It is especially important to handle this problem tactfully when dealing with children who have malignant diseases.

The concept of death is not understood by young children. The professional should answer children's questions honestly, but a discussion of the possible fatal outcome of their disease is usually not appropriate. If an older child asks if he will die, one should strive to be both honest and reassuring at the same time. Although what one says to a child makes a difference, it is more important that the adult recognize the need to listen to the hospitalized child with a fatal disorder.

Allergies

About 15 per cent of the childhood population is "atopic," that is, sensitive to substances that do not cause symptoms in the normal population. Hereditary factors contribute, and one often gets a family history of "allergies." The allergic symptoms change with age. Allergic eczema commonly has its onset in infancy and usually improves during the preschool years. At this age it is encountered as a localized skin condition, commonly in the flexure areas of the arms and the legs. This type of eczema is not particularly responsive to the removal of either foods or inhalants. The most common allergic symptoms in childhood are respiratory: a chronically stuffy nose, frequent colds, nosepicking, coughing, serous otitis, and later sinusitis. Seasonal hay fever in response to pollen is unusual in the younger child (in contrast to nonseasonal hay fever) but may occur in later childhood. Allergic asthma frequently has its onset after 3 years of age, seldom after 10 years of age, and usually improves at puberty. True gastrointestinal allergies are extremely rare during childhood. In contrast, nonspecific vomiting and diarrhea are common, as is abdominal pain as a psychosomatic symptom (as discussed previously).

Nutritional and Metabolic Disorders

Obesity. A common problem in adolescence (see Chapter 8), obesity often has its onset in childhood. Some children never lose their "baby fat," continue to be chubby through childhood, and almost imperceptibly develop into fat adults. In some children obesity has its onset in the early school age years, but most commonly it starts in preadolescence, when there is a physiological increase in the accumulation of adipose tissue prior to the adolescent growth spurt. At this time boys frequently accumulate fat around the mammary region, enough to suggest breast development (Fig. 7–20). This phenomenon is more common in boys who are truly obese. It is a temporary condition of great embarrassment to the boy, who should be reassured of its harmlessness.

Successful prevention of obesity in childhood would help to solve a major health problem in adults, as 15 per cent of adult obesity has its onset in childhood. Approximately 70 per cent of children who are overweight will be obese adults. There is increasing evidence that genetics plays an important role in the development of childhood obesity, but family eating patterns and availability of highly caloric foods also contribute to the problem.

Malnutrition. Caloric and vitamin deficiencies are seldom seen in children in the United States. However, it is important to recognize that some children exposed to serious environmental deprivation are actually underfed — a form of child abuse. These children may present as growth failures, with weight more affected than height. A clue to the reason for poor growth is to be found in a history of bizarre eating habits, such as the rifling of garbage cans. Underfed children will gain in height and weight when offered food and tender loving care in a hospital or a foster home (the ultimate diagnostic test).

Iron deficiency anemia can occur during the preschool years, and more subtle forms of nutritional disturbances are common. An adequate supply of calories, vitamins, protein, and iron is probably available in the average American diet, but as a result of ignorance and the use of convenience foods, satisfactory nutrition is by no means universal during the childhood years. Snacking on high carbohydrate foods and consumption of "empty calories" (soda pop and potato chips, for example) is common in children in our society.

Vitamin Excess. It is a sad reflection on our pill oriented society that children's major problem with vitamins is one of excess. Vitamin A and D intoxication occurred in the past mostly as a result of ignorance. Recently megavitamin treatment, i.e., large dosages of supposedly harmless vitamins, are being perpetrated as treatment for a host of behavior and learning problems in children without any scientific proof of their efficacy. Even if they are not toxic after prolonged use (which is unproven), they still tend to distract the family and child from concentrating on the difficult work needed to control the behavior problem.

Diabetes. About 5 per cent of all cases of diabetes mellitus have their onset during childhood. This endocrine disorder has a multifactorial etiology, but genetic factors are important, as most cases are familial. The presenting symptom in children may be diabetic coma, but the classical symptoms of malaise, thirst, excessive urination, and weight loss are also seen.

Management of childhood diabetes, like that of other chronic illnesses in childhood, is complicated by the fact that growing up means becoming increasingly independent. When special diet, regulated activity, and daily medications are part of children's lives, the growing up process is complicated. Professionals dealing with chronically ill children and their families should be particularly sensitive to social and emotional aspects of child development in order to guide the family toward letting children assume an increasingly greater responsibility for the management of their disease.

Cystic Fibrosis. The symptomatology of this recessively inherited disorder of the exocrine glands ranges from gastrointestinal obstruction by meconium plugs in the newborn to infertility in the adult male, but it is usually considered a disease of childhood. Its basic pathophysiology is still not well understood, but it is considered a metabolic disorder. Repeated respiratory tract infections, intestinal symptoms in the form of malabsorption and an excessive loss of salt during perspiration are some of the most prominent symptoms. It is a disease currently without a cure, but symptomatic treatment continues to increase longevity. In the past, afflicted individuals died in infancy or early childhood; now many reach adulthood. As a result, when dealing with this disorder professionals and families are continually faced with new medical and psychosocial problems.

Phenylketonuria (PKU). This recessively inherited inborn error of metabolism is a model for what can be accomplished in screening and treatment to prevent a serious childhood handicapping condition (mental retardation). With an incidence of 1:15,000 births, it is common, compared to similar diseases. The enzymatic defect is quite well understood. The screening is simple and inexpensive and consists of a routine blood test done soon after birth. The treatment, use of a milk substitute, is relatively easy in infancy. The outcome — prevention of mental retardation — is almost a certainty. The successful treatment of this disorder does require adherence to a strict diet through most of childhood, which has many psychosocial implications. But, PKU is a success story offering hope that other inborn errors of metabolism will also eventually be conquered.

Handicapping Conditions

Handicapping conditions are those which have a significant detrimental effect on a child's entire lifestyle, such as mental retardation, sensory handicaps, and cerebral palsy. In the modern vernacular, these conditions are frequently referred to as developmental disabilities. Approximately 6 to 8 per cent of the childhood population is so afflicted. The etiologies of these conditions are varied. Most are due to frequently undeterminable prenatal factors, while some are caused by birth trauma or serious disturbances later in life. Sometimes purely social and environmental factors result in a truly handicapping condition such as mental retardation. More than one etiological factor may contribute to the handicap in a child. For example, children with Down syndrome growing up in institutions have a significant I.Q. deficit compared to home reared children with the same condition. Here, environmental deprivation adds to a handicap with a basic, organic etiology.

Most handicapping conditions are due to static lesions, and affected children are expected to gain skills and to learn, albeit at their own rate. A few are caused by disorders resulting in progressive deterioration, as in the case of metabolic disorders affecting the central nervous system. These disorders need to be considered in children who are losing ground developmentally. Medical conditions with physical defects are usually diagnosed at birth, and one can then often anticipate that an affected child will become handicapped. But many conditions have mainly central nervous system manifestations, and the presence of the handicap only becomes apparent as the child grows older and the brain matures.

It is important to realize that the most commonly used classifications of developmental disabilities (to be used below) constitute a list of significant symptoms with no relation to basic etiology. Data concerning the prevalence of handicapping conditions are presented in Table 7–4. Many children exhibit more than one handicapping symptom; many known etiologies of developmental disabilities affect multiple organs. For example, the child exposed to rubella in the first trimester of pregnancy may be deaf, blind, mentally retarded, cerebral palsied, and have seizures, or have any of these symptoms singly or in combinations. Similarly, many children whose conditions have no basic identifiable etiology, exhibit a combination of handicapping symptoms.

TABLE 7–4 HANDICAPPING CONDITIONS IN CHILDHOOD*

	Prevalence per 1000	
Mental retardation (MR)		30
I.Q. below 50		
Moderate MR	1.8	
Severe MR	0.9	
Profound MR	0.3	
Hearing handicaps		15
Deaf	1	
Visual handicaps		0.5
(legally blind)		
Totally blind	0.1	
Light perception only	0.05	
Congenital malformations		15
Congenital heart disease	2.0	
Club foot	1.5	
Down's syndrome	1.3	
Neural tube malformation		
(meningomyelocele)	1	
Cleft lip and palate	1	
Polydactyly	0.5	
Anal and rectal malformations	0.2	
Cerebral palsy		5
Epilepsy		10
Childhood psychosis		0.5
Total		More than 75 per 1000

*From a variety of sources, see bibliography.

Mental Retardation. This condition is usually considered to be present when a person has an intelligence quotient more than 2 standard deviations below the mean on a standardized psychological test, usually an I.Q. of less than 70. In addition, to be properly labeled mentally retarded, a child should show evidence of delays in adaptive skill development. A child's responses on psychological tests are fairly predictive of academic achievement, and most children with significantly subaverage results need special consideration for education. Approximately 3 per cent of school age children fall in this category. It should be emphasized, however, that a large number of these children are functionally retarded because of socioeconomic and environmental causes, and that the degree of their impairment is mild. They have the potential to function as fully contributing members of society as adults, and should then no longer be considered retarded. Most children with a more severe degree of retardation (I.Q. less than 50) function this poorly because of some specific disorder which has resulted in inadequate development of the brain. In this group other associated handicaps are common.

Hearing Handicap. Most hearing losses found on routine screening in children are temporary, mild, and amenable to medical treatment. Conditions muffling the air waves through the external ear canal, tympanic membranes, and middle ear cause so called conductive hearing loss. (See Figure 7–32.) These conditions are common in children, but fortunately only rarely result in permanent middle ear destruction and handicap. Sensorineural hearing loss is caused by conditions affecting the cochlea, the eighth nerve, and the neurologic pathways relaying hearing impulses to the cerebral cortex. Most congenital hearing losses are of the sensorineural type. They are not medically remediable but may improve with hearing aids; they vary in degree and are rarely progressive. Approximately 1.5 per cent of the childhood population has sufficient hearing loss of one type or the other to be considered handicapped. Most of these children are "hard of hearing." They can be taught in regular school programs with the use of hearing aids, preferential seating, speech therapy, and special attention to their educational needs. Only 1 child per 1000 or less has nonfunctional hearing even with hearing aid and should be considered deaf.

Visual Handicap. Visual problems are very common in childhood (Fig. 7–31); they include near and far sightedness, astigmatism, and strabismus. However, very few children are truly visually handicapped (defined as a visual acuity of 20/200 or less in the better eye with the best possible correction); the incidence is less than 0.5 per 1000. Of these, less than one third are totally blind. Some legally blind children have sufficient vision to read large print and can move around in society like a sighted person. Most children who are visually handicapped need special educational training in sight saving classes, or if more severely impaired, need training to read Braille.

Congenital Malformations. Extensive examinations of infants and young children will reveal an incidence of congenital malformation as high as 4 to 5 per cent. However, many have single and remediable malformations of no serious consequence. Severe malformations contribute substantially to mortality during the first few years of life, and kill more children than infections in the 5 to 14 year old age group (Fig. 7–30). Significant congenital malformations probably affect from 1 to 2 per cent of the childhood population. Only a small percentage of these children have congenital malformations involving the central nervous system and are considered developmentally disabled. Such malformations include neural tube defects (e.g., meningomyelocele), hydrocephalus, congenital brain cysts, and others. These congenital malformations have early prenatal origin and their presence is usually recognized in infancy. However, the medical care and management of the behavioral and psychosocial aspects of these children during the childhood years will determine the quality of life in adolescence and adulthood.

Cerebral Palsy. A variety of symptoms of motor dysfunction (increased or decreased muscle tone, incoordination, involuntary movements) due to a lesion or disorder of the central nervous system are commonly grouped under this heading. Cerebral palsy may have pre-, peri-, or postnatal origin. *Pre*natal etiologies include a host of genetic and sporadic syndromes plus a number of "unclassifiable" children with a constellation of signs and symptoms pointing to prenatal origin of their symptoms. Prematurity is the most common *peri*natal etiology of cerebral palsy. At this time approximately one third of children with cerebral palsy in childhood were born prematurely. Fortunately, improved neonatal medical care seems to have reduced the number of children who have spastic diplegia (increased muscle tone in the legs with minimal hand involvement), the classical cerebral palsy syndrome of prematurity (Fig. 7–33). It seems likely that improved obstetric care will continue to decrease the occurrence of another perinatal antecedent, fetal asphyxia (lack of oxygen, shock, and acidosis). Head injuries and central nervous system infections constitute *post*natal causes.

Even though the brain lesion is static in cerebral palsy, the symptoms exhibited by the child will change over the years because of maturation of the central nervous system. During the first few weeks or even months of life, most children with cerebral palsy, except for the severely involved (who usually show hypotonia, or occasionally, increased muscle tone) will appear normal or have nonspecific problems with feeding or sleeping. Towards the end of the first year, the cerebral palsied child will show delayed or asymmetric motor development (e.g., early hand preference), but it usually takes months and years of maturation before the

Figure 7–33 Two year old monozygotic twins born prematurely. The left twin has spastic diplegia.

full degree, type, and distribution of the motor handicap emerges. The degree of disability varies from gross and fine motor incoordination to total physical dependence.

Additional handicaps are common in more severely affected children. Fifteen per cent have visual disorders, 50 per cent have speech defects, and about 50 per cent have general mental retardation. Even if they can handle a regular school program, most children with cerebral palsy need additional services, such as physical and speech therapy, in order to reach their full potential for functioning. They will need close medical supervision all through their growing years because of the high frequency of orthopedic and other complications.

Epilepsy. Convulsions are relatively common in children, especially at a young age, and are associated with a variety of underlying causes (breath holding and fever, for example). Epilepsy is defined as convulsions of basically unknown etiology and it afflicts approximately 0.5 per cent of the childhood population. It is included among developmental disabilities only when encountered in combination with other symptoms of abnormal brain function (cerebral palsy and mental retardation).

Several types of seizures are encountered in childhood, and both type and frequency of seizures change with maturation. Some forms of seizures are peculiar to the childhood years. Petit mal seizures (absence spells) consisting of brief episodes of staring, often with rhythmic blinking, and accompanied by specific changes in the electroencephalogram, is a seizure disorder with onset commonly between 3 and 5 years of age. Daily medication keeps most epileptic children free of seizures. It is usually not necessary to restrict children's activity except when control is difficult and a sudden loss of consciousness would be dangerous, such as during unsupervised swimming.

Childhood Psychosis. Behavior and learning disorders in varying degrees of severity are common in childhood (Fig. 7–31) and have been discussed previously. A small number of children with childhood psychosis or autism are seriously handicapped in social development, often associated with abnormal language development. They exhibit a constellation of frequently bizarre behavioral characteristics: tiptoe walking; hand waving; stereotyped play behavior with preoccupation with strings, shiny or spinning objects; and an aloofness toward other human beings. These actions set them apart from other children even though frequently no physical or neurologic abnormalities may be demonstrated. Many of these children function in the retarded range on intelligence tests. Some show "islands" of normal cognition. Children with autistic childhood psychosis in its "pure" form (which is rare) demonstrate a difference in social development from early infancy (lack of responsiveness to parenting), but their developmental disability is usually not recognized until age 2 or later. The etiology is assumed to be organic and probably variable. Treatment is difficult, time consuming, and unrewarding.

The bizarre behaviors described above are sometimes referred to as "autisms." Autisms occur in a variety of brain disorders, e.g., untreated PKU and congenital rubella. Some children with such symptoms show abnormal neurologic findings and others are relatively mildly affected. The question of exactly whom to include in this "spectrum of autism" is controversial, but most of these children are truly handicapped for life.

Multiple Handicaps.   Categorization of developmental disabilities are needed primarily for the provision of educational and other services. The present trend is to keep persons with developmental disabilities in the community and out of institutions. This has made it necessary for public schools to develop educational programs for severely disabled children. Such services must now be available: "Education for all" is federal law. These changes have brought an awareness that many children cannot be properly placed in any one of the traditional educational categories. As mentioned in the beginning, many children have more than one handicapping symptom, and these are usually the most severely affected ones. The "deaf-blind" rubella children of the 1964 epidemic (Fig. 7–34) would probably have ended up on the back wards in our institutions for the mentally retarded in the past. Instead, educational programs are now available in the community for them and other children with "multiple handicaps," recently recognized as an official category of developmental disabilities.

The medical and educational care of handicapped children is expensive for society. It also poses similar, overwhelming problems for the families of such children, regardless of the nature of the child's handicap. Strong emotions in the parents, such as guilt, anger, frustration, and depression, are frequently encountered. The family's childrearing practices are often distorted with respect to their handicapped child, creating a variety of behavioral complications. Any remedial program,

Figure 7–34 Ten year old youngster with the congenital rubella syndrome. (Note thick glasses and close-up vision to compensate for cataract surgery, and the hearing aid.)

whether medical or educational, should take parental feelings into consideration. Handicapping conditions influence all aspects of a child's development. They may provide distorted sensory input or cause a lack of normal social experiences. The child often has to learn to live with pain and discomfort. The child's own reaction to the handicap varies with the type and degree of limitation, but almost invariably the older child's sense of self worth is shaken. How to minimize these problems and assist children with developmental disabilities to reach their potential for human development are issues our society has just begun to face fully.

PREVENTIVE HEALTH MEASURES

Preventive health measures for the childhood years include immunizations and screening procedures to detect asymptomatic but potentially curable disorders and developmental deviations.

Immunizations. "Booster shots" after the initial immunizations given in infancy, are needed periodically during the childhood years. Up to date recommendations are published by the American Academy of Pediatrics and additional suggestions are available from local health departments. These recommendations cover the age at which immunizations should be given, time intervals between boosters, and which diseases require immunization. At the present time, it is most important to provide booster inoculations against diphtheria, tetanus, and poliomyelitis during the childhood years. However, with advances in medical knowledge, recommendations for immunizations can be expected to change periodically. Some children do not receive preventive immunizations in infancy, the percentage varying greatly between communities and depending on the availability and use of health care facilities. An immunization program in the school (with parental permission) is one way to provide this preventive care for unprotected children. Such programs are also effective in halting community epidemics, as communicable diseases are quickly transmitted among children in school. All but 2 states now have laws requiring immunizations for school entry, but unfortunately such laws have not been particularly effective. Compliance with recommended immunization schedules still is low, and inquiries about a child's immunization status need to be a routine part of all child health evaluations.

Screening Procedures.   The following are some of the most common screening procedures used for children at the present time by physicians and nurses in private offices, public health departments, and schools.

VISION SCREENING.   Approximately 25 per cent of all children will eventually need glasses, at least part time, to correct for myopia or astigmatism. A surprising number of these children make no complaints and will only be found through routine screening. Many discover how much they previously have missed only after their visual deficit has been corrected. Periodic reevaluations of visual acuity for both asymptomatic children and those who wear corrective lenses are recommended until growth ceases in adolescence (Fig. 7–29). Because of the importance of good vision for education, annual screening starting in kindergarten, is provided in most schools.

HEARING SCREENING. Children with language delay or possible hearing loss should have hearing tests by a competent professional person as soon as a problem is suspected. In addition, all children need periodic hearing screening, which is done regularly in most school systems. Over 5 per cent of school children will not pass the usual hearing screen, but in many the decrease in hearing acuity is mild and due to a temporary upper respiratory tract infection. However, long term collection of sterile fluid in the middle ears (serous otitis media) is a relatively common occurrence (as previously discussed), and is especially prevalent around 4 to 7 years of age. Allergies may be a contributing factor, but frequently there are no associated symptoms. Long standing serous otitis media and chronic infectious otitis media (usually associated with earaches and drainage) are accompanied by fluctuating hearing losses. Untreated, these conditions might lead to permanent conductive hearing loss. There is also evidence that periodic mild hearing loss, even fluctuating, has an adverse effect upon learning, another impetus for routine hearing screening in public schools.

HEIGHT AND WEIGHT MEASUREMENTS. Nutritional deviations (most commonly obesity), chronic illnesses, and endocrine disorders are just a few examples of important conditions which will be discovered when adequate height and weight measurements are obtained. The importance of collecting these data over a period of time and comparing them to population and family standards has been discussed in Chapter 1, but needs to be emphasized again. Many schools keep height and weight records on their pupils.

SCOLIOSIS SCREENING. Screening for spinal abnormalities has recently been added to the school health program in some communities and the method has been described previously (Fig. 7–28). It qualifies as a screening procedure because it is inexpensive, reliable, and results in identification of a condition that benefits from early treatment. Progressive scoliosis can usually be arrested by appropriate bracing, avoiding painful and expensive surgery.

SCREENING FOR TUBERCULOSIS (TUBERCULIN TESTS). The aim of tuberculin skin testing is to find the individuals who convert from a negative to a positive test, indicating recent exposure to someone with active tuberculosis. At the present time, the child with a positive reaction is usually treated with antituberculosis drugs, even though asymptomatic, to prevent the later occurrence of symptomatic tuberculosis. A secondary gain from tuberculosis screening in children is that the source of infection usually is found among the child's immediate adult contacts, so this person can be treated before spreading the infection further in society. Tuberculin testing programs are sometimes carried out in schools. The yield of routine screening is low, approximately 1 per cent (higher in some racial groups and in low socioeconomic populations), but still considered worthwhile.

URINE ANALYSIS. Routine urine analysis is customary in most medical settings. The main purpose is to find silent urinary tract infections, common in girls. Approximately 1 per cent of school girls have active urinary tract infections but are often asymptomatic. Simple screening techniques for urinary tract infections are now available. Chronic renal disease, which is a serious health hazard to the adult female, probably has its onset in childhood. Unfortunately, it is not known at the present time if treatment of silent urinary tract infection in girls will result in a decrease in chronic renal disease in the adult female. Other abnormal urine findings such as the presence of sugar (glycosuria) or protein (proteinuria) are less helpful for screening. They might indicate serious disease, but the conditions they reflect (juvenile diabetes, nephrosis, glomerulonephritis) are seldom, if ever asymptomatic. Instead, these latter findings (especially proteinuria) are sometimes present without significant disease.

BLOOD TESTS. Hemoglobin or hematocrit determinations are fre-quently included in routine medical screening of children. They might disclose the presence of iron deficiency anemia, a common asymptomatic problem in several groups of children such as young preschoolers, children from economically depressed areas, and menstruating girls.

DENTAL AND PHYSICAL EXAMINATIONS. The need for early detection and treatment of dental caries is obvious. Caries can develop rapidly in young children, and checkups once or twice a year are recommended. Naturally or artifically fluoridated water supplies are now available to approximately half of the United States population. Topical fluoride treatment provides additional protection against caries for young children. The prevalence of dental caries is 80 per cent during childhood. Fluoridation of water has cut this figure in half in some communities.

Routine physical examinations are usually recommended yearly or every other year. Few additional significant, unsuspected physical conditions will be found in older children if the above screening tests have been performed. An example would be elevated blood pressure, a very unusual but highly significant finding in a child. Routine physical examinations serve mainly to reassure the child and his family regarding the degree of significance of minor physical deviations, and to provide health education.

DEVELOPMENTAL ASSESSMENT. The Denver Developmental Screening Test (DDST), is the most commonly used tool to assess development in the preschooler; but other tests, such as the Goodenough Draw a Man Test, or Peabody Picture Vocabulary Test, can also be used. Developmental delays are common, but some that are environmental rather than inherent in the child may be remediable. More and more communities are developing rehabilitation programs for the young, developmentally deviant child, thus early recognition becomes important. In the older child the school takes on the task of developmental screening, comparing the child's achievement with that of age mates. The child who, after being observed and screened, shows suspected or apparent deviation in development may need to be referred to clinics specializing in developmental disorders, to school psychologists, or to other professionals for further evaluation.

Inquiry about problems of behavior of concern to parents or teachers is also part of developmental assessment. If present, behavior problems could indicate significant adjustment difficulties needing professional intervention in order to prevent later mental health problems. One must remember, however, that some worries about childhood behaviors are unjustified and reflect a lack of knowledge of normal variations in child development.

COMMENT: The listed preventive health measures needed during childhood can be provided in many ways — by personal physicians, dentists, and their specially trained health aides. A new health professional, the pediatric nurse practitioner, is taking on this task in many settings. This new health career has developed rapidly and its practitioners enjoy strong support by pediatricians and the public. This development may indicate that the maintenance of health in childhood is finally a recognized priority item in our society.

REFERENCES

American Academy of Pediatrics, Committee on School Health: School Health: A Guide for Health Professionals. Evanston, Ill., American Academy of Pediatrics, 1977.

American Academy of Pediatrics, Committee on Standards of Child Health Care: Standards of Child Health Care. 3rd ed. Evanston, Ill., American Academy of Pediatrics, 1977.

Bee, H.: The Developing Child. 2nd ed. New York, Harper and Row, 1978.

Brazelton, T. B.: Toddlers and Parents: A Declaration of Independence. New York, Dell, 1974.

Chinn, P. L., and Leitch, C. J.: Child Health Maintenance: A Guide to Clinical Assessment. St. Louis, C. V. Mosby Company, 1974.

Dreikurs, R.: Children: The Challenge. New York, Hawthorn Books, 1964.

Erikson, E.: Childhood and Society. 2nd ed. New York, Norton, 1963.

Frailberg, S. H.: The Magic Years: Understanding and Handling the Problems of Early Childhood. New York, Scribners, 1959.

Frankenburg, W. K., and Camp, B. W.: Pediatric Screening Tests. Springfield, Charles C. Thomas Company, 1975.

Gardner, H.: Developmental Psychology. Boston, Little, Brown and Co., 1978.

Ginsburg, H., and Opper, S.: Piaget's Theory of Intellectual Development: An Introduction. Englewood Cliffs, N.J., Prentice-Hall, 1969.

Hobbs, N.: The Future of Children: Categories, Labels and Their Consequences. San Francisco, Jossey-Bass, 1975.

Kennedy, W. P.: Epidemiologic aspect of the problem of congenital malformations. Birth Defects Original Article Series, Vol. III, 2, December, The National Foundation-March of Dimes, 1967.

Pless, I. B., and Douglas, J. W. B.: Chronic illness in childhood: Part I. Epidemiological and clinical characteristics. Pediatrics, 47: 405, 1971.

Richardson, W. P., and Higgins, A. D.: A survey of handicapping conditions and handicapped children in Alamance County, North Carolina. Am. J. Public Health, 54:1817, 1964.

Vaughan, V. C., McKay, R. J., and Nelson, E. W. (Eds.): Nelson Textbook of Pediatrics. 10th ed. Philadelphia, W. B. Saunders Company, 1975.

Whipple, D. V.: Dynamics of Development: Euthenic Pediatrics. New York, McGraw-Hill, 1966.

8

Adolescence

S. L. HAMMAR

Adolescence is defined as the period of psychobiologic maturation during which the secondary physical growth spurt is completed and sexual maturity and the ability to reproduce are achieved. Puberty connotes the development of the secondary sexual characteristics and sexual maturation. In the average girl, these physical, physiological, and psychosocial changes occur during the period from 10 to 18 years; in boys, from 12 to 20 years. Chronological age is a poor measure of biologic maturation because of the wide range of individual variations in the onset and completion of these changes. It is important to consider each adolescent individually in terms of his own biologic age and stage of maturation.

LIFE SITUATION

Physical Changes

The increased production of testosterone in the male and estrogen in the female triggers a sequence of changes. At puberty, there is a marked change in the growth rate, resulting in an increase in body size, a change in body shape, and rapid development of the gonads. The mechanisms which initiate puberty are not entirely understood. Under the influence of control centers in the hypothalamus, gonadotropins (FSH and LH) begin to increase markedly 2 to 3 years before puberty, stimulating an increased production of sex hormones. Pubertal changes are the result of increased secretions of these sex hormones by the gonads and the adrenal cortex.

While the timing of the adolescent growth spurt is variable, the sequence of events once it occurs is fairly predictable. Nearly every muscular and skeletal dimension of the body takes part and exhibits a characteristic pattern of growth. The average boy begins his growth spurt around 12 years of age, reaching his maximum velocity in height growth at about 14 years of age. At this time he will be growing at nearly twice his childhood or preadolescent rate. Girls begin puberty approximately two years earlier (8 to 10 years) and will reach maximum velocity in their height growth around 12 years of age. The maximum rate of growth for the girl will be somewhat less than that exhibited by the boy. Although children have been getting progressively taller and heavier and maturing earlier over the years, this two-year difference between the sexes in the timing of the adolescent growth spurt has remained unchanged.

Figure 8–1 shows the "typical" individual velocity curves. Velocity is defined as the rate of growth per year. The velocity curve of human growth illustrates that even though the child is making significant gains from birth through childhood, his rate of growth is decelerating until he reaches puberty. The greater adult height in the male has been attributed to the longer period of preadolescent growth and the greater velocity rate during the adolescent spurt. The growth pattern for body weight is similar.

Although we are most aware of the growth changes in height and weight during puberty, a similar growth spurt can be seen in other body parameters, such as pelvic and shoulder diameters, hand and foot length, and head circumference.

The pubertal spurt in height and weight is accompanied by rapid development of the reproductive organs and the appearance of the

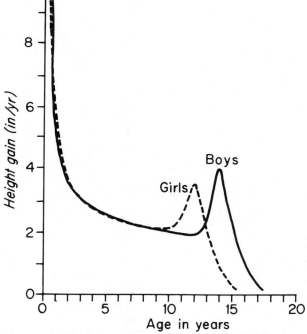

Figure 8–1 Typical-individual velocity curves for supine length or height in boys and girls. (From Tanner, J. M.: Growth at Adolescence. Oxford, Blackwell Scientific Publications, 2nd ed., 1962.)

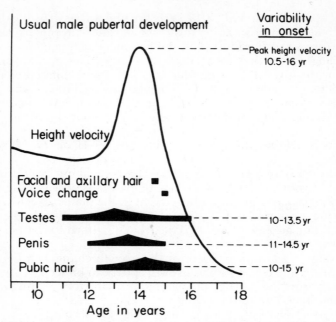

Figure 8–2 Diagram of sequence of events at adolescence in boys. (Adapted from Hammar S. L.: Adolescence. *In* Kelley, V. C. (ed.): Brenneman's Practice of Pediatrics. Hagerstown, Maryland, Harper & Row, Publishers, Inc., Vol. I, Chapter 6, 1970.)

secondary sexual characteristics. The sequence of events, as well as the average age of occurrence of these changes in the male, is shown in Figure 8–2. The first sign of the onset of puberty is the appearance of axillary sweating, increased testicular sensitivity to pressure, an enlargement of the testes, and reddening and stippling of the scrotum. An increase in the length of the penis occurs about the time the spurt in height begins. Axillary hair, facial hair, and voice changes are later manifestations of puberty and appear after the peak growth in height has passed. The first ejaculations of seminal fluid generally occur about a year after the penis has begun the adolescent spurt in growth. Nocturnal emissions usually begin at about age 14.

Most of the secondary sexual characteristics in the male are completed within two years after the onset of puberty, though shape changes, growth of body hair, and muscle development may continue at a slower rate until age 19 to 28. Although the greater part of the growth in stature for most North American males is complete by 18 to 19 years of age, an additional 1 to 2 cm in height can be expected during the third decade of life through continued growth of the vertebral column.

The sequence of pubertal changes in the girl is shown in Figure 8–3. The appearance of the breast bud occurs in the average female at about age 10, coinciding with the onset of the height spurt. Menarche occurs about 9 to 12 months after the peak height velocity has been achieved. For the average North American girl this will take place around 12.8 years of age. Although achievement of the menarche represents a ma-

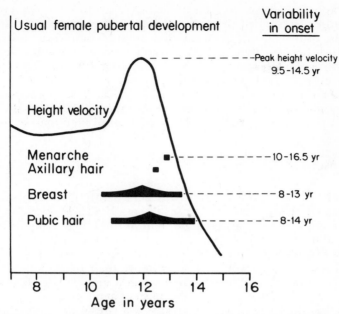

Usual female pubertal development

Variability in onset

Peak height velocity
9.5-14.5 yr

Height velocity

Menarche — 10-16.5 yr
Axillary hair

Breast — 8-13 yr

Pubic hair — 8-14 yr

Age in years

Figure 8–3 Sequence of events at adolescence in females. (Adapted from Hammar, S. L.: Adolescence. *In* Kelley, V. C. (ed.): Brenneman's Practice of Pediatrics. Hagerstown, Maryland, Harper & Row, Publishers, Inc., Vol. I, Chapter 6, 1970.)

ture stage of uterine development, it does not signify full reproductive capacity, since the earlier ovarian cycles are usually anovulatory. This period of adolescent sterility may last for 12 to 18 months after menarche.

Variations in pubertal development are not uncommon. Gynecomastia or benign adolescent breast hypertrophy affects approximately 60 per cent of males during their pubertal growth period. Asymmetrical breast development is present in approximately 8 per cent of girls and variations in the growth of pubic hair and axillary hair in relation to the onset of menarche affect about 3 per cent of normal girls. These pubertal variations may cause adolescents to question their normality and require interpretation and reassurance.

Physiological Changes

Also as a consequence of the appearance of sex hormones, many physiological as well as physical parameters change. Knowledge of these changes helps us to understand some of the common disorders found in this age group. One important change to note is the rise in gastric acidity. Abdominal pain is a common complaint during adolescence. Occasionally, frank ulcer symptoms appear; these may well relate not only to the life stresses and concerns of the patient but to this physiological rise in gastric acidity.

The apocrine glands in the skin begin to produce large amounts of thick sebum resulting in plugging of hair follicles and the picture of acne. Some of the reasons for acne may lie in the adolescent's life style, one in which hectic activity prevents frequent skin cleansing. Nevertheless, the physiological fact of the excessive sebum must be considered.

Red cell mass and hemoglobin rise during late adolescence, in the male under the effects of testosterone. In girls, these changes are less striking; a mild decrease in hemoglobin and red cell mass usually occurs several years after menarche, which persists until menopause.

Cardiovascular Changes

Pulse Rate.   The pulse rate drops persistently from birth until 10 years of age. The pulse rate decreases in both boys and girls during the adolescent period, more in the male than in the female, this sex difference becoming apparent during the late preadolescent period.

Blood Pressure.   The systolic blood pressure rises during the adolescent period in both sexes. Girls experience their rise in systolic blood pressure earlier, but adolescent boys exhibit a greater rise than that of girls. This sex difference becomes established at adolescence. Accompanying the rise in systolic blood pressure is a rise in the pulse pressure. The diastolic pressures show little change during adolescence and no sex difference.

Heart Size.   The heart size increases during childhood. From 12 years on, boys have larger values for the transverse cardiac diameters. In most girls an increase in cardiac size is closely related to the time of menarche.

Pulmonary Function.   The increase in vital capacity is fairly constant during childhood, but increases rapidly during adolescence. The vital capacity of the lungs is constantly greater in boys than in girls, even when corrected for differences in body size and surface area. This sex difference increases rapidly from ages 13 through 19 years. In contrast to other parameters, the respiratory rate under basal conditions decreases steadily throughout childhood and continues to do so during puberty, but no sex difference is apparent.

Psychosocial Changes

NANCY ROBINSON

The physical and physiological changes of adolescence described above act as a catalyst for psychological maturation. There are vast differences in the way in which adolescents handle the significant tasks of this period. While there are inevitable stresses — some of them the product of sexual maturity which occurs long before the young person is educated, employed, and/or otherwise ready to assume adult status — they need not prove overwhelming.

Erikson, whose description of earlier life tasks we considered in

Chapters 6 and 7, describes the major task of adolescence as the establishment of *a firm sense of identity* (as opposed to role confusion). Certainly one of the major tasks of this era is experimentation with, and awareness of, one's self-image, the roles one plays with respect to others, and a sense of the "type of person" one is. Erikson also emphasizes the need to experience diverse roles, culminating in what he terms *fidelity* — a consistent, mature commitment to one's community. These tasks take place in the context of others which are occurring at the same time: adjusting to a sexual role, establishing some degree of independence from the family unit, and making a vocational or career choice. For the half or more of the population who pursue higher education after completing high school, completing these tasks may be delayed into the early years of young adulthood. In general, this tends to make them harder, not easier, to resolve.

Cognitive Development. At about age 11 or 12, most adolescents become capable of functioning at a new cognitive level, that of *formal operations.* A new elegance of thought appears, and truly logical, scientific reasoning emerges. Adolescents enjoy their new ability, testing ideas by reasoning them out mentally, evaluating all possible outcomes and permutations. The world of abstract ideas opens up. In school, abstract systems such as historical schemes, mathematics, physics, and chemistry may become interesting. As this occurs, adolescents begin to see "here and now" reality as only one possible world among many alternatives. Enlightened by this exciting new insight, many become impatient with their parents and other adults, who have created, or at least accepted, an imperfect world. As a consequence, they become involved with groups demanding rapid social change, but in the process, they may fail to take into account conflicting principles or to see that one idea they hold dear runs counter to another. For example, they may campaign against violence on television without noting how their solutions would violate the principle of free speech. In the long run, though, their concern and agitation are probably good for the society as a whole.

Social Development. We have noted the marked individual differences in the ages at which adolescent growth spurts and puberty are attained. It is clear that in both the short run and the long run, early maturers, especially among the boys, have the advantage. They tend to be more self-assured, poised, matter-of-fact, and restrained in their behavior, and more attractive to and popular with their peers. Later maturing boys tend to have more body concerns and to react to their delayed puberty by withdrawal, restlessness, or acting out attention seeking behavior. They tend to be less well accepted by their peers and to be more insecure. Studies have shown that these behavioral differences can be detected even during the adult years, long after maturity has been attained. For girls, the difference tends to be in the same direction but less marked. Indeed, early maturing girls may at first be considered a bit out-of-step and sexually overprecocious, but by junior high school they generally come into their own.

During adolescence, membership in a group or clique assumes more importance than at any other time of life. The peer group provides a stabilizing influence for young people who are questioning their own identities and breaking away from their families. It can also provide at least some temporary answers to the adolescent's questions about identity and belonging.

Teenagers feel an overwhelming need to conform in order to be accepted. They want to dress like others, talk with them, listen to the same music, engage the same issues and ideas, carry out the same "anti-establishment" behaviors. Since in the United States there tends to be quite a broad split between the values of adults and those of adolescents, this may well lead to conflicts with adults who respond negatively to slavish conforming and (correctly) sense the "put down" of adult values.

Establishing Intimate Relationships.   Much of the ease with which an adolescent accepts sexual changes and the accompanying sexual drives is determined by previous preparation. Although sexual identification becomes firmly established during adolescence, early childhood is probably a more critical period. Successful identification appears to result from a combination of parental conditioning and reinforcement, parental role models, role models provided by other adults, and (as yet poorly understood) biologic factors.

Adolescents tend to be sexually active, a fact which disturbs most parents. Masturbation, heterosexual experimentation, and sometimes homosexual experience are common. Earlier maturation, in addition to changing cultural attitudes toward sex, may be producing a significant change in sexual behavior in this age group. Data regarding normal adolescent sexual behavior are incomplete. Since the 1960's, there has been a change in sexual attitudes among teenagers. Whether these changes reflect an increase in adolescent sexual activity is unclear. The double standard related to sex behavior for the male is declining. The percentage of sexually active males and females is similar. Sexual activity among adolescents is occurring at an earlier age and is affecting all socioeconomic segments of the teenage population. Major health problems related to teenage sexual behavior are a rising incidence of venereal disease, increasing teenage pregnancies, abortions, and ineffective pregnancy prevention. Teenagers usually channel sexual drives partly into their studies, sports, and hobbies as a means of handling some of their anxieties about their developing sexuality. Most adolescents learn to accept their own sexuality. Some, however, withdraw from their peers, become preoccupied, exhibit excessive modesty, or deny their sexual changes. Often they gravitate toward a younger, less mature, and therefore less threatening peer group. Frequently such adolescents could profit from professional attention.

Today, there is an overall trend toward a more liberal view of sexuality. Even "unsophisticates" are constantly exposed to sexual information, sexually provocative music and films, and a growing trend toward sexuality even on the (previously prudish) TV screen. It is not surprising that in the United States, more than half of girls have engaged in intercourse by age 19. Yet, responsibility has not kept pace with sexual awakening. Unwanted pregnancies, venereal disease, and exploitation of young men and women have been the result. (See Chapter 3.)

Establishing Independence. By age 15, most adolescents show some signs of emancipating themselves from their families. Appropriately, their families tend to reduce limits on their behavior as the young people grow away from the nuclear family. They put distance between themselves and their parents in a variety of ways, such as becoming involved in outside activities, selecting a different religion and/or different political orientation, and spending time with their peers and friends who are unknown to the family. Communication between the adolescent and parents often breaks down, although the teenager may be able to establish positive relationships with other adults whose support, advice, and confidence he or she values. During this period, young people need more privacy, as well as respect as worthwhile young adults.

Making a Vocational, Educational, and/or Career Choice. During the adolescent years, teenagers begin to think about their future. Pressures in our society unfortunately require teenagers to commit themselves and to make these decisions progressively earlier. Even so, adolescence provides considerable room for "role testing" and changing of goals. It is characteristic of poorer students and those from lower socioeconomic groups that few vocational alternatives are considered; many teenagers either drop out of high school or take the first job after graduation that comes along. Young people who, by reason of their own academic capabilities or the orientation of their families, realize the number of alternative paths open to them, may feel overwhelmed by their freedom to choose the "one best" life path for themselves. Some young people opt for, and effectively use, a period of thoughtful retreat from the academic milieu before returning to higher education and preparation for a career. Other young people "opt out" of the system, finding ways of maintaining themselves without reaching the potential which they and their families recognize to be theirs. It is important to keep doors open for young people so that they need not abandon hope of a productive and satisfying adult role by their temporary retreat.

MORBIDITY AND MORTALITY DURING ADOLESCENCE

The major causes of death in the adolescent age group are violent ones. Accidents, homicide, and suicide account for 73 per cent of all deaths in this age group. (See Figure 8–4.) For the past decade suicides in adolescents have shown a steady increase and reflect such prevailing factors as chronic family problems, reactive depression, social alienation, and a climate of violence. Adolescent girls make more suicidal gestures than boys, but the adolescent male is more successful in his suicidal attempts and is less likely to give warnings or seek professional help.

The leading nontraumatic causes of death during adolescence are malignant neoplasms and cardiovascular disorders.

Accurate morbidity data on the adolescent age group are very difficult to obtain. Few medical problems are unique to adolescents, with the exception of acne, Osgood-Schlatter's disease, and delayed puberty. The most common complaints seen in student health services relate to

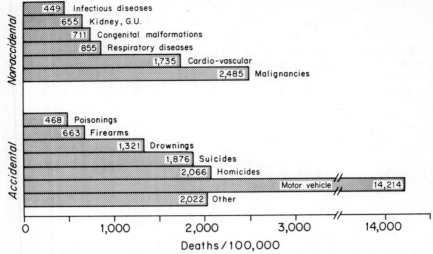

Figure 8–4   Causes of death in the United States in the 15- to 24-year age group, based on World Health Organization statistics.

upper respiratory tract infections, various types of traumatic disorders, gastrointestinal disorders, and emotional upsets.

In special medical referral facilities for adolescents, the most common problems seen are: school underachievement, obesity, behavior disorders, growth and metabolic disorders, seizures, infectious diseases, and mental retardation. Obviously, patients seen in these clinics represent a select population, but they reflect areas in which physicians dealing with this age group need to develop expertise.

COMMON DISORDERS

Infectious Diseases

The incidence of the usual childhood diseases, such as rubella, rubeola, mumps, and chickenpox, has continued to decline in the adolescent age group as a result of effective immunization programs or childhood exposure. Many older adolescents, however, have not been adequately protected against rubella, giving rise to a susceptible population of older teenagers and young adults. The incidence of pulmonary tuberculosis tends to increase during adolescence. Though adolescents are susceptible to all types of bacterial and viral infections, only two will be discussed.

Infectious Mononucleosis.   Infectious mononucleosis is an acute infectious disease most commonly diagnosed in older children, adolescents, and young adults. It is generally felt to be related to the Ebstein-Barr virus, although other viruses such as cytomegalovirus can produce an infectious mononucleosis-like picture. Generally, it is a disease of low communicability. The peak incidence occurs in the spring and autumn; the incubation period is generally from 4 to 14 days, with the onset being acute or gradual.

This disease often is characterized by chronic fatigue or generalized malaise, and should always be considered in a teenager who complains of feeling tired and listless, even though obvious emotional reasons for these symptoms may be present. The cardinal signs are fever, sore throat, enlarged lymph nodes, and splenomegaly. The febrile phase is variable, lasting one to three weeks. The pharyngitis may appear as a late rather than an early manifestation and may be characterized by the presence of an exudate and a thick, white, shaggy membrane.

The lymphadenopathy usually makes its appearance during the febrile stage, beginning with the cervical nodes and gradually becoming generalized. The enlarged nodes are usually tender, discrete, and firm, rarely becoming suppurative. Splenomegaly occurs in about 50 per cent of cases. Other findings may include hepatitis, skin eruptions, central nervous system involvement, and pneumonitis. Hepatitis is relatively frequent, with abnormal liver function tests present in about 80 per cent of patients. Skin rashes, which occur in 10 to 15 per cent of cases, typically appear as an erythematous maculopapular eruption similar to that of rubella, and often are present from the fourth to the tenth day.

Central nervous system involvement may occur early or late in the course of the disease, and such suggestive symptoms as stiff neck, blurred vision, mental confusion, weakness of the extremities, and depressed reflexes may be present.

The blood smear usually shows an absolute increase of greater than 20 per cent atypical lymphocytes peaking, in most cases, around the seventh to the tenth day of the illness. A positive Monospot test and a rise in serum heterophile antibody titer depend on the phase of the illness. The serum heterophile antibody titer usually rises by the end of the first week or early in the second week, but may subsequently fall rapidly, making it easy to miss a positive titer.

Venereal Disease. Once thought to be conquered, venereal disease has again become a major health problem. Since 1957, the incidence of gonorrhea has continued to rise at an alarming rate and has reached pandemic proportions. At best, the reported cases represent only a small portion of the actual number, since many patients are treated by private doctors. Because of the social stigma involved and concern for secrecy, many cases are unreported. Over half of the cases reported in this country and in Western Europe involve the 15 to 24 year age group. The increased incidence appears to be directly related to changing sexual mores and behavior among young adults and is not peculiar to any particular social class or stratum. The apparent increase in male homosexuality is also of significance in the spread of venereal disease among older adolescents and young adults. Male homosexuals appear to have several times as many contacts as heterosexuals in a shorter period of time. The confirmed adult homosexual poses the greatest public health threat because of his mobility and transient encounters, often with a multiplicity of unknown partners, which make an epidemiological approach to case finding extremely difficult.

Serological tests for syphilis are routinely performed in many hospitals, clinics, and physicians' offices. However, gonorrhea poses a greater threat to this age group in many more ways than syphilis because of the difficulty of diagnosis, particularly in the female. In adolescent girls the diagnosis is easily missed since girls seldom complain of pain, discharge, or other symptoms until the infection spreads to the uterus and fallopian tubes, and pelvic inflammation develops.

Acute gonorrhea in the male generally appears as a urethritis or urethral discharge and is diagnosed by culture or by finding organisms in the smear of the exudate. When prostatitis develops in males, homosexual practices should be suspected.

Because of difficulties in diagnosis, all sex partners of males who have gonorrhea should be treated regardless of culture or smear.

Chronic Diseases

Juvenile Obesity.   Obesity is a major health problem of the adolescent. It has been estimated that over 10 million teenagers, or between 16 and 20 per cent of the adolescent population are obese. Juvenile onset obesity rarely begins at puberty, but rather dates from the early childhood years. In those cases where the weight problem is long-standing, not only does the patient have a greater body weight for age, but often an advanced height age, moderately advanced bone maturation, and a greater lean body mass. These adolescents often develop pubertal changes slightly earlier than the non-obese. In adolescent cases with early onset obesity, at least 65 per cent of the parents and 40 per cent of the siblings are also obese, suggesting a genetic predisposition towards the development of obesity. A susceptibility to the later development of obesity in childhood has been related to feeding practices in early infancy and rapid weight gain during the first year of life. Hypernutrition during sensitive periods of adipose cell replication may be a major factor in the development of juvenile obesity. In any event, the present methods of treatment are largely unsuccessful and usually fail to bring about a permanent reduction in body weight. Ninety-five per cent of this population appear to have exogenous obesity; rarely can an endocrine cause be found.

Obesity in the adolescent is complicated by social and psychological factors. In part, this may be due to society's attitude in viewing obesity as a moral defect rather than as a chronic disease.

The psychosocial characteristics of the obese adolescent are important and affect the success of any therapeutic efforts. Many obese teenagers feel socially ostracized, ugly, and unacceptable. Depression is frequent. Severe environmental stress and intra-family conflicts often potentiate the weight problem, since many obese patients tend to react to anxiety and stress by eating compulsively. Motivation for weight loss is frequently limited in the adolescent. His goals for weight reduction are often unrealistic. If weight loss is to be achieved and maintained by our present methods, careful attention must be given to emotional adjustments, self-image, sexual feelings, social adaptation, and activity patterns, as well as to the diet. Providing adequate nutritional education to the adolescent is extremely important. The group therapy approach to managing obesity has been successful in some cases. Fad diets, high protein liquid diets, and starvation regimens are inappropriate for treating adolescent obesity. Behavioral modification has been useful in selected, highly motivated cases. Ileal bypass surgery has generally been reserved for only the most refractory patients with medical indications for rapid weight reduction. Every obese adolescent deserves a thorough medical and psychosocial evaluation as part of an initial workup.

Seizure Disorders. The actual incidence of seizure disorders in the adolescent and young adult populations is difficult to establish because of the reluctance of families to reveal this affliction. It is often quoted that one in every 100 persons in the United States suffers from some type of seizure disorder. Most seizure patients are diagnosed, or experience their first seizure, before they are 20 years old. Grand mal is the most common type of seizure encountered in the adolescent. Petit mal epilepsy, although usually tending to disappear as puberty approaches, is also not uncommon in this age group. Temporal lobe (psychomotor seizures) epilepsy is often difficult to diagnose; the clinical picture is varied and may include automaton-like behavior, lip smacking, chewing movements, confused psychotic attacks, nocturnal fears, and sleepwalking. Seizures are only a symptom of a disease and not a disease in themselves; therefore, every adolescent with a seizure problem requires a thorough evaluation in order to rule out possible underlying disorders such as hypoglycemia, brain tumor, vascular anomaly, or atrophic lesions which may be treatable.

Seizures often become difficult to control at the time of puberty. Adolescent girls may experience seizures just before the onset of their menstrual period. This may be related to the complex hormonal changes that occur during the menstrual cycle or to the increased fluid retention which may irritate the central nervous system and lower the seizure threshold. Hyperventilation, water loading, sudden environmental changes, stressful and highly charged emotional situations, or family disruptions have been known to increase seizure activity.

The adolescent with seizures usually has many anxieties and concerns which require patience, understanding, and skillful handling. Excessive restrictions are unnecessary, and the adolescent should be encouraged to become as self-sufficient and independent as possible. Physical activity and participation in sports should be encouraged, while some activities, such as mountain climbing, should be discouraged. Other activities, such as swimming and sailing, may be permitted in the company of others rather than as a solitary activity. Physical and peer group activities are important to the overall development of the teenagers, and restrictions should be kept to a minimum.

In many cases, the epileptic adolescent must learn to conduct his life and social activities without the use of a car. This is usually upsetting to the adolescent boy, unless he is well prepared in advance. Many epileptic adolescents are concerned about the advisability of marriage. There is no contraindication to marriage for most seizure patients, provided they are otherwise able to assume the responsibilities which marriage involves. Girls are often concerned about the possible adverse effects of pregnancy upon their seizures. In some instances, seizures occur more frequently during pregnancy, particularly when complicated by fluid retention, excessive weight gain, or toxemia. Some anticonvulsant medications have been shown to have teratogenic effects upon the developing fetus. Adolescent girls with epilepsy require careful counseling regarding the advisability of pregnancy and the risks involved. Teenagers with epilepsy require occupational counseling in order to steer them into an appropriate vocation. The seizure patient is undoubtedly best employed in a business or vocation which allows some flexibility. Workmen's compensation laws and industrial insurance vary from state to state at the present time and may greatly limit occupational choices.

Behavior Disorders

NANCY ROBINSON

For many young people, the teenage years are marred by uncertainty, inconsistency, conflict, and frequent loneliness, although in most instances these feelings occur in a context of success and progress which make them tolerable and even conducive to growth. Too many youngsters, however, become casualties. Approximately 25 per cent of teenagers drop out of school before graduation. Schizophrenia, depression, drug abuse, and suicide become appreciably more frequent during this period. Accident rates are high. Teenage marriage (and frequently, subsequent divorce), early pregnancies (see Chapter 3), and juvenile delinquency complete the gloomy picture.

School Underachievement. Poor school achievement may stem from a variety of causes. Retarded and slow learning young people who have functioned with reasonable comfort in the self-contained classrooms of the elementary school may become spectacular failures in junior high school (especially as their nonretarded peers enter the cognitive era of formal operations); such young people need special programming to minimize their feelings of failure and to maximize their achievement. Adolescents with specific deficits in learning to read or master other school subjects despite normal intelligence will also need attention, as in the earlier years of school. Many of these students will give evidence of visual-perceptual problems, soft neurological signs, or other findings suggestive of mild central nervous system dysfunction; they are also likely to show behavior problems resulting from years of frustration, repeated school failures, and consequent disturbed peer relationships.

There is also another group of teenagers whose school failures are psychogenic; these may or may not have been underachievers in elementary school. They may be preoccupied with family stresses or with their own internal conflict. School refusal or inconsistent school attendance in an adolescent who is bright, sensitive, overanxious, and unable to cope with the school situation represents a serious type of school problem which usually requires prompt intervention. The parents are often unable to cope constructively with the problem. They may set standards which are unrealistically low or may make demands for scholastic achievement that are too intense. Sometimes, then, the school failure may be an effective passive-aggressive method of retaliation against parents. In other instances, cultural expectations, peer group values, and familial patterns of underachievement may be largely responsible.

Rebelliousness.   Because the maturing process is at times painful and unsettling, some adolescents try to define their identities in a negative fashion by opposing values and persons they have previously admired. Many parents feel uncertain and threatened by the developing independence of the adolescent and respond by trying to establish tighter limits and firmer controls, thereby encouraging rebellion rather than the compliance or growth they desire. Some rebelliousness during adolescence must be considered "par for the course," but when the pattern becomes consistent and self-destructive, counseling is advisable. The professional must take extra care with such young people not to assume an authoritarian or judgmental role, but rather to become a trusted ally. Although the professional is a member in good standing of the society at large, and is interested in effecting a reconciliation with the family, he or she should have a basic respect for and trust in the worth of the adolescent, and should consider their needs and perceptions.

Antisocial Behavior.   Antisocial behavior in teenagers appears to be increasing, although there is also some tendency toward more complete reporting of offenses. Referrals to the juvenile court system indicate that the antisocial boy is most frequently involved in car theft, running away, and stealing; girls are usually referred for sexual acting out or running away. In dealing with such situations, it is important that the teenager understand his or her responsibility for the transgression, and that at the same time basic, underlying causes be brought to light. In some instances, the lawbreaking is an expression of rebellion; in some, a common activity of the peer group; in others, it is the only way the teenager knows to call attention to his or her unhappiness and need for assistance outside the family.

Drug Usage.   The medical profession and the pharmaceutical industry must share much of the blame for drug abuse today. The idea that every ill, anxiety, and worry which besets people can be cured with a pill, and the overprescription of potent pharmacologic agents as a substitute for spending time with patients to find out what is really bothering them, have both been factors in the increasing use and abuse of drugs in all age groups.

Drug usage among teenagers and young adults has become an increasing health hazard. Adolescents who use drugs are not necessarily alienated, in rebellion, or even emotionally disturbed, though they may be. Many are "experience seekers." Some take drugs to prove their courage by risk taking, to relieve loneliness, to provide an emotional experience, or to seek meaning in life.

Marijuana users often report experiencing freedom from anxiety, distortion of sensation and perception, release of inhibitions, and freedom from hunger. Limited or casual marijuana use probably should be considered today a "normal" activity, at least among older adolescents, although like any other escape activity (even watching television), it can occur to excess. Alcohol also is in widespread use, although here the degree of abuse is greater. Alcohol related problems far exceed the problems related to other drugs, perhaps as much as tenfold. Alcoholism among teenagers is becoming widespread. The mixture of automobiles and alcohol is particularly lethal. Our society in general has failed to acknowledge the degree to which alcohol is abused by all ages, and retains an ambivalent attitude toward the drunk who is seen as "funny" or "pitiful," depending upon the circumstances. Although there are clearly biologic and cultural predisposing factors, the problem is basically why an individual's life is so painful that escape is sought. The problem is rampant. One carefully done study in a suburban community showed that among high school students in the early 1970's, 82 per cent reported regular use of alcohol compared with 40 per cent reporting regular use of marijuana. In a middle school population in the same community, the figures were an astonishing 50 per cent for alcohol and 6 per cent for marijuana. In addition to these broadly used drugs, smaller proportions of the teenage population make use of barbiturates, amphetamines, heroin, morphine, and hallucinogenic drugs. These drugs may lead to dangerous side effects such as nausea, anorexia, vasomotor changes, headaches, palpitations, tremors, and even grand mal seizures. Amphetamines in particular may lead to sensitivity and suspiciousness bordering on paranoia.

Role Confusion.   Erikson, as we noted, has pointed to inadequate role identity as the major crisis of adolescence. Without a firm sense of self, a direction, a commitment, young people often continue a futile search for the fantasied "real self" which might be better than the present self they know. Failure to establish role identity may lead, among other outcomes, to (1) continued bewilderment, often with depression; (2) alienation, a sense of belonging nowhere; (3) temporary overidentification with a political, religious, or other group which demands total devotion and furnishes a ready-made identity in place of one painfully hewn from personal growth; and (4) ill-considered entry into the adult world, out of school and into the first job and/or intimate partnership that comes along.

Depression.   Although depression is much more frequent in older patients (see Chapter 10), episodes of depression and acute anxiety reactions are not uncommon in adolescents. Often these occur when an individual experiences separation and loss — for example, a broken love affair, separation from home upon going to college, departing for another city, or joining the armed services. Ordinarily such episodes are self-limiting, but suicide or self-destructive risk taking is always a danger. In some adolescents, these depressive episodes represent exaggerated tendencies toward mood swings which will eventually become apparent as bipolar or unipolar affective disorders. An underlying depression may be masked by "depressive equivalents" or other problem behaviors such as drug abuse, sexual promiscuity, a drop in school performance, temper outbursts, boredom and listlessness, a negative or delinquent self-image, attention problems, obesity, excessive sleep, or hyperactivity.

Recognition of the depression and the potential for suicidal behavior is important in proper management. Brief hospitalization is often appropriate.

Adolescent Reaction to Physical Illness.   Adolescents tend to be very self-conscious about their appearance, their physical status, and anything which sets them off from others. Illness, particularly a chronic illness which requires medication, diet, or any other special regimen, may be very threatening. Often, one sees denial, anger, and depression. For example, children with diabetes may reject medical regimes they have previously accepted, ignore their diets, refuse medication and urine checks, and so on. It is important that health professionals understand these reactions and react supportively, while letting the parent know the risks being run and the fact that hospitalization may become necessary if the regime is not resumed.

Schizophrenia.   Initial episodes of schizophrenia often appear in adolescents and young adults. A broad variety of behaviors are called schizophrenic, suggesting that there may be many schizophrenias. The most important aspect of the disorder is a disturbance in basic thought processes. There is a tendency toward a loosening of associations (disjointed expressions that run on in a scattered way and fail to reach a logical conclusion) with cognitive "slippage," autistic thought processes (determined by personal needs, not reality), and disturbances in emotional expression. Affect is often either inappropriate (e.g., tears, anger, or laughter unwarranted by the situation) or bland and flat (lackluster mood) and lacking empathy or a "sense of community" with others. Massive anxiety and marked withdrawal may be seen. The patient may experience delusions (false ideas, misinterpreted perceptions) and hallucinations (experiences occurring in the absence of an appropriate external stimulus). No one of these symptoms by itself necessarily indicates schizophrenia, but taken together, especially when they represent a change from the adolescent's previous status, they may well indicate psychosis.

Some schizophrenics exhibit a lifelong pattern of underachievement, withdrawal, and increasingly bizarre and/or retarded behavior. Others erupt in a more acute fashion, often appearing to be escaping from reality in response to a very threatening precipitating event. The former type, called process schizophrenia, carries a somewhat more pessimistic prognosis than the latter, called reactive schizophrenia, even though in reactive schizophrenia there is a strong tendency for episodes to recur throughout life. There are several theories about the origins of schizophrenia. Recent studies suggest a strong hereditary factor or at least a familial predisposition, with evidence implicating biochemical abnormalities in the amount and/or receptor functions of dopamine systems in the central nervous system. Experiential factors include family disturbances, conflicting demands from parents, and other stresses. Early treatment with appropriate antipsychotic medication can help to avert blatant psychotic reactions, to lessen their severity and perhaps their recurrence, and/or to maintain the individual as a functioning member of society despite deviant affective and cognitive behavior.

SUMMARY

Adolescence is a period of dynamic growth and development involving physical, physiological, and psychosocial changes. Human growth, however, is not a static process; many of the processes begun during this decade continue into adulthood at a slower rate and in a much less dramatic manner. Likewise, much of groundwork for the completion of adolescent tasks, particularly in the psychosocial areas, is laid in early childhood.

While the adolescent period is generally a healthy one, many adult illnesses and disorders may well begin during the teenage years. Any adolescent who deviates from his peers, shows a different pattern of growth and maturation, or has a chronic disease or a handicap, is potentially at risk and requires special understanding. Major health problems such as accidents, teenage pregnancy, venereal disease, depression, school failure, and teenage unemployment relate to many of the developmental issues of adolescence in our society and demand increasing knowledge and attention from health care professionals.

REFERENCES

Conger, J. J.: Adolescence and Youth: Psychological Development in a Changing World. 2nd ed. New York, Harper and Row, Inc., 1977.
Daniel, W. A., Jr.: The Adolescent Patient. St. Louis, C. V. Mosby Company, 1970.
Erikson, E.: Identity, Youth, and Crisis. New York, Norton, 1968.
Gallagher, J. R., Heald, F. P., and Garell, D. C.: Medical Care of the Adolescent. New York, Appleton-Century-Crofts, Inc., 1976.
Gardner, L. I. (Ed.): Endocrine and Genetic Diseases of Childhood. 2nd ed. Philadelphia, W. B. Saunders Company, 1975.
Hammar, S. L.: Adolescence. In V. C. Kelley (Ed.): Brennemann's Practice of Pediatrics. New York, Harper and Row, Inc., Vol. II, 1975.
Matteson, D. R.: Adolescence Today: Sex Roles and the Search for Identity. Homewood, Ill., Dorsey, 1975.
Smart, M. S., and Smart, R. C., (Eds.) Adolescents: Development and Relationships. New York, MacMillan, 1973.
Sorenson, R. C.: Adolescent Sexuality in Contemporary América. New York, World Publishing, 1973.
Tanner, J. M.: Growth at Adolescence. 2nd ed. Oxford, Blackwell Scientific Publications, 1962.
Usdin, G. L. (Ed.): Adolescence: Care and Counseling. Philadelphia, J. B. Lippincott Company, 1967.

9

The Young Adult

ELAINE D. HENLEY
JEFF ALTMAN

LIFE SITUATION

Young adulthood spans roughly the years from 18 to 35. It is the unique life stage when the descending curve of physical growth intersects the ascending curve of aging. It is also a time of unrivaled and often stressful psychosocial transitions. Major changes that confront the young adult include separation from parents, siblings, and close friends, establishment of new relationships, marriage, first pregnancy, and beginning parenthood. Other significant changes include completion of formal education, transition into occupational roles, and migration precipitated by a job or career.

Physical and Physiological Changes

For most young adults, full physical and reproductive maturity has been achieved. Many physiological functions have increased to peak levels (Fig. 2–4). In addition, parameters such as lean body mass, recall ability, reaction time (Figs. 9–2, 9–3, and 9–4), and bone density (Fig. 10–1) also reach their peak during this stage. Relative to body fat, muscle mass has also increased but without significant change in height or weight. Physical performance involving strength and endurance now unfortunately is destined toward a steady decline with continued aging. In contrast, psychosocial growth erupts with renewed vigor and velocity as the young adult strives to attain total emotional independence.

Psychosocial Changes
NANCY ROBINSON

The initial period of young adulthood in many lives is an era of high drama; by ages 30 to 35, however, most people have determined

187

Figure 9–1 The young adult: vigor, stamina, peak performance, and risk taking. Brad, the biker; Karen, the climber.

Figure 9–2 The percentage of body fat increases gradually with age. At age 75 it is double that found in the young adult. (Adapted from Finch, C. E., and Hayflick, L., (Eds.): Handbook Biology of Aging. New York, Von Nostrand Rheinhold Co., 1977, p. 685.)

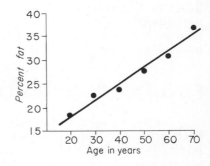

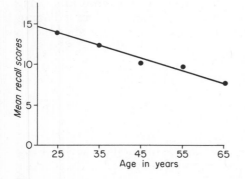

Figure 9–3 Mean recall scores gradually decrease with increasing age. After age 60, scores fall to about half those found in the young adult. (Adapted from Schonfield, D.: Memory changes with age. Nature, *208* (918): 169, 1965. In Finch, C. E., and Hayflick, L., (Eds.): Handbook Biology of Aging. New York, Von Nostrand Rheinhold Co., 1977, p. 676.)

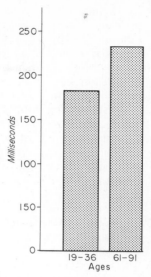

Figure 9–4 Simple auditory reaction time involving finger movement increases with advanced age. Similar delays in response have been demonstrated with jaw and foot movement. (Adapted from Birren and Botwinick, J. Geront., *10*:429, 1955a. In Finch, C. E., and Hayflick, L., (Eds.): Handbook Biology of Aging. New York, Von Nostrand Rheinhold Co., 1977, p. 701.)

the pattern of their lives, their personalities, their interests, their careers, their families, and their friends. Many life changes occur at the beginning of this period, far fewer occur toward its end.

Psychosocially, "young adulthood" is determined by role rather than physiology, beginning when one leaves school and assumes a productive, rather than a dependent, place in society. For the high school dropout, then, adulthood may begin abruptly as early as age 16. For the highly educated young person, true adulthood may be postponed until well into the 20's. Those who attend college enjoy a kind of moratorium period which has been called *youth* by Keniston. This period, which is considerably more characteristic of middle than lower socioeconomic groups, permits a gradual assumption of responsibilities. It allows for protracted preparation for adult roles and encourages a period of "shopping around" for an "identity-in-depth" and a value system warranting a set of commitments. The tyranny of the peer group, so strong during adolescence, subsides; youth provides a buffer period for individual exploration and experimentation with even the outlandish. Parents and others who overreact to temporary adaptations fail to get the point: it is mainly by successive approximations, trying on and discarding unsatisfactory roles, that many young people "find their way." That emerging identity usually expresses a strong continuity with the past, although it may not seem so at the time. The professional who keeps a long range perspective may be able to allay parental anxieties and suggest optimistic outcomes.

The significant conscious decisions which must be made by the young adult exceed in number and impact those which occur at any other time of life. This process has, of course, begun during adolescence, but it accelerates at this time. Few, if any, of the decisions are actually irrevocable, but that fact is not always apparent from the viewpoint of the young person. Among the developmental tasks are those which follow.

Separation from Family.   Most young people move out of the parental home during this period, abruptly losing an important source of emotional support and suddenly confronting unaccustomed loneliness, financial concerns, and the myriad details of self-care. Many young people move into a transitional relationship with a roommate, a heterosexual partner, or a communal group, before coping alone, and many never reach the "solo stage."

Establishing Intimate Relationships.   For Erikson, whose work we have met in previous chapters, the primary task of young adulthood is the establishment of *intimacy,* as opposed to its negative opposite, *isolation.* Erikson maintains that only an individual who has as an adolescent established a firm sense of identity, can risk the experience of intimacy, which requires "losing oneself in another." Intimacy implies an openness and depth in one's relationship, not only with sexual and conjugal partners, but with selected friends and family members.

Long Term Partnerships.   From adolescence onward, mating becomes a major goal for most young people. Relationships become less diffuse, longer lasting, more exclusive, and more sexualized. "Living together" has recently become an accepted stage of the courtship pattern, with only 1 out of 3 or 4 such relationships culminating in marriage. These cohabitational relationships are not, as often thought, specifically characteristic of middle class young adults, although it may be that more lower class partners remain unmarried for economic reasons rather than for reasons of preference. One recent survey by Clayton and Voss of 2500 males representative of the general population, ages 20 to 30 years, demonstrates that the basic pattern is still marriage oriented. Of this sample, only 5 per cent were living with a woman to whom they were not married (although 18 per cent had done so at some time for a period of six months or more); 52 per cent were married; 32 per cent were living alone or with roommates; and 11 per cent were living with parents.

All but 2 to 5 per cent of American adults marry at some time in their lives. There is a strong tendency toward assortative mating, that is, partner resemblance. This similarity is detectable in physical characteristics, education and intelligence, social and ethnic background, religion, temperament, and life outlook. The degree of partner similarity relates to the stability of the marriage.

In modern Western society, the shrinking family has lost many of its former functions, its geographic stability, and its relatedness to an extended family network. Its functions are largely reduced to procreation (see Chapters 3 through 6), friendship of husband and wife, and maintaining the emotional equilibrium of the family members. It is no longer economic bonds but primarily emotional bonds on which the existence of the family depends — an oasis in a stress producing, technologically sophisticated, competitive, and imperfect society.

Sexual Relations.   Sexual activity is very much a part of the lives of most young adults, married or unmarried. Indeed, by age 19, some 40 per cent of white never-married women and some 80 per cent of black never-married women report that they have engaged in intercourse, according to Kantner and Zelnik; comparable figures for males are higher. Greater sexual activity in lower income groups does not, however, necessarily imply greater "sexual freedom." Middle class individuals, on the average, express less stereotyped and more mutual, egalitarian, and caring attitudes toward sexual activity and the sexual partner. Poorer working class women are much more likely to feel "anti-sexual" or desexualized, while males in that group are expected to dominate the sexual relationship. In nonsexual aspects of the marital relationship as well, there is apparently more segregation and isolation in low income families in family life, child rearing, work, and leisure time activities. But with greater freedom and mutuality come higher aspirations, and it is more likely to be the sexually dysfunctional middle class patient who seeks advice from the health professional.

Cognitive Changes. Cognitive changes are usually minimal during this period. Although there is some indication from recent research that an even higher order stage than formal operations (see Chapter 8) may emerge during young adulthood, on the whole, cognitive behavior tends to be very stable in early adulthood. The declines in efficiency to be noted later on are imperceptible during this period, learning is rapid, and an expanding knowledge base usually enables the young adult to function at the peak of his or her cognitive powers.

Vocational Changes. As discussed in Chapter 8, high school dropouts and even high school graduates are likely to take the first job that comes along without much consideration of a lifetime career; college educated youth, aware of many more alternatives, may agonize over the decision. For this reason, many "stop out" of college for a year or so along the way. Yet, with rapidly increasing technology, extended education guarantees neither a job opening nor job security. Retraining and even significant occupational shifts may be necessary more than once during one's working life.

Work, including housekeeping, consumes more waking hours than any other category of human activity. Moreover, the occupational status of the family head largely determines social status of the family, which in turn relates to a wide network of values, customs, and expectations. The job or jobs held by family members (or lack of them) determines in large part the family's standard of living; where it lives; how often it moves; who takes care of the children; hours of waking, eating, and sleeping; evening and weekend activities; church and other organizational membership; and so on.

Stabilizing. By the late 20's, most of the initial choices and changes have occurred. Education is complete and young families are established. To older people who have married, these years often seem in retrospect the most satisfying of all. (The unmarried tend to look back on childhood as happiest.) The pattern begins to fall into place, steps on the career ladder are begun, and a view of oneself as a stable, worthy, productive, "self-actualized" individual emerges.

Readaptation. Somewhere around age 30, many young adults (especially those in the middle class who still see alternatives as open) undergo a reassessment, modifying their early choices. Sometimes this means a job switch, a career switch, a return to school, dissolving a marriage, or moving to a different city. This may be a particularly difficult time for couples who married before only one of them went to college or trained for a profession.

"Rooting and Extending."   This phrase of Gail Sheehy's refers to the settling down which tends to occur in the early 30's. Life becomes more predictable and conventional. Most people settle down, buy houses, rear children, become members of a community, and pursue their careers. The children become the true focus of family life, with consequently less attention for the husband and wife, and frequently a decline in marital satisfaction. Yet, most people see these as good, productive, and even comfortable years.

COMMON PROBLEMS

Relative to other life stages, especially childhood and senescence, young adulthood is generally a time of well-being, of good health and freedom from serious illness. Even with the overall low morbidity and mortality characteristic of this age span, significant problems and diseases do occur which demand care and treatment. These health conditions can be categorized in the following way:

(1) Diseases that originate earlier in life but continue to exist, or first manifest themselves, in young adulthood.

(2) Diseases that are latent, or first recognized during young adulthood, but have their major impact later in life.

(3) Diseases that are unique to the period of young adulthood.

Although most of the developmental problems and crises of the growing years have resolved, the acute infectious diseases of childhood are still seen with frequency. Some illnesses such as rheumatic heart disease or glomerulonephritis, although beginning earlier in life, become major health problems in the young adult. Conversely, not only do diseases typical of middle age appear, but degenerative changes not yet clinically manifest have already begun. From autopsy studies of American soldiers, of average age 22, killed in the Korean and Vietnam wars, about half already had gross or microscopic evidence of coronary artery arteriosclerosis. Other problems, such as sexually transmitted diseases, hepatitis B, or testicular cancer are more characteristically found in the 20's and 30's.

Important concerns and goals for health professionals caring for this age group must include not only the treatment of chronic and acute diseases, but health education, health maintenance, and disease prevention.

Behavioral Problems

NANCY ROBINSON

The attainment of adulthood, while viewed as rewarding by most people, brings unprecedented responsibility and stress. Admissions to

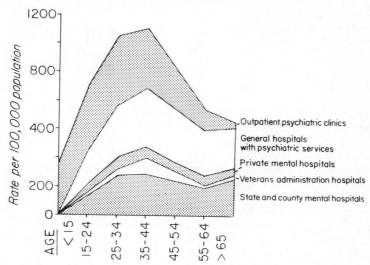

ADMISSIONS TO MENTAL HOSPITALS DURING 1966 BY AGE

Rate per 100,000 population

1200
800
400
200
0

AGE < 15, 15-24, 25-34, 35-44, 45-54, 55-64, > 65

Outpatient psychiatric clinics

General hospitals
with psychiatric services

Private mental hospitals

Veterans administration hospitals

State and county mental hospitals

Figure 9–5 From Kramer, M., Taube, C. A., and Redick, R. W.: Patterns of Use of Psychiatric Facilities by the Aged: Past, Present and Future. In Eisdorfer, C. and Lawton, P. M., (Eds.): The Psychology of Adult Development and Aging. Copyright 1973 by the American Psychological Association. Reprinted by permission.

mental hospitals and outpatient psychiatric clinics increase dramatically during the early adult years. (See Figure 9–5.) (The decline in admissions with increasing age reflects longer term hospitalization patterns.)

Risk Taking. Risk taking behaviors of adolescents and young adults bear special emphasis. Despite their fears of inadequacy with respect to life's larger goals, young people are often blatantly unrealistic about ordinary risks. (See final section of this chapter.) They often fail to consider the limits of their physical endurance. Wear and tear injuries to muscles and tendons may therefore constitute a considerable shock to their self-image.

Aftermath of Precipitous Decisions. The pressures of the early adult years often lead to decisions which later prove inappropriate. Yet, there are age norms and a kind of "social clock" that make it difficult later on to correct earlier errors. Interruption of education, impulsive marriage and/or childbearing, unwise choice of vocation, and/or financial overextension create situations that make later escape difficult. Poverty and unemployment increase stress and feelings of helplessness and fatalism. The result may be any of a variety of behavior disorders: intractable anxiety, depression, feelings of alienation and lack of commitment, obesity, drug dependency, and so on. Today's young adults in particular include some victims of the myths of the early 1970's, who "dropped out" of conventional society to "do their own thing," and are still drifting without a satisfying direction.

Divorce. Rates of divorce have taken a dramatic upswing in recent years. In 1977, the marriage rate was 9.6 per 1000 population; the divorce rate was 5.0. While the former has remained reasonably stable over the years, ranging only from 9.0 in 1890 to 12.2 in 1945 (immediately after World War II), divorce rates have risen from 0.5 in 1890 to the present level, with a rate of 2.5 as late as 1965. Divorce has, then, reached essentially epidemic proportions. We must begin to view it not as "abnormal" but as reflecting a change in the form of the family from a permanent entity to one which may include a succession of partnerships. Social scientists are naturally concerned about the possible failure of families to cope with the primary responsibility of child rearing under such circumstances, but as yet there is surprisingly little evidence about the effects of the successive-family pattern on children's adjustment.

Sexual Dysfunction.   Anxiety about sexual performance and/or inability to please one's partner, together with previous learning of negative or conflicting attitudes towards sex, produce in many adults mild to severe impairment in sexual response. In men, this often takes the form of either premature ejaculation or impotence (inability to achieve or maintain erection); in women, vaginismus (involuntary spasm of the outer portion of the vagina), inability to experience orgasm, or orgasms limited to a particular situation such as masturbation. Successful treatment can often be achieved by systematic densensitization (counterconditioning of sexual inhibitions) and graduated practice under the guidance of specially trained counselors.

Variations of Sexual Behavior.   Although heterosexual activity between consenting men and women is clearly the norm in all societies, variations in sexual behavior are increasingly accepted. Homosexuality, in particular, is currently viewed not as abnormal but primarily as the opposite end of a continuum from heterosexuality. Abnormal forms of sexual behavior include, however, transsexualism (experienced sexual identity of the opposite sex), fetishism (sexual interest focused on a part of the body other than the genitalia, or on an object), transvestism (cross-sex dressing), voyeurism (pleasure in viewing nude persons or the sex act), exhibitionism (pleasure in exposure of the genitals), sadism (sexual pleasure from inflicting pain), and masochism (sexual pleasure from experiencing pain). These variations may or may not be punishable by law, depending upon circumstances. Completely illegal forms usually leading to arrest after detection are pedophilia (sexual gratification with children) including incest between adult and child, and rape (an act of aggression or coercion). Referral to specialized programs for the sexually deviant, when available, is called for in cases of clearly abnormal behavior.

Psychosis.   The prevalence of psychosis is moderate in this period. Psychosis implies a severe psychological disturbance, including personality disorganization and loss of contact with reality. See discussions of schizophrenia (Chapter 8) and the affective disorders (Chapter 10).

Character Disorders.   As the name implies, character disorders are long-standing personality disorders which are not episodic but represent "the way the person is." While the manifestations are present during childhood and adolescence, it is mainly when people are expected to assume a responsible role in society that the disorders become more disturbing to others. Generally speaking, persons with character disorders cope with their problems and relate to other people in ways that seem troublesome, unusual, or "strange," but not bizarre. They generally do not experience a great deal of anxiety except when they encounter special crises. Some show lifelong adjustments that resemble in mild form more serious behavior disorders; these include people labeled as paranoid personalities, schizotypal personalities, or compulsive personalities.

Individuals with an antisocial personality pattern (sometimes labeled a psychopathic or sociopathic personality) behave as if a special set of rules, or no rules, should apply to their behavior; they seem to show a disorder of "conscience." They tend to use other people for their own ends and to show great skill in short term interactions, with an uncanny knack of saying just what others want to hear, and often convince health care professionals that they are genuinely repentant, desire to reform, and/or have been wrongly accused. Some persons with such personalities are "con men," forgers, embezzlers, or drifters.

Individuals (usually women) with a histrionic personality tend to be immature, self-centered, dramatic, and attention-getting. They often get others to do their bidding through indirect, "Southern belle" behaviors and useful illnesses, while denying the presence of any psychological problems as well as the sexual connotations of their seductive behaviors. Individuals with this pattern may show the somatoform disorders discussed in Chapter 10.

Nutritional and Metabolic Disorders

Diet. The body and health consciousness of the adolescent becomes a way of life for many young adults. Attention is focused on the

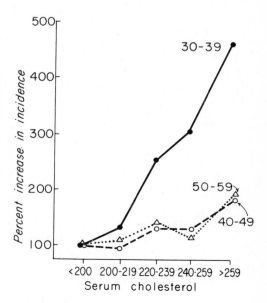

Figure 9–6 Increase in incidence rate of coronary heart disease in males in Framingham during a 22 year period in relation to the initial serum cholesterol level. A cholesterol level over 260 mg/dl (levels are considered normal up to 220) increases coronary risk in the 30 to 39 year age group more than twice as much as in the 40 to 49 or 50 to 59 year age groups. (From Bierman, E. L., and Ross, R.: Aging and Atherosclerosis. In Paoletti, R., and Gotto, A. M., Jr.: Atherosclerosis Reviews. Vol. II. New York, Raven Press, 1977, p. 89.)

types of foods consumed and often on losing excess weight. Dieting to the point of emaciation results in abnormal water and temperature regulation, and deranged hormonal secretion. When weight loss is progressive and severe, death may ensue. These individuals, almost invariably women, have starvation amenorrhea or anorexia nervosa. For those who remain obese, related morbidity continues to accumulate.

The "junk food" generation often loses interest in "empty calories" and becomes enamored with "natural foods," often at the risk of commercial exploitation, but in hope of a healthier body and future. Others tune in to dietary and lifestyle changes hoping to decrease future cardiovascular risks. This emphasis is timely in view of the atherosclerosis prevalent in autopsied soldiers. Current information certainly suggests that factors which bring about cardiovascular disease in later years are already operative and subject to intervention (Fig. 9–6). Similarly, the unseen effects of hypertension accumulate in young adults. Surveys have disclosed that 6 percent of young adults have significant blood pressure elevations. In young black males this figure rises to 18 percent. Since young adulthood is a time when people establish lasting lifestyle changes, it affords a singular opportunity to influence or alter dietary patterns.

Thyroid Disease. Although abnormalities of function and/or anatomy of the thyroid gland can be found from the neonate to the elderly, the peak incidence occurs in the young adult, especially in women during the childbearing years. Over- or underproduction of thyroid hormone may occur in the absence of clinical thyroid gland enlargement, but it is often the development of a goiter that causes the individual to seek medical attention. The production of hormone by these multinodular or diffusely enlarged glands may meet metabolic needs or be abnormally low or high. When excessive amounts of thyroid hormone are secreted, the individual becomes hyperthyroid.

Hashimoto's disease, also called autoimmune thyroiditis, is another common cause of goiter in the 20's and 30's. Although the production of thyroid hormone is initially normal, or even elevated, deficient levels of hormone ultimately ensue as the disease progresses, despite the increasing size of the gland. In this disease, as well as others associated with goitrous hypothyroidism, thyroid enlargement occurs as the result of faulty or inadequate synthesis of thyroid hormone.

There is a distinct familial predisposition to thyroid disease, and in addition, relatives are often found to have other disorders of autoimmunity such as pernicious anemia, rheumatoid arthritis, and myasthenia gravis.

Chemical Agents

Not only do we ingest increasing quantities and types of chemical substances, but our living and working environments expose us to additional known and unknown agents. Society has minimal capability for ascertaining and monitoring the toxic potential of chemicals. While most toxic manifestations will only be revealed when they cause disease later in life, the harmful effects of drugs and chemicals will nonetheless continue to accumulate during the young adult years. Some of the hazardous effects which have been identified will hopefully be susceptible to intervention.

The short and long term effects of alcohol and tobacco are known. Alcohol is the most abused drug in the United States. It is a factor in 50 per cent of all highway deaths and 50 per cent of all homicides, both of which are significant causes of mortality in the young adult (Fig. 9–13, p. 205). Consumption begins in adolescence and peaks in the young adult. In our culture, intake is tightly intertwined with social activities and other behavioral patterns, as exemplified by the "two-fisted drinking man" image. Some young adults, chiefly male, enter the spectrum of alcoholism; they may have life problems secondary to drinking and may become incipient or frank alcoholics as early as their 20's. Alcoholism can be intercepted and successfully treated at this stage, before social and medical complications ensue (Chapter 10).

Smoking tobacco follows the same pattern of young adult use and middle aged sequelae. Smoking has been linked to peptic ulcer disease, lung cancer, coronary heart disease, and the vascular complications of oral contraceptives.

The Oral Contraceptive Pill. Some 7 million American women, most of them between the ages of 18 and 35, are currently taking birth control pills. Users of this uniquely effective, reversible contraceptive method should be aware that they are taking chemical agents that are not without potential hazard (Fig. 9–7).

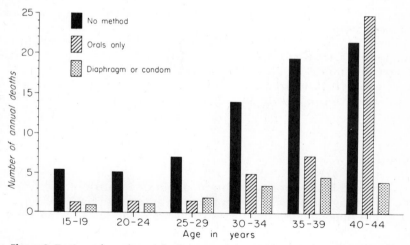

Figure 9–7 Annual number of deaths associated with control of fertility and no control per 100,000 nonsterile women. Contraceptive risk has two parts: (a) the risk associated with the method itself, and (b) the risk associated with method failure. The risk of death from all methods of birth control is low compared to the risks of childbirth, except for oral contraceptives in women over 40. At any age, the risk of death (due to unexpected pregnancy) from use of the diaphragm or condom is generally the same as, or less than the risk of death from the use of oral contraceptives *per se*. The mortality from diaphragm or condom failure can be further reduced if backed up by early therapeutic abortion. (Adapted from Patient Package Insert: Oral Contraceptives. Rockville, Maryland, U.S. Food and Drug Administration, 1977.)

TABLE 9–1 ANNUAL DEATH RATES PER 100,000 HEALTHY WOMEN*

Cause	Ages 20 to 34	35 to 44
Blood clots		
Pill users	1.5	3.9
Nonusers	0.2	0.5
Pregnancy, all related causes	17.2	47.2
Abortion	5.6	10.4
Motor accidents	4.9	3.9
Cancer	13.7	70.1

*Adapted from Inman, W. H. W., and Vessey, M. P., Br. Med. J., 2:193, 1968.

As early as 1968, only 8 years after "the pill" was marketed, studies from Great Britain indicated that the risk of death from blood clots was probably increased in women who used these compounds, especially if they were over the age of 40. More recent reports in 1977 have confirmed these earlier findings and added deaths and illness from high blood pressure, strokes, and heart attacks to those from blood clots. Although the risk from these cardiovascular diseases is 5 excess deaths per 100,000 in women between the ages of 15 and 24, it increases dramatically with age, to 143 excess deaths per 100,000 in women ages 45 to 50. The risk is associated with other risk factors for cardiovascular disease such as cigarette smoking, high blood pressure, diabetes, obesity, and elevated blood lipids. Use of the pill for more than 5 years is also related to excess mortality.

Other significant conditions that are associated with oral contraceptives include liver tumors, gall bladder disease, hepatitis, and urinary tract infections.

To date, the reported increased incidence of these diseases, including the very serious adverse effects on cardiovascular mortality, is based on a small number of affected women. In the young adult, these risks must be weighed or balanced against pregnancy and abortion, both of which carry more risk to life than use of birth control pills (Table 9–1).

Infections

As noted in the morbidity graph, about one fourth of all physician visits in this age group are precipitated by infection (Fig. 9–8).

Acute Appendicitis. Acute appendicitis is the most frequently occurring acute abdominal condition requiring surgery and is most common in the 20's and 30's.

Infectious Mononucleosis. Infectious mononucleosis, the "kissing disease," is an acute illness caused by the Epstein-Barr virus (Chapter 8). Once considered a disease primarily of those of college age, it is now seen more often in adolescence. Currently in the United States, by age 18, some 85 per cent of blacks and 55 per cent of whites are already immune to the disease from prior symptomatic or asymptomatic infection.

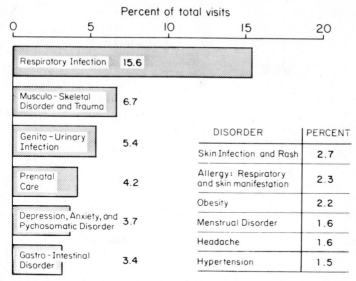

Percent of total visits

	PERCENT
Respiratory Infection	15.6
Musculo-Skeletal Disorder and Trauma	6.7
Genito-Urinary Infection	5.4
Prenatal Care	4.2
Depression, Anxiety, and Pychosomatic Disorder	3.7
Gastro-Intestinal Disorder	3.4

DISORDER	PERCENT
Skin Infection and Rash	2.7
Allergy: Respiratory and skin manifestation	2.3
Obesity	2.2
Menstrual Disorder	1.6
Headache	1.6
Hypertension	1.5

Figure 9–8 All visits to 118 family practitioners across the state of Virginia were coded into 607 problems over a two year period, 1973–75. Patients age 15 to 34 years old made 159,050 visits. (Adapted from Marsland, D. W., Wood, M., and Mayo, F.: A data bank for patient care, curriculum, and research in family practice: 526,196 patient problems. J. Family Practice, 3(1):24, 1976.)

Sexually Transmitted Diseases (STD) Within the past decade remarkable changes in human sexual behavior have occurred. Some of our puritanical taboos have been shed and premarital sexual activity, usually stripped of its attendant guilt and the threat of pregnancy, is now generally accepted as a cultural norm. Associated with this rise in coital activity, which often includes multiple sex partners and oral-genital contact, is a striking increase in sexually transmitted diseases.

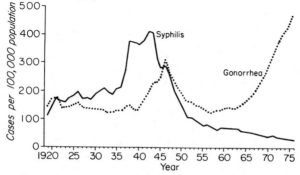

Figure 9–9 Reported cases of gonorrhea and syphilis (all stages) per 100,000 population by year, United States, 1919–1976. (From Annual Summary: Reported morbidity and mortality in the United States, 1976. Morbidity and Mortality Weekly Report, 25(53):67, August, 1977.)

Gonorrhea, nongonococcal urethritis and vaginitis, venereal warts, trichomoniasis, and genital herpes have seemingly reached epidemic proportions. Syphilis, however, as the result of diagnosis, treatment, and tracing of sexual contacts, has decreased in frequency following World War II and since 1960 has had a low and relatively stable reported prevalence (Fig. 9–9). The endemic reservoir is found predominantly in prostitutes and in the male homosexual community.

Conversely, the incidence of gonorrhea has progressively increased (Fig. 9–9). In the United States, it is currently the most common communicable disease that must be reported. Of the estimated 3 million cases treated in 1975, 90 per cent were under age 30. Transmission is usually via an asymptomatic female or male carrier. Aside from genital infections, gonorrhea can cause disseminated disease or can involve the eye, pharynx, rectum, or any of the pelvic and abdominal organs. In women, infertility secondary to pelvic inflammatory disease (PID) is a major threat.

At the present time in the United States, only about one third of all cases of urethritis are gonococcal. *Chlamydia trachomatis* and *Ureaplasma urealyticum* (T mycoplasma) are presumptively the major responsible etiologic agents in the remainder. In women about one half of the cases of PID are caused by organisms other than the Gonococcus.

Herpes Simplex.   Antibody studies indicate that 50 to 75 per cent of the world's population is infected with herpes simplex virus (HSV), but only about 25 per cent of those harboring the virus will have overt disease. Transmission is by direct contact, infecting any area of the body of a susceptible host.

Two distinct varieties of HSV are now recognized, type I and type II. Primary infection with HSV-I occurs most frequently in children and is generally followed by recurring perioral "fever blisters" or "cold sores." HSV-II, on the other hand, has its peak incidence as genital lesions in the adolescent and young adult, coincident with sexual activity. However, genital or oral lesions can be caused by either type. Genital herpes is now considered to be the third most common sexually transmitted disease.

Newborns are at high risk for disseminated herpes infection, if their mothers shed the virus at the time of delivery.

The herpetic whitlow, a digital infection, is a recognized occupational disease of dentists and other medical personnel.

The possible link between cancer of the cervix and HSV has been a recent cause of great concern. The epidemiologic association is clear and definite but whether or not there is a direct cause and effect relationship is still speculative.

Viral Hepatitis.   Viral hepatitis is an acute infection of the liver caused by several different viruses. Only in the last decade have the two major responsible viruses been specifically identified and found to be epidemiologically and serologically distinct. In 1976 some 600,000 cases were reported to the Center for Disease Control but it is estimated that 10 times that number remain unreported (Fig. 9–10).

Hepatitis A, previously called infectious hepatitis, is primarily transmitted by the fecal-oral route (including via contaminated food and

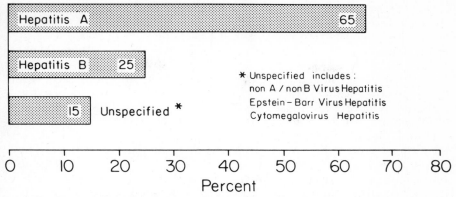

Figure 9–10 Hepatitis cases reported to Center for Disease Control, 1976. EB virus is the etiologic agent causing infectious mononucleosis. Cytomegalovirus infection is a major cause of birth defects. Non-A/Non-B hepatitis virus is an as yet unidentified hypothetical virus(es) which is now the most common cause of post-transfusion hepatitis in the United States.

water). It can also be transmitted by blood and bile. Preliminary studies have recently documented that over half of the population in the United States have serologic evidence of past infection by midadult life.

Hepatitis B, formerly called serum hepatitis because of its association with transfusions or needle punctures, is now known to be transmitted not only by blood and blood products but also by saliva, stool, bile, urine, breast milk, and semen. Unlike hepatitis A, which has no known carrier state, about 10 per cent of individuals infected with hepatitis B will become asymptomatic carriers who can transmit the virus to susceptible contacts.

Viral hepatitis occurs most commonly between the ages of 15 and 30 with a peak incidence between the ages of 20 and 24, predominantly in urban white males (Fig. 9–11). The reported rate of hepatitis has not changed markedly since 1973, although there has been a steady decrease in the incidence of Type A, especially in children, which is at least in part

Figure 9–11 Specific rates for hepatitis cases reported to the Center for Disease Control, 1972–1975. (From Center for Disease Control: Hepatitis Surveillance Report No. 40. Phoenix Laboratories Division, Center for Disease Control, 1977.)

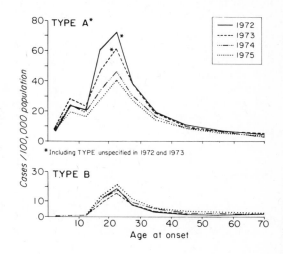

related to improved sanitation and hygiene. During the same period there has been a concomitant rise in Type B hepatitis, which was thought to be due primarily to transmission via parenteral drug abuse. Recent information indicates that sexual transmission, especially in homosexual males, is a major cause for the increase.

Urinary Tract Infections (UTI). Urinary tract infections are common in young women, the frequency increasing with sexual activity. Although data on prevalence vary, it is estimated that 10 to 20 per cent of all women will have at least one symptomatic episode during their lifetime, while an additional 5 per cent will have an asymptomatic infection. In a given year, dysuria, or burning on urination, is experienced by 20 per cent of all women. One third of these, or 7 per cent of the female population, will have culture-proven urinary tract infection. Those with a negative urine culture have a urethral syndrome which is probably the female counterpart of nongonococcal urethritis in the male.

Recurrences are frequent and may be due to relapse (same organism) or reinfection (different organism). Fecal bacterial flora colonizing the vulva provide the major reservoir of pathogens. Routine bladder hygiene, consisting of proper wiping, voiding four or more times each day, and voiding before and after sexual intercourse is a possibly effective preventive measure.

Uncomplicated UTI's are rare in young men and, when they occur, an anatomic abnormality should be suspected.

Immunologic Disorders

Although occurring less frequently than in the child or adolescent, eczema and asthma are still common and sometimes disabling problems in the young adult. Allergic rhinitis (hay fever) and allergic sinusitis reach peak incidence in this age group.

Medications, infections, and other agents may trigger a group of immunologic aberrations which typically produce disease in young adults. These include idiopathic thrombocytopenic purpura, which involves the immunologic destruction of platelets, and two distinctive skin conditions, erythema nodosum and erythema multiforme.

Under current investigation are a group of genetically determined and immunologically mediated diseases. These disorders are found to correlate with human gene locations called HLA antigens. These gene complexes were originally identified as determinants of tissue compatibility for organ transplant surgery. Diseases in this group include two types of arthritis found in young adults, Reiter's syndrome and ankylosing spondylitis.

Neoplasms

Nineteen per cent of total deaths in all ages combined are from cancer, whereas between the ages of 20 and 34 cancer deaths comprise 9 per cent of the total. Furthermore, the death rate from cancer in white

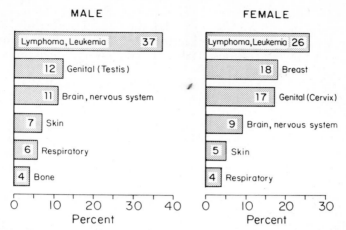

Figure 9–12   Death from various types of cancer as a percentage of total cancer deaths, age 20 to 34. The three most common types of cancer causing death in men in this age group represent 60 per cent of the total, and in women 61 per cent. (Adapted from Vital Statistics of the United States, 1973. Vol. II, Part A: Mortality. Rockville, Maryland, National Center for Health Statistics, 1977, pp. 1–194 to 207.)

Americans 20 to 34 years old fell 16 per cent from 1964 to 1974. Distinct from other age groups, these malignancies are concentrated among a few types (Fig. 9–12). Clinicians and patients need to direct efforts toward early detection, including self-examination for testicular and breast cancer. A high index of suspicion and rapid initiation of coordinated multidisciplinary treatment will continue the downward trend of cancer mortality in this age group.

Cancer of the Uterine Cervix.   The incidence of death from cancer of the cervix is low in the young adult and is about 5 per cent of total (all ages) cervical cancer deaths. However, in 20 to 34 year old women, 17 per cent of all deaths from malignancy are caused by cervical neoplasia (Fig. 9–12). The frequent recognition of pre-malignant cell changes remains a cause of concern, despite the epidemiologic evidence that carcinoma of the cervix evolves slowly over many years. This disease has recently been called a late developing, sexually transmitted cancer because of its epidemiologic association with early onset of coital activity, multiple partners, use of the birth control pill, and trichomoniasis and genital herpes simplex infection.

Testicular Cancer.   Nearly 40 per cent of total (all ages) testicular cancer deaths occur in the young adult. These tumors account for 12 per cent of all cancer deaths in males from age 20 to 34 (Fig. 9–12). Between the ages of 29 and 35, they are the most common malignant tumors in men. Malignancy in undescended testes, including those surgically placed in the scrotum, has been variously reported to be 10 to 40 times higher than in normally descended gonads. Self-examination should be taught and encouraged in an attempt to identify small palpable tumors.

Late Sequelae Neoplasms.   Late sequelae malignancies are associated with exposure decades earlier to substances not then considered carcinogenic. Recognition of the teratogenic effects of toxins, infections, drugs, and irradiation on the developing fetus has now broadened to include serious concern regarding the later development of cancer, not only in the individuals exposed *in utero,* but also in those exposed during infancy and childhood.

Two such neoplasms are those of the vagina and of the thyroid. These tumors were found previously only in older individuals, but are now increasingly prevalent in young adults.

CLEAR CELL ADENOCARCINOMA OF THE VAGINA AND DIETHYLSTILBES-TROL (DES). As recently as 1971 the link between maternal DES therapy during pregnancy and occurrence of cancer of the vagina in female offspring 1 to 3 decades later became known. DES or similar chemical compounds were used extensively during the 1940's and 1950's in an attempt to improve fetal salvage in problem pregnancies, particularly when there was a high risk of spontaneous abortion. Use was gradually discontinued a decade ago when studies revealed such therapy to be less effective than was originally believed.

Although it is estimated that 2 million pregnant women received DES type hormones, only about 300 cases of vaginal cancer had been reported by 1977. Abnormal but noncancerous changes in the vagina and cervix are more commonly found. The significance of these unusual developmental lesions is unknown at the present time. To date, no DES related cancers have been reported in male offspring, but the incidence may change as exposed individuals grow older.

IRRADIATION RELATED THYROID CANCER. Treatment with x-rays or radium for noncancerous conditions of the head, neck, or upper chest in infancy and childhood is now identified as a cause of both benign and malignant tumors of the thyroid.

Beginning in the early 1920's and continuing until the mid 1960's, radiation therapy was recommended as a highly effective treatment modality for a large variety of common conditions. Indications included enlargement of the thymus gland in infancy, chronic tonsillitis, sinusitis, mastoiditis, ear infections, swollen lymph nodes in the neck, facial scars or birthmarks, ringworm of the scalp, acne, and even whooping cough. About a decade ago, when published reports began to reveal the association between thyroid tumors and a past history of irradiation, this type of treatment was generally discontinued. Although countless patients will remain unidentified because of destroyed or lost records, approximately 1 million exposed individuals in the United States have been recognized thus far.

About 25 per cent of these individuals will have abnormal thyroid glands on palpation. Of these, some 33 per cent will have cancer, yielding an overall rate of malignancy of 5 to 7 per cent. At present the highest incidence (up to 15 per cent) has been found in the 20 to 35 year age range. Since these tumors can occur as early as 5 years or as late as 35 or more years after irradiation, identification and follow-up of exposed individuals is important. The tumors tend to be slow growing and are curable if diagnosed early. Health professionals are currently being alerted to watch not only for these thyroid tumors, but also for malignancies of the salivary glands, skin, parathyroids, breasts, and brain in this group of exposed patients.

Trauma

Until their mid 20's, many young adults unrealistically perceive their bodies not only as having unlimited physical capabilities, but also as being nearly indestructible. This attitude is associated with a wide spectrum of trauma related disabilities. "Shin splints" or periostitis, an annoying but self-limited condition, results from excessive demands placed on the musculoskeletal system. Inflammation of the deep surface of the kneecap known as chondromalacia patellae is another common exercise related problem. Such conditions are harbingers of the generally more severe, more lasting degenerative diseases of middle age.

As already implied, much of the trauma experienced by young adults is sports related, involving the entire spectrum of activities from hang gliding to boxing to scuba diving. Serious and often fatal trauma results from auto and motorcycle accidents, half of which are alcohol related.

Suicide and homicide together account for 21 per cent of all deaths in this age group (Fig. 9–13). Even when these destructive attempts do not achieve their objective, they frequently result in serious and sometimes permanent disability. Crime, with its associated aggression and violence, is also a significant cause of young adult injuries and deaths.

Throughout our history, wars have been a major cause of mortality and lifelong disability of young adults. From 1940 through 1974, 27 per cent of male deaths in the 20 to 34 age group were war related.

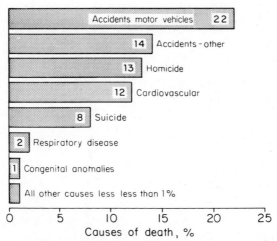

Figure 9–13   Common causes of death in the young adult as percent of total deaths between the ages of 20 and 35. (Adapted from Vital Statistics of the United States, 1974. Vol. II, Part B: Mortality. Rockville, Maryland, National Center for Health Statistics, 1976, pp. 150–167.)

MAJOR CAUSES OF MORBIDITY AND MORTALITY

Young adults seek medical care primarily for the reasons depicted in Figure 9–8. Infections and injuries are responsible for the largest percentage of patient contacts. In contrast, traumatic events monopolize death statistics (Fig. 9–13).

PREVENTIVE HEALTH MEASURES

The fortuitous convergence, in this age group, of a high level of health concern plus the ability to consider and make lifestyle changes, could result in the successful establishment of important preventive health measures. Additionally, since most of the potentially susceptible degenerative and metabolic derangements of middle and old age (Chapters 10 and 11) have yet to cause significant or irreversible structural or functional change, primary prevention rather than secondary intervention could yield the most impressive results.

Some of the risk factors and preventive health measures listed in Tables 9–2 and 9–3 are discussed in detail in Chapters 7 and 10. Although it is clear from the data presented that smoking and alcohol intake are the two most important established risk factors which demand intervention, other measures can have a favorable impact on health in the young adult.

TABLE 9–2 PREVENTIVE MEASURES WITH CLEARLY ESTABLISHED IMPACT*

Condition	Primary Risk Factor Modification
Some Viral and Bacterial Diseases...............	lack of immunization
Motor Vehicle Accidents	alcohol, speeding, failure to use seat belts
Homicide..	alcohol, guns
Hypertension	obesity
Congestive Heart Failure ⎤	
Stroke }	hypertension
Renovascular Disease ⎦	
Coronary Artery Disease	smoking, hypertension
Cirrhosis of the liver...............................	alcohol
Cancer [lung larynx]	smoking, alcohol
........[mouth esophagus]	
Chronic Obstructive Pulmonary Disease	smoking
	Secondary Detection
Hypertension	blood pressure measurement
Testicular Cancer	palpation
Breast Cancer..	palpation, mammography
Cervical Cancer	pap smear

*Adapted from Louria, D. B., et al.: Primary and secondary prevention among adults: an analysis with comments on screening and health education. Preventive Medicine 5:549, 1976.

TABLE 9–3 PREVENTIVE MEASURES WITH IMPACT NOT YET FULLY
ESTABLISHED*

Condition	Primary Prevention Measure
Periodontal Diseases	flossing, deplaquing
Sexually Transmitted Diseases	condom use
Hypertension	minimal sodium intake
Coronary Artery Disease	regular exercise, stress management; control of obesity, hyperlipidemia, diabetes mellitus
Various Tumors	minimize radiation exposure
	Secondary Preventive Measure/Detection
Maturity Onset Diabetes Mellitus ⎤ Hyperlipidemia ⎦	weight loss – in the obese
Active Tuberculosis	tuberculin skin testing
Female Urinary Tract Infections	hygienic measures

*Adapted from Louria, D. B., et al.: Primary and secondary prevention among adults: an analysis with comments on screening and health education. Preventive Medicine 5:549, 1976.

SPECIAL COMMENTS

A common thread through the adolescent and young adult years, especially in males, is risk taking behavior. Attitudes of bravado, of "it can't happen to me," and acculturation bring this about. The risk taking ranges from passive failure to contracept and flirting with sexually transmitted diseases, to smoking and drug experimentation, to participating in hazardous sports, motorcycling and reckless driving with and without alcohol, and to crime and unintentional suicide. The result of this behavior is that 57 per cent of the deaths in this age group are violence related (Fig. 9–13).

More positively, young adulthood is a time of flexibility and openness. The willingness, if not eagerness, to question old cultural values, explore new directions, and seek information is enhanced by direct and effective communication, new and varying relationships, and a receptiveness to change.

REFERENCES

Enos, W. F., Jr., et al.: Pathogenesis of coronary disease in American soldiers killed in Korea. JAMA, 158:912, 1955.

Evans, A. S. (Ed.): Viral Infections of Humans, Epidemiology and Control. New York, Plenum Medical Book Company, 1976.

Keniston, K.: Young Radicals: Notes on Committed Youth. New York, Harcourt Brace Jovanovich, 1968.

Luker, K.: Taking Chances: Abortion and the Decision Not to Contracept. Berkeley, University of California Press, 1975.

McNamara, J. J., *et al.*: Coronary artery disease in combat casualties in Vietnam. JAMA, *216*:1185, 1971.

O'Donoghue, D. H.: Treatment of Injuries to Athletes. 3rd ed. Philadelphia, W. B. Saunders Company, 1976.

Sheehy, G.: Passages: Crises of Adult Life. New York, Dutton, 1976.

Steele, B. F.: Violence in our society. Pharos of Alpha Omega Alpha *33*:42, 1970.

Thorn, G. L., *et al.* (Eds.): Harrison's Principles of Internal Medicine. 8th ed. New York, McGraw-Hill, 1977.

World Health Organization. Expert Committee on the Health Needs of Adolescents: Health Needs of Adolescents. Geneva, WHO, 1977 (WHO Technical Report Series No. 609).

10

Adulthood — The Middle Years

EDWIN L. BIERMAN
WILLIAM R. HAZZARD

LIFE SITUATION

After young adulthood, "middle age" is reached, spanning the ages of about 35 to 65. It is not a fixed plateau period of life, but rather "passages" of continuing physical, physiological, behavioral, and social adaptation. It represents the age of maturing, the years of major economic productivity, and family and social responsibility. Demographically, there are fewer individuals in each successive decade of life; however, almost half of the U.S. population falls within this age span.

Physical Changes

Following completion of growth, and attainment of mature adult stature, there is a gradual loss of musculoskeletal integrity. A progressive decrease in bone density (Fig. 10–1) and mass occurs, and gradual vertebral compression results in a decreasing ratio of body height to arm span. In addition, the lack of regenerative capacity of articular cartilage, and the accumulated insults to joint surfaces, aggravated by excessive weight, make arthritic complaints progressively more common in middle age. With assumption of a sedentary way of life and continued intake of calories in excess of those expended, adipose tissues expand and weight increases (Fig. 10–2), despite a decrease in lean body mass. Acquired obesity, subtle or obvious, is a hallmark of life's middle years in developed cultures. Since such phenomena as "aches and pains" and the "middle aged spread" are commonly accepted as inevitable consequences of aging and even worn with pride as badges of hard work and

209

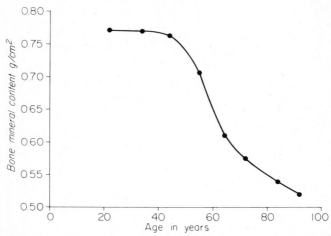

Figure 10-1 Bone mineral content, adjusted for variation in bone size, as a function of age in normal females. Estimated by bone mineral analyzer along the shaft of the left radius; 29 to 134 subjects were measured in each decade. (From the Proceedings of the International Conference on Bone Mineral Metabolism. R. B. Mazess, (ed.), p. 239, 1973. DHEW Publication Number (NIH) 75-683.)

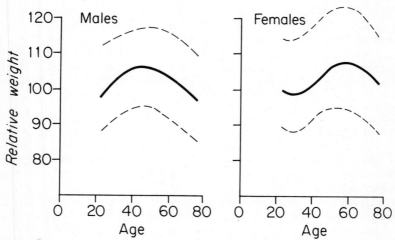

Figure 10-2 Relationship between age and relative body weight (ideal = 100) in males and females in an American community — Tecumseh, Michigan. Solid lines are 50th, dashed lines 20th (lower) and 80th (upper) percentiles. (From Epstein, F. H., et al.: Prevalence of chronic diseases and distribution of selected physiological variables in a total community. Tecumseh, Michigan. Am. J. Epidemiol. *81*:307, 1965.)

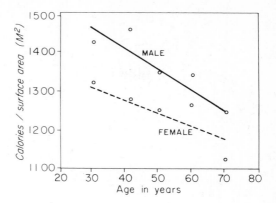

Figure 10–3 The effect of age and sex on caloric requirement during energy balance. For males, the downward trend with age was 43 calories per square meter surface area per decade, and for women, 27 calories. (Adapted from E. H. Ahrens, Jr., Liquid formula diets in metabolic studies. In Advances in Metabolic Disorders. Vol. 4, p. 297, 1970.)

success, the distinction between "normal" and "abnormal" with regard to arthritis and obesity may become blurred.

Physiological Changes

The linear decrease in the functional capacities of various organ systems (see Chapter 2, Fig. 2–7) becomes more evident with each passing year. The decrease in basal energy expenditure necessitates a decreased food intake, since there is a continuing decrease in caloric requirement with age (Fig. 10–3). The actual decrease in caloric intake is usually not adequate, however, to avoid fat accumulation.

Peak reproductive and sexual activity in early adulthood gives way to a decrease in fertility and sexual function, the latter declining at a much more gradual rate than has often been suggested.

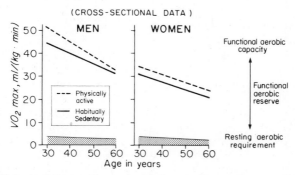

Figure 10–4 Variations with age in relative aerobic requirements. For a young man, usual energy expenditure represents only a small proportion of maximal capacity. This proportion increases with age, and is a major reason that a universal symptom of middle age is the perception that ordinary activities performed at the rate or pace achieved in youth now seem harder. Physically active individuals maintain higher functional aerobic capacities throughout life. (Adapted from Bruce, et al.: Am. Heart J. 85:546, 1973.) Longitudinal studies (Dehn and Bruce) suggest that the rate of decline in maximal aerobic capacity with age is more rapid in sedentary than in physically active persons.

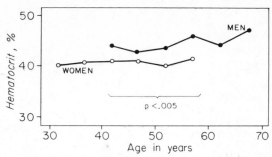

Figure 10–5 Variations with age in hematocrit in U.S. men and women (unpublished data obtained in Seattle). Note that women have about a 10 per cent lower value than men throughout the middle years.

The capacity for physical work declines. Functional aerobic capacity, which defines the power limits of aerobic metabolism available for muscular exercise or physical work, declines with age (Fig. 10–4). It is usually limited by the functional capacity of the cardiovascular system to deliver the maximal amount of oxygen, not by skeletal muscle mass or function, lung function, or a decline in oxygen carrying capacity of blood (hemoglobin concentration) (Fig. 10–5). Physically active individuals maintain higher aerobic capacities throughout the middle years than do sedentary individuals, emphasizing the need for a shift from spectator sports to participatory activities.

Psychosocial Changes

NANCY ROBINSON

The middle adult years tend to be the most stable and productive in the life span. Major developmental tasks of this period include attaining career goals, taking on social and civic responsibilities, developing mature leisure-time activities, adjusting to a possible caretaking role with one's aging parents, relating to one's adolescent children, and adapting to their departure.

For Erikson, the major developmental task of this period is "generativity vs. stagnation." Generativity constitutes the ability of the mature individual to pass wisdom and substance on to the young. Generativity leads to sustained plans for the future, investment in long range tasks, and a sense of continuity with future generations. Without a sense of generativity, one tends to go mechanically through the routines of work and one's necessary daily activities, preoccupied with self rather than others.

Many people do undergo a kind of reevaluation and renewal between ages 35 and 45, experiencing a now-or-never push in their careers, the knowledge that if success does not become attainable during these years, it never will. One's children are usually reaching the junior high and high school years, releasing parents from the demands of 24 hour surveillance but requiring greater financial expenditures and more astute kinds of parenting. Parents who have relied on authoritarian relationships with their children may find them in rebellion during the adolescent years; parents who have employed more democratic and warmer approaches are not so likely to have to deal with sustained conflict, although the growing pains of the adolescent years require thoroughgoing changes in the relationships. The same parents who thrive on the rearing of children when they are tiny and totally dependent may be unable to cope with them as the children mature. Just when parent-teenager conflicts reach their apex, the retired grandparents may begin to place emotional and financial demands upon the parents. Both younger and older generations may evoke conflicts over the issues of dependence and independence, responsibility and nonresponsibility, which may go unresolved. As a result, the parents may feel less like the "middle generation" than the "generation in the middle."

Interpersonal Changes. The current urban living pattern in which adults are geographically separated from their departed children, their own parents, and their siblings, demands intimacy and dependence of both marital partners. Paradoxically, this occurs at a time when cultural patterns allow substantial autonomy and independence to both men and women. The shift in middle life to an isolated marriage pair thus represents a major challenge to the stability of the marriage bond. Small wonder, then, that the phenomenon of divorce in the middle years, often after a relatively long marriage, has become so prevalent.

Provided that the couple remains together, a new phase of adulthood emerges, the latter half of the married life span. After a time of critical challenge, with its opportunity for new or reclaimed intimacy (and its threat of increasing distance and chronic loneliness), the majority of couples report that marital happiness increases after the departure of the children. Often to their surprise, the "empty nest" is far more pleasant and releasing than they had anticipated.

Cognitive Changes. Conventional wisdom once held that after age 25, one's intellectual course was a steady downhill decline. While tasks requiring swift reaction time and cognitive flexibility or "fluency" do show mild declines over the middle years, the overall picture is not a negative one. In fact, in functions which reflect continued learning, such as reasoning and vocabulary, mild increases are observed throughout adulthood.

Career Progression. Job development takes different paths in different segments of society. For most blue collar workers and those whose upward mobility is limited (housewives, for example), job progression is essentially horizontal. One's pay may increase with seniority; one may change jobs for extrinsic reasons such as locale, working hours, or noise levels; but qualitative progression is minimal. For professional and upwardly mobile groups, however, job development during this period is vertical, in the sense of increasing skill, status, and power. Perhaps a third of adult workers are engaged in an orderly career progression, moving upward in some status hierarchy. A person may shift from one orderly progression to another, but when the shifts become frequent and lose direction, career progression is said to be disorderly.

Today, the forces and conflicts related to careers reach their peak in the years between ages 40 and 50. During these years, particularly for the business and professional person, this may be the decade of greatest opportunity and productivity. Women who have worked halfheartedly while their children were growing may now invest more of their energies into job attainment. It is also the time for crucial decisions: promotion or stagnation, leader or perpetual "also-ran," realization of youthful ambition or of dwindling mediocrity. For the woman with an initial career of nursemaid and mother completed, this age is often one of searching for a new identity through a new career or style of living. For both men and women, this decade is one of continual adjustment to change.

Personality and Sexual Changes.　Changes occur in personality and in its sexual expression throughout adulthood. During young adulthood, men usually manifest the stronger sexual drives, whereas women most often experience their greatest sexual drive and satisfaction during the middle years of marriage. As a result, the opportunity is afforded for an optimal sexual relationship in middle life when husband and wife share equally in the intimacy and satisfaction of their sexual lives. However, the strong emphasis on youthful sexual attractiveness and performance in contemporary culture may provoke doubts over sexual adequacy in the middle aged person. Because of this, the doubting adult may trade his or her sense of poise, self-respect, and acceptance of the aging process for the usually vain attempt to recapture the vigor of youth through extramarital sexual exploits or the acquisition of a new, youthful marriage partner.

Other personality changes also occur in middle life. Men often become less aggressive and thus more nurturing, more concerned with the feelings and needs of others, less domineering and less consumed with the conquest of the world. Women, on the other hand, become freer as their children become less dependent; often this results in their becoming more assertive, demanding, and self-generated.

PREVENTIVE MEASURES FOR HEALTH MAINTENANCE

Possible preventive measures for health maintenance entail the personal rejection of most aspects of a way of life which is still enthusiastically accepted by the vast majority of society. Furthermore, given the complex, often subtle association between a risk factor such as tobacco smoking and its attendant disease, *e.g.,* cancer of the lung, it becomes very difficult to prove a causal relationship between the two. It is even more difficult, but not impossible in this case, to demonstrate conclusively that the correction of the risk factor will prevent the associated disease. Considerations both of personal freedom of choice and of a lack of conclusive proof of cause and effect, as well as powerful economic forces, leave the burden of the reversal of a popular way of life upon the individual. If he chooses to attempt that reversal, he can expect to be subjected to powerful social and economic pressures to conform to contemporary living patterns. The problems of preventive health maintenance in middle age appear to have been largely identified and are the same as those that should be initiated in young adulthood and earlier (Chapter 9). The means of their correction, except at a very high price of personal sacrifice and determination, often have not.

Most disorders of middle age, such as osteoarthritis and obesity, are both common and chronic. They are so common that they are often accepted as the price of having achieved middle age and are therefore not even considered abnormal. Furthermore, it is unusual for such disorders to have a single obvious cause. The response of a given individual to a certain set of circumstances usually reflects a complex interaction between environmental forces and his unique genetic makeup. Most often, these common disorders are designated as "multifactorial" in origin and are looked upon as the consequence of our way of life. As such, they are associated with its most obvious characteristics: a sedentary existence, high economic productivity, psychological stress, high caloric intake — especially of foods derived from animal sources — the consumption of alcohol, tobacco, and drugs, and chronic exposure to environmental pollutants including radiation and the emission from internal combustion engines.

Obesity is the single most common preventable factor associated with excess mortality and morbidity in this age group. Excess mortality in men who are 30 per cent overweight exceeds 40 per cent and is due mainly to atherosclerosis, hypertension, and the complications of diabetes. Morbidity is also excessive among the obese from disorders of the digestive system (gallstones and hepatic dysfunction), respiratory system (hypoventilation syndromes), and musculoskeletal system (osteoarthritis). An enormous proportion of adult Americans are overweight: 20 per cent of men are more than 10 per cent overweight and 5 per cent of men are at least 20 per cent above average; corresponding proportions for women are somewhat higher, 25 per cent being more than 10 per cent above average, and 12 per cent at least 20 per cent above average. Furthermore, the "ideal" or "best" weight for lowest mortality and health maintenance may lie below the present average weight of the population. This problem is probably totally amenable to preventive measures which simply involve reduction of caloric intake. But this restriction must take place in the face of increasing availability and attractiveness of food. Alternatively, a solution could be found through an increase in energy expenditure by regular exercise. However, this would have to occur in spite of progressive automation and availability of labor saving devices.

Other preventive dietary measures for minimizing the risk of atherosclerosis through decreased cholesterol and saturated fat intake, and of

osteoporosis through adequate calcium and protein intake are also war-
ranted. The intake of particular foodstuffs may produce conflicts in the
achievement of certain goals in adults. For example, though milk is a
rich source of calcium and protein, it is also high in saturated fat and
calories. Modified foodstuffs, such as skim milk, in this example, may
provide appropriate compromises.

Regular exercise may improve cardiovascular status to the extent
that the risk factor of sedentariness associated with coronary artery
disease (see below) is significantly reduced. Furthermore, exercise may
increase cardiovascular efficiency and allow the individual with a limited
cardiovascular capacity to function adequately in his daily activities. The
ancient principle of Maimonides, i.e. that one should exercise to the
point of breathlessness each day, is even more urgently applicable to our
highly mechanized society.

The adverse health consequences of chronic cigarette smoking, and,
to a lesser degree, cigar and pipe smoking, become manifest during this
phase of life. Well-documented excess morbidity and mortality stem
from lung cancer, oral cancers, chronic bronchopulmonary diseases
(commonly diagnosed as chronic bronchitis or pulmonary emphysema),
cardiovascular disease, particularly coronary heart disease, and gangrene of the lower extremities. Cigarette smoking is the most important
cause of chronic bronchopulmonary diseases in the United States; even
younger smokers have demonstrable reduction in ventilatory function.
The ratio of overall death rate of smokers to that of nonsmokers is
highest during the age decade from 45 to 55, more than a twofold
increase. Futhermore, cessation or appreciable reduction of cigarette
smoking has been shown to decrease excess morbidity and mortality.

Excessive exposure to external radiation is usually preventable,
since, barring a nuclear catastrophe, exposure from diagnostic and
therapeutic radiology constitutes the major source of radiation in the
environment. In these disciplines, efforts are made to minimize risks of
morbidity, and maximal permissible levels of exposure are rarely
reached. Other environmental hazards not controllable by the single
individual appear to be under ever-increasing public surveillance and
control owing to the collective efforts of concerned citizens.

The health problems related to chronic excessive intake of alcohol
are multifaceted (psychological, sociological, medical) and constitute a
major concern during this age span. In the United States there are
currently at least four million alcoholics, where alcoholism is defined as a
dependence on alcohol to a degree sufficient to interfere with health,
interpersonal relations, and social and economic positions. The secondary effects of chronic excessive alcohol intake in terms of decreased
productivity, accidents, crime, mental and physical disease, and disruption of family life, are also preventable through efforts to curb alcohol
abuse.

The consequences of drug addiction (narcotics) and drug dependence (tranquilizers and stimulants) assume increasing importance during this age, not only through effects upon the middle aged addict or
habitué, but through influence upon other, usually younger family
members.

COMMON PROBLEMS OF THE MIDDLE YEARS

Behavioral

NANCY ROBINSON

Many people simply do not make a success of adult life. Those who were deviant, withdrawn, or underachieving children and young adults may become crashing failures in the middle years. Spotty job histories with periods of unemployment are, for many adults, signs of poor adjustment. Mental illness, alcohol abuse, and marginal adjustment because of long-standing character disorders become more frequent. The incidence of admission to mental hospitals is at a peak. (See Figure 9–5.) Emotional and behavioral disorders which are prevalent during the middle years include the affective disorders, paranoia, sexual conflicts, and somatization of anxiety.

Affective Disorders. The main characteristic of the affective disorders is a severe disturbance of mood, which causes abnormalities of thought and behavior related to mood. Only a minority of affected persons experience bipolar episodes (mania and depression); most experience only one type, depression being more frequent than the excited, hyperactive episodes. Depression is characterized by underactivity; a poverty of verbal and gestural expression; and vegetative changes including sleep disturbance, decreases (sometimes increases) in appetite, fatigue, energy loss, and often chronic pain such as headache. There is a pervasive feeling of helplessness, and a lack of pleasure in things and activities the person used to enjoy. Alcoholism, especially in women, is often associated with depression. Suicide is a real threat, 80 per cent of suicides being long term depressed persons.

In some older persons, depression appears as a midlife phenomenon termed "involutional depression" that may be transient and nonrecurring. In depressions which occur somewhat earlier, the pattern is more likely to be repetitive, with episodes spontaneously ending and reappearing with little apparent life stress. Both learning and biochemistry appear to play important roles in the etiology of the affective disorders, but a variety of medications including the tricyclics (such as imipramine) and lithium carbonate are effective with various subtypes, both in treating the current manic or depressive episode and in preventing subsequent cycles.

Somatoform Disorders. This group of disorders is distinguished by symptoms which take, or at least mimic, a physical form. Prominent is Briquet's disorder, found much more frequently in women than in men. Its typical picture is a history of multiple vague somatic complaints. These are often described in dramatic terms but are not associated with identified disease states. The pattern may or may not be associated with a histrionic personality pattern — immature, self-centered, seductive, attention getting, manipulative behavior. (See Chapter 9.) The professional must be on guard against initiating unwarranted somatic treatment (often "fishing expeditions") for the somatoform disorders. Many such patients have histories of multiple surgeries. Unfortunately, the disorder is often easier to diagnose retrospectively than prospectively.

With increasing age and the gradual decrease in physical prowess, there may be added concern with bodily functions which borders on the normal and should not be confused with the more pervasive and characterological somatoform disorders. Normal adults' concerns may take the form of minor hypochondriases, vague or generalized pain problems, and more especially, the concern over adequacy of body functions. As old age approaches, this is reflected in a preoccupation with food and bowel functions. Too, as midlife brings increased anxiety over sexual performance, menopause, and the climacteric, both men and women may develop either hyposexual symptomatology (impotence, inorgasmia) or hypersexual symptomatology (interest in sexual experimentation, compulsive sexuality).

Psychological Factors Affecting Physical Conditions. These disorders reflect physiological damage to some organ or organ system, thereby differing from the "somatoform" disorders in which no physical damage can be discerned. There a number of serious and even life threatening conditions in which psychological factors are thought to play an important role. These include, among others: gastric ulcers, diarrhea, colitis, neurodermatitis, eczema, migraine headache, hypertension, bronchial asthma, hyperventilation, and diabetes insipidus. Although the psychological dynamics in each condition are thought to vary, the common strain is a response to psychic stress and anxiety.

Paranoid Reactions. Full-blown paranoid reactions are marked by delusions of grandiosity or persecution, but except for their elaborate delusion systems, paranoid psychotics typically show no other marked disorder of thinking. Milder forms of paranoid reactions are seen in persons who are hypersensitive, irritable, and suspicious, but not psychotic. Degrees of paranoid reactions are frequently seen in middle aged women, apparently related to increased marital strain in the middle years of a conflictual marriage. The disease is by no means limited to women, however. Paranoid reactions are sometimes seen in persons with arteriosclerosis (more common in old age) and persons of any age taking amphetamines and some other psychoactive drugs. In fact, "pure" paranoid reactions are less common than is paranoid schizophrenia (see Chapter 8), characterized by nonencapsulated basic and pervasive thought disorder.

Nutritional and Metabolic Disorders

These include obesity, gallbladder disease, and anemia. Obesity itself leads to morbidity because of its aggravating effect on a variety of other disorders such as hypertension, diabetes mellitus, atherosclerosis, varicose veins, hernia, gallstones, uterine cancer, and osteoarthritis. A combination of obesity with these other disorders may appreciably compound the problem, as is evident in the increased mortality risk noted in the presence of *both* moderate overweight and slight elevation of blood pressure. Adiposity secondary to weight gain in adult life may have different implications from adiposity present since early childhood. Adult-onset obesity appears to be less chronic and therefore potentially more reversible. However, pound for pound, perhaps it may be more ominous insofar as cardiovascular risk is concerned. The overweight patient undergoing surgery offers special problems, both to the anesthesiologist because of inadequate respiratory exchange, poor airway, and large anesthetic dosage requirements, and to the surgeon because of increased frequency of postoperative thromboembolism, infection, and wound breakdown. In addition, the overweight woman incurs an extra risk during pregnancy from toxemia and increased fetal mortality. Reduction of overweight in these circumstances has been clearly associated with reduction of morbidity.

Gallstones occur with gradually increasing frequency after age 30 and are particularly common in multiparous women; the overall female-male ratio below age 65 is 4 to 1. By age 75, 1 of every 3 persons will have gallstones, though symptoms of colicky pain and/or complications of infection, obstruction, liver damage, or neoplasm may not necessarily follow. Although some gallstones are composed mainly of bile pigments and/or insoluble calcium salts, most contain at least 70 to 80 per cent cholesterol, which crystallizes in the gall bladder in the setting of inadequate bile acids and/or phospholipids. The pharmacologic correction of this imbalance among biliary cholesterol, bile acids, and phospholipids as a means of preventing (or dissolving) gallstones is presently under evaluation.

Non–iron related nutritional anemias are not common among adults in the United States except in association with alcoholism. Females are particularly prone to develop iron deficiency anemia related to iron intake inadequate to compensate for chronic periodic blood loss associated with normal menses or excessive menstrual bleeding, which is common in the peri-menopausal years. Menstrual loss partially accounts for lower hemoglobin levels in women than men during this age span (Fig. 10–5).

Chemical Agents

Alcohol is the most common toxic external agent involved in morbidity and mortality in this age span. In addition to cirrhosis of the liver, pancreatic dysfunction and neurologic disorders (such as peripheral neuropathy, cerebellar degeneration, and encephalopathy) are prominent. Mortality from alcoholic cirrhosis peaks in the fifth and sixth decades at 50 per 100,000 in the United States. It is markedly higher for males than females at all ages, and is higher for nonwhites below age 45. Even when consumed in socially acceptable and nontoxic levels, alcohol contributes significantly to caloric excess and obesity. Recent data suggest that in U.S. males, an average of 10 per cent of total daily calories is derived from alcohol. Aside from caloric excess, limited regular alcohol consumption has been associated with a reduction in mortality from coronary atherosclerosis.

Trauma

The mortality rate from all types of accidents is roughly comparable to that from alcohol. In addition, nonfatal, severe trauma affects a large segment of this group. On a more subtle but more universal level, chronic or acute trauma often causes musculoskeletal problems that occur as the initial clinical manifestations of aging in connective tissue.

Bone mass declines in a linear fashion during middle age (Fig. 10–1). "Pathologic" fractures, due to inapparent or minor trauma, are uncommon in this age group, but trauma which earlier in life would be insignificant, such as stepping off a curb or tripping on the front steps, may result in major osseous injuries. Whereas in the young adult injuries to joints frequently result in ligamentous disruption, similar injuries in middle age usually result in fractures.

Articular (arthritic) complaints are also progressively more common in the middle years. Growth of articular cartilage ceases at maturity while attrition continues. Articular cartilage has no inherent capacity to repair or renew itself. At maturity, mitotic activity ceases and, with aging, there is a steady decline in cell density. Attrition, however, continues throughout the life of the joint. The rate of such attrition appears to be influenced by the stress to which it is subjected, since optimal pressures seem to be necessary for normal cartilage nutrition. Areas of cartilage subjected to either too little or too much pressure degenerate, and, once the process has been initiated, it appears to be self-perpetuating.

The frequency of joint disease at all ages and its progressive increase with age illustrate the common problem of making the distinction between specific disease processes and physiological aging. Arthritis of all types accounts for a significant proportion of the problems encountered in adult medical practice, afflicting an estimated 14 per cent of males and 23 per cent of females beyond the age of 45, and trailing only heart disease as the leading cause of restricted activity among adults. The social and economic burdens imposed by joint diseases therefore loom very large. The frequency of disorders of periarticular tissue (capsule ligaments and bursae) is readily apparent clinically, but the pathogenesis of these degenerative conditions is poorly understood. Repetitive trauma, as in a baseball pitcher's elbow, unusual activity, as in the shoulder of a weekend ceiling painter, or infrequent vigorous activity, as in the once-a-week squash player, may result in painful, inflammatory lesions of the periarticular structures. According to the site of involvement, these conditions are called tendinitis, fasciitis, bursitis, or capsulitis. Presumably the additive effect of unusual stress in the presence of preexisting degeneration produces an irritative inflammation that results in pain and limitation of motion.

Infection

Viral illness, particularly respiratory, is a common cause of intermittent, transient disability in this age span. Individuals of this age, unless disabled by coexistent heart or lung disease, are not likely to develop serious complications of viral agents, such as influenza. Viral exanthems are rare because of immunity developed during childhood; however, when they are contracted in adulthood, complications are more frequent and serious, and may include encephalitis, orchitis, pancreatitis, or myocarditis. Viral hepatitis of both infectious and serum varieties, although past peak incidence (Fig. 9–10), may affect adults throughout the age span.

Bacterial infection is a problem of lesser importance during adulthood. In those individuals whose host defense mechanisms have become impaired through a coexisting disorder, such as cancer or alcoholism, a bacterial infection may be disastrous. This is particularly true of tuberculosis, which remains an important cause of morbidity and mortality among the socioeconomically disadvantaged and immunologically vulnerable.

Immunologic Disorders

The allergies of childhood carry over into adulthood mainly as allergic rhinitis (hay fever) and bronchial asthma. Approximately half the cases of asthma are associated with hypersensitivity to specific environmental antigens and are referred to as extrinsic asthma; the remainder are called intrinsic asthma and are of unknown origin, but may result from repeated infections and hypersensitivity to bacterial products or pollutants. The latter frequently has its onset during the middle years, may become chronic, and is a common cause of disability. Persistent asthma from any cause may produce pulmonary emphysema and permanent ventilatory insufficiency.

An important, relatively recent phenomenon is the emergence of drug allergies among adult populations. The widespread, often indiscriminate use of pharmacologic agents, notably sedatives and antibiotics and especially penicillin, makes inquiry into past drug reactions an important part of the medical history and a critical determinant in the choice of treatment.

The rapid decrease in the incidence and severity of streptococcal infections coincident with improved socioeconomic conditions and the widespread use of antibiotics has led to a dramatic decline in the prevalence of two formerly very common immunologic disorders related to streptococcal antigens — rheumatic valvular heart disease and chronic glomerulonephritis. Although reparative valvular heart surgery and renal dialysis and transplantation have ameliorated early mortality risk in afflicted persons, morbidity related to these disorders still remains a major task for medical and paramedical personnel and family members, and is a large economic burden.

Neoplasms

Cancer accounts for one fourth to one third of the deaths during this age span (Fig. 10–6). The types of malignancies differ strikingly for

DEATH FROM CANCER

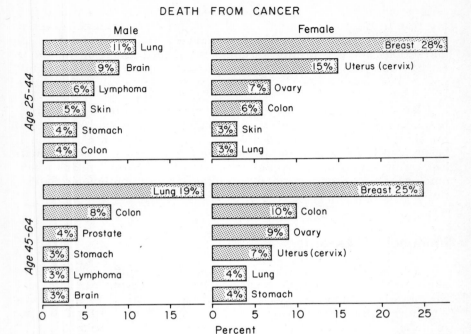

Figure 10–6 Death from various types of cancer as per cent of the total in younger and older middle-aged males and females. (Adapted from World Health Organization: Mortality from Malignant Neoplasms, 1955–1965. Part I. Geneva, Switzerland, 1970. pp. 78–101.)

males and females owing to the high prevalence of breast and uterine cancer among the latter. Skin cancer, although frequent, has a high cure rate so that lung cancer is currently the leading cause of death from cancer in men.

OTHER PROBLEMS: MULTIFACTORIAL DISORDERS

The most striking difference in types of disorders between youth and adulthood is the shift toward chronic diseases with advancing age. These diseases, such as coronary heart disease, hypertension, and peptic ulcer, tend to be common and either progressive or recurrent. Therefore the aim of medical treatment of these disorders is more often to arrest or control rather than to cure, and prevention remains the ultimate goal. Since these disorders are both common and time-related, it is not surprising that they are felt to be largely multifactorial in origin, the result of many interacting forces, both genetic and environmental. In the United States, more persons die from coronary heart disease (30 per cent of all deaths) than from any other single cause. The risk of death from this disorder dramatically increases with age — over age 45 the risks from one decade to the next double for males and triple for

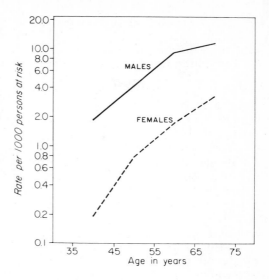

Figure 10–7 Average annual incidence rate of myocardial infarction. Data from a 16 year follow-up of individuals in the Framingham study. (Adapted from Arteriosclerosis: A Report by the National Heart and Lung Institute Task Force on Arteriosclerosis. DHEW Publication Number (NIH) 72–219, 2, June, 1971.)

females (Fig. 10–7). Since males have a relatively higher incidence of this disorder earlier in middle age, the mortality differential between the sexes becomes less as age advances. This approximation of the female toward the male mortality curve in later life, however, may reflect more the earlier removal of many high-risk males than a true equivalence in risk between the sexes at advanced ages.

Coronary heart disease appears to be a "disease of affluence" and is appropriately considered a modern epidemic in the United States. Risk factors toward coronary disease that have been firmly identified include hypertension, cigarette smoking, and elevated blood levels of cholesterol-rich and triglyceride-rich lipoproteins. Less well-defined and -understood associated factors may include certain personality traits such as aggressiveness and conscientiousness, hyperglycemia, certain dietary habits, including increased saturated fat, cholesterol, and caloric intake, and decreased physical activity. It is not surprising that several of these risk factors — hypertension, hypercholesterolemia, hypertriglyceridemia, hyperglycemia, and a sedentary existence — are most common in persons who are obese. Genetic predisposition to many of these risk factors has been demonstrated, and such propensities may underlie the well-known tendency of heart disease to run in families. Although preventive genetics may not be currently practicable, prevention of obesity and cigarette smoking may yield important advantages not only for the individual at special genetic risk but also for the entire affluent population in Western societies. In the recent decade ending in 1975, a dramatic decline in death rates from coronary and cerebrovascular disease occurred in the United States for the first time, associated with a drop in per capita consumption of cigarettes and animal fats among adults. Thus it appears that coronary atherosclerosis may be eminently preventable.

Just as routine body weight increases with age (Fig. 10–2), so do blood pressure (Fig. 10–8), serum cholesterol (Fig 10–9), and blood glucose following an oral glucose challenge (Fig. 10–10). These age-related changes pose important diagnostic problems which are discussed in detail in Chapter 11. The epidemiologic implications of these changes are clear, but their importance in a given person remains largely conjectural. For example, according to insurance company statistics, approximately 10 per cent of the United States' population have blood pressures greater than 140 mm Hg systolic and 90 mm Hg diastolic by the age of 40 to 50. Some individuals with chronic blood pressure elevations develop hypertensive vascular disease, arteriosclerosis of the smallest arteries of the kidney, retina and brain and/or large vessels. However, many hypertensive individuals never develop significant ischemia and therefore remain asymptomatic. Thus, as with all risk factors, the significance of hypertension in the individual adult cannot be assessed with a high degree of precision.

Primary hypertension, exclusive of renal disorders and other causes of secondary increases in blood pressure, remains a disorder of unknown etiology and is thus not yet preventable. However, exacerbating factors, such as obesity and perhaps chronic excessive salt intake, are correctable. Regardless of etiology, treatment to lower blood pressure does appear to prevent untoward cardiovascular sequelae in hypertensive patient groups, as demonstrated in recent clinical trials.

Peptic ulcer is a common, presumably multifactorial disorder which may affect as many as 10 to 15 per cent of adults. The disorder is more common in males than in females and occurs at all ages; but symptoms most often develop between the ages of 20 and 40 and reach a peak

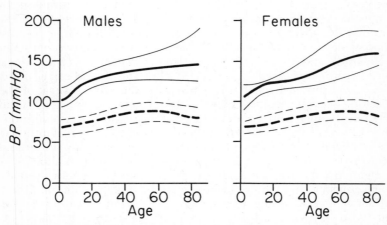

Figure 10–8 Relationship between age and systolic (upper, solid lines) and diastolic blood pressure (BP) (lower, dashed lines) in males and females in an American community—Tecumseh, Michigan. Heavy lines are 50th percentile; light lines are 20th (lower) and 80th (upper) percentiles. (Adapted from Epstein, F. H., et al.: Prevalence of chronic diseases and distribution of selected physiological variables in a total community. Tecumseh, Michigan. Am. J. Epidemiol. 81:307, 1965.

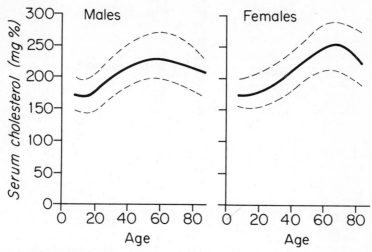

Figure 10–9 Relationship between age and serum cholesterol concentration in males and females in an American community—Tecumseh, Michigan. Solid lines are 50th percentiles; dashed lines are 20th (lower) and 80th (upper) percentiles. (Adapted from Epstein, F. H., et al.: Prevalence of chronic diseases and distribution of selected physiological variables in a total community. Tecumseh, Michigan. Am. J. Epidemiol. 81:307, 1965.

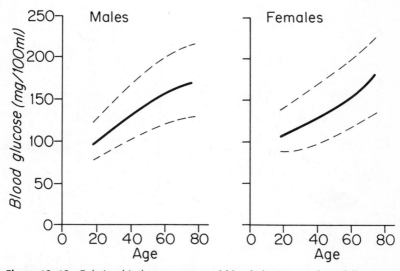

Figure 10–10 Relationship between age and blood glucose one hour following a 100 gm oral glucose challenge in males and females in an American community—Tecumseh, Michigan. Solid lines are 50th percentiles; dashed lines are 20th (lower) and 80th (upper) percentiles. (Adapted from Epstein, F. H., et al.: Prevalence of chronic diseases and distribution of selected physiological variables in a total community. Tecumseh, Michigan. Am. J. Epidemiol. 81:307, 1965.

DISORDERS OF MIDDLE AGE

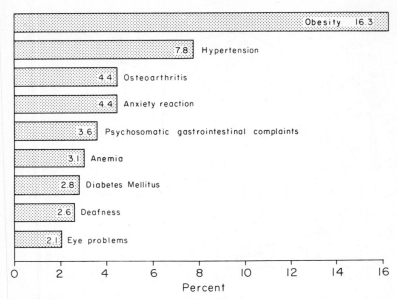

Obesity 16.3
7.8 Hypertension
4.4 Osteoarthritis
4.4 Anxiety reaction
3.6 Psychosomatic gastrointestinal complaints
3.1 Anemia
2.8 Diabetes Mellitus
2.6 Deafness
2.1 Eye problems

Percent

Figure 10–11 Prevalence of various disorders detected in screening examinations of ostensibly healthy middle-aged American members of a prepaid health care plan. (Adapted from Collen, M. F.: Automated Multiphasic Screening, Chapter 2, pp. 25–66. *In* Sharp, C. and Keen, H.: Presymptomatic Detection and Early Diagnosis. London, Pitman Medical Publication Company, Ltd., 1968.)

COMMON CAUSES OF DEATH IN MIDDLE AGE

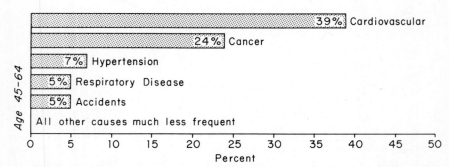

39% Cardiovascular
24% Cancer
7% Hypertension
5% Respiratory Disease
5% Accidents
All other causes much less frequent

Age 45-64

Percent

Figure 10–12 Common causes of death in middle age, as per cent of total deaths between ages 45 and 64. (Adapted from Vital Statistics of the United States, 1968. Vol. II, Part B: Mortality. Rockville, Maryland, United States Department of Health, Education and Welfare, 1971, pp. 114–126.

incidence between 45 and 55. The disease is more frequent among people whose occupations involve administrative responsibility, competitive effort, and nervous tension. It is usually duodenal in location, though all sites along the human upper digestive tract are responsive to "ulcerogenic" influences that affect the balance between tissue resistance and secretory products, mainly acid and the acid-activated proteolytic enzyme, pepsin. There appears to be a genetic predisposition and an increased incidence in people with blood type O. The disorder occurs in association with practically all diseases except those characterized by complete absence of gastric acid, and is particularly frequent in patients with chronic pulmonary disease and chronic alcoholism.

COMMON CAUSES OF MORBIDITY IN MIDDLE AGE

Revealing figures relating to disorders peculiar to this age have been obtained from diagnoses made on ostensibly healthy patients who have come to a large prepayment medical group (Kaiser) for screening (Fig. 10–11). It can be appreciated from the figure that many of these disorders may produce no symptoms until a complication, usually cardiovascular in nature, occurs.

COMMON CAUSES OF MORTALITY IN MIDDLE AGE

The commonest causes of mortality in the middle years are depicted in Figure 10–12 and clearly reflect the shift toward chronic disease in this age group.

The health spectrum is broad in the middle years, ranging from individuals who are completely free of both symptoms and risk factors to those who are gravely ill and dying. Since most of the causes of morbidity and mortality in this age group are intimately connected with processes which appear to be universal and age-related, the varied health of middle aged adults serves to emphasize the highly variable rate of aging in individuals who may share in common only their chronological age.

REFERENCES

Bierman, E. L., and Ross, R.: Aging and Atherosclerosis. In Paoletti, R., and Gotto, A. M., Jr. (Eds.): Atherosclerosis Reviews, New York, Raven Press, 1977, Vol. II, 79.
Bray, G. A.: The Obese Patient. Philadelphia, W.B. Saunders Company, 1976.
Clayton, R. R., and Voss, H. L.: Shacking up: Cohabitation in the 1970's. Journal of Marriage and the Family, 39(2):273, 1977.
Dehn, M. M., and Bruce, R. A.: Longitudinal variations in maximal oxygen intake with age and activity. J Appl Physiol, 33:805, 1972.
Erikson, E. H.: Identity and the Life Cycle. Psychological Issues. Monograph I, Vol. I, No. 1, 1969.

Kantner, J. F., and Zelnik, M.: Sexual experience of young unmarried women in the United States. Family Planning Perspective, 4:9, 1972.

Kramer, M., Taube, C. A., and Redick, R. W.: Patterns of use of psychiatric facilities by the aged: Past, present, and future. In Eisdorfer, C., and Lawton, P. M., (Eds.): The Psychology of Adult Development and Aging. Washington, D.C., American Psychological Association, 1973.

Lurie, H. J.: Clinical Psychiatry for the Primary Physician. Nutley, New Jersey, Roche Laboratories, 1976.

Neugarten, B. (Ed.): Middle Age and Aging. Chicago, University of Chicago Press, 1968.

Schmidt, G.: Working-class and middle-class adolescents. In Money, J., and Musaph, H., (Eds.): Handbook of Sexology. Amsterdam, Elsevier/North-Holland Biomedical Press, 1977.

Sheehy, G.: Passages: Crises of Adult Life. New York, Dutton, 1976.

Simon, A. W.: The New Years: A New Middle Age. New York, A.A. Knopf, 1968.

Stander, J., and Epstein, F. N.: Coronary heart disease: Risk factors as guides to preventive action. Prev Med, 1:27, 1972.

Troll, L. E.: Early and Middle Adulthood. Monterey, California, Brooks/Cole, 1975.

11

Old Age

WILLIAM R. HAZZARD
EDWIN L. BIERMAN*

"Age only matters when one is aging. Now that I have arrived at a great age, I might just as well be twenty."

Pablo Picasso

"I will never be an old man. To me, old age is always fifteen years older than I am."

Bernard Baruch

LIFE SITUATION

When does old age begin? Clearly no simple answer can be given. Not only do individuals age at differing rates, but also no single physical or physiological characteristic demarcates old from middle age. The date most commonly chosen as the onset of old age has been the 65th birthday. Hence "the problem of the elderly" is most often described in terms of the numbers or proportion of the population who have reached that milestone. In 1973 every tenth American was over the age of 65, nearly 21 million in number, a figure which presumably will rise by 100 a day to 25 million by 1985.

From a physical or physiological standpoint only rarely does the 65th birthday herald a dramatic change. The same cannot be said from a social and economic standpoint, however, since age 65 frequently signals the beginning of retirement. Retirement requires major adjustments in standard of living, marital relationship, and the activities of daily life. These adjustments in turn exert a major influence upon the physical and mental health of the aging individual. Hence in old age perhaps more than during any other epoch of life, the mutual interrelationships of physical, emotional, social, and economic factors are critical determinants of health and function.

229

Physical Changes

The physical characteristics of old age are perhaps best brought to
mind when one thinks of an elderly aunt or neighbor woman about 85
years old. The choice of sex in this illustration is intentional (and in this
chapter the female rather than the male gender has been used in
descriptions of the general characteristics of this age). The ratio of
women to men above 65 years of age is 139 to 100 (roughly 12 million to
8 million) in the U.S. Furthermore, this sex ratio in favor of females
progressively increases with advancing age: the average life expectancy
at age 65 is 12.2 years for men vs. 16.1 years for women (England, 1973).
Moreover, this sex differential appears to be growing, since those life
expectancies rose between 1901 and 1971 by only 11 per cent in men as
compared to 24 per cent in women (Fig. 11–1).

Picture this elderly woman as an illustration. Her skin is deeply
lined, reflecting the loss of skin elasticity and the wasting of subcutaneous fat and supporting tissues, sometimes called "senile atrophy." This
loss of connective tissues may increase skin fragility, and trivial trauma
may cause cutaneous bleeding, leaving purplish spots sometimes called
"senile purpura." (The use of the term "senile" should be avoided
wherever possible because of its perjorative connotations, which call to
mind pictures of the decrepit and demented rather than the sprightly,
plucky elderly who are much more typical of this biological age.) Returning to our elderly aunt, the common loss of teeth may accentuate the
wrinkling and indentation about the mouth and lips. Brown areas,
usually benign "age spots" ("senile keratoses") dot the face, hands, and
other sun-exposed areas. Other cutaneous tumors are common, ranging
from benign, small red spots ("cherry angiomas") about the trunk, to
lesions on the face with rolled edges that are technically malignant basal
cell carcinomas, but which rarely metastasize and are readily eradicated
by surgical treatment.

By this age the hair is usually gray or white, reflecting the lack of
pigment production by hair follicle cells. Hair loss is common among

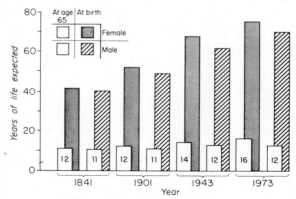

Figure 11–1   Life expectancy at birth and at age 65 for males and females for different
years in England. (Adapted from Coni, N., Davison, W., and Webster, S.: Lecture Notes on
Geriatrics. Oxford, Blackwell Scientific Publications, 1977.)

women as well as men, though this is general rather than a sex determined or inherited balding pattern and is rarely extensive.

The stature is typically stooped forward, reflecting chiefly the dorsal kyphosis or "dowager's hump," but also loss of the normal lumbar lordosis. There is also loss of height due to thinning and sometimes anterior wedging and collapse of the intervertebral discs. The vertebral bodies themselves may be compressed as the skeleton becomes demineralized (Fig. 10–1) to the point of osteoporosis, a phenomenon especially pronounced in women. In addition the normally obtuse angle between the neck and the shaft of the femur may become more acute, accentuating the bent over posture (and increasing the risk of fracture at this point).

At the same time the large joints are frequently undergoing the loss of cartilage and proliferation of subjacent bone which produce the chronic and often painful condition of osteoarthritis. Hence the gait of the elderly is often stiff and awkward. Changes in the nervous systems of the aged also contribute to difficulties in ambulation. Coordination is slow and imperfect, and reflexes which minimize sway in the erect posture become sluggish and blunted. Visual defects aggravate the problem, and often the person attempts to compensate by adopting a slow, shuffling gait as well as utilizing mechanical aids such as canes or walking sticks.

In addition to these more obvious changes, closer examination often discloses fluid filled cysts or extra folds about the eyes and white, ringlike deposits of cholesterol ester just inside the edge of the cornea (arcus corneae or arcus "senilis"). The pupils are often small, a miosis which might be accentuated by drops used in the treatment of glaucoma, a common condition among the elderly. Visual acuity is frequently also impaired by cataracts and/or retinal degeneration. The farsightedness or presbyopia caused by the loss of lens elasticity is nearly universal, though it has usually reached its peak in the middle years.

All too often there are few if any remaining teeth, reflecting not only the consequences of poor dental hygiene and care from earlier years but also gingival diseases and ill-fitting dentures. The latter is aggravated by bone loss in the jaw and that in turn by the lack of chewing caused by the lack of teeth, and so on. Thus poor dentition often represents both a major cause of disability in the elderly and a major barrier to their return to health.

Examination of the neck of the aged person reveals a limited range of motion, especially in lateral planes, reflecting the changes of osteoarthritis in the cervical spine. Listening with the stethoscope over the carotid bifurcation may reveal murmurs indicative of atherosclerotic disease. Examination of the thyroid gland is especially important, since a goiter may assist in the detection of hypo- or hyperthyroidism, diseases of special importance and subtle presentation in the elderly.

The chest reflects the skeletal changes in the dorsal spine. In addition, the chronic, progressive increase in lung volume and decrease in respiratory excursion characteristic of emphysema may add to the increased anteroposterior chest diameter. Heart sounds and rhythm are not necessarily affected by aging, but systolic murmurs (often of no physiological importance) and arrhythmias are common, even in the healthy elderly.

The abdomen of the elderly may protrude owing to the loss of muscle tone, the dorsal kyphosis, and the frequently large, fixed lung volume with consequent displacement of the subdiaphragmatic organs, notably the liver. Hard feces in the descending colon may make this organ palpable along the left lateral abdominal margin of the constipated elderly patient. At the same time a scaphoid (concave) abdomen in the recumbent position is common, since obesity is less frequent. Whether the relative lack of obesity among the elderly reflects the earlier death of the obese or a true loss of adipose mass is unclear. Perhaps a combination of both factors is more likely. It is clear, however, that obesity is not a general phenomenon among the aged (and is particularly uncommon among elderly men).

The male genitalia usually do not show age-distinctive changes; specifically, striking testicular atrophy is uncommon in elderly men. Pelvic examination of the elderly female frequently discloses atrophy of the vaginal mucosa, partially attributable to estrogen deficiency. Parenthetically, such changes in the physical aspects of sexuality need not be accompanied by functional changes, although changes in appearance and fears of declining sexuality often pose serious problems. Men are especially prone to worries about loss of sexual potency, not only as a source of pleasure but also as a symbol of masculinity and personal worth. For the woman, loss of sexual attractiveness may threaten her marital security as well as her self-esteem. Perhaps the most important determinant of sexual activity among the elderly is their pattern of earlier sexual practice. The timid, prudish, and inhibited may welcome a decline in sexual powers and interest in old age. However, those with a previously vigorous and healthy sex life often continue that pattern, maintaining sexual activities into their seventies and eighties. As sexual vigor is more openly espoused among today's younger generations, one can predict that the elderly of the future will continue to enjoy sexual activity well into old age albeit with less frequency and male potency.

Returning to our elderly aunt, the lower extremities often reveal the bony and articular changes of the hips previously described. The knees are often knobby, reflecting the proliferative bone changes of osteoarthritis. Varicose veins are very common in this age group. This may simply produce dialated and tortuous superficial veins. However, when the deep veins are affected, ankle swelling and brown skin pigmentation, stasis dermatitis, may occur. The skin of the dependent leg may also be a dusky red color if the arterial circulation is compromised by atherosclerosis, in which case the lower extremity is cold, the hair over the feet and lower leg is usually absent, and thick, discolored toenails (reflecting fungal overgrowth called onychomycosis) are common.

Evidence of the gradual, progressive loss of muscle bulk with age may be absent, although with use, aging muscle retains its capacity to regenerate by hypertrophy. Histologically, muscle tissue from the elderly reveals increased interstitial fat, and large round lipid droplets may occur within the muscle fibers. Functionally, muscle strength decreases with age. The individual muscles of the 65 year old retain about 60 per cent of the strength of those from a 25 year old, while grip strength is 77 per cent. There is great variation among individuals in these measurements, however, and some 65 year olds are stronger than some 25 year olds. Most authorities have suggested that age changes in muscle size and strength reflect decreased use with age. However, decreased strength and atrophy of hand muscles used throughout life is also seen among the aged, suggesting a more fundamental decline as a function of aging *per se*.

Neurological examination frequently discloses not only impaired coordination and position sense (for instance, using rapid finger to nose pointing or heel down shin testing) but also deep tendon reflexes are often diminished or absent, especially ankle jerks. Among tests of cranial nerve function, taste discrimination (olfactory nerve, I) is frequently reduced, vision diminished (optic nerve, II), and hearing grossly impaired (auditory division of VIII): the latter two defects particularly aggravate the isolation of the aged person. Vestibular function (vestibular division of VIII) is also often imperfect, adding to problems of instability and susceptibility to falls which plague the frail elderly. Other

Figure 11–2 A 74 year old woman and a 75 year old man who met two years previously in a retirement apartment house. They have been steady companions since, enjoying a variety of activities together.

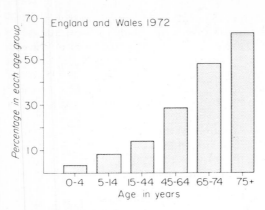

Figure 11–3 Percentage of individuals in each age group reporting long standing, chronic illness (England and Wales, 1972). (Adapted from Coni, N., Davison, W., and Webster, S.: Lecture Notes on Geriatrics. Oxford, Blackwell Scientific Publications, 1977.)

sensory deficits include decreased perception of light touch, vibration, temperature, and pain. Psychomotor responses are generally retarded, apparently owing to slowing of higher integrative functions. Hence the more complex the response, the more markedly is it slowed.

The composite picture of this fragile elderly woman may be quite misleading. Most aged persons lead independent, vigorous lives. Ninety-five per cent live in their own homes or apartments, either alone or with spouse, relatives, or friends. This independence and relatively good health is especially characteristic of the "young-old," those between 65 and 75 years of age (Fig. 11–2). This group is rapidly growing in Western societies, by virtue of the general aging of the population (Fig. 2–5).

However, the most rapidly growing segments of the population (in percentage as opposed to absolute terms) are those over 75 and even above 85. And it is especially in these groups that the disabilities and diseases of the elderly are so prevalent and, given survival, ultimately inevitable. Those over 65 account for a disproportionate amount of disability, especially major disability. And this disproportion increases with age beyond 65, being especially great among the "old-old" above 75 and 85 years of age. Thus the majority of those above age 75 report at least one chronic disease (Fig. 11–3) and many of the "frail elderly" are beyond that age.

Physiological Changes

The age-dependent decline in physiological control common to nearly all organ systems often reaches clinically significant proportions in this age (Chapter 2, Figure 2–7). When the decline in one particular function proceeds at a faster rate than others and reaches a threshold resulting in clinical symptoms, we usually call that decline a disease, especially if a reasonably clear-cut cause can be found. This tends to be particularly true if the disorder presents in youth or middle age. On the other hand if a decline results in no significant functional disability, such as graying of the hair, we tend to call it "physiological aging." Between these two extremes are a multitude of age-related changes that may produce minor dysfunction, especially in situations of stress requiring adaptation. Many of these relative defects would be considered pathological in a younger person and would initiate a search for a specific disease entity. Among the elderly, while the physiological basis of such dysfunction may be the same as that in a younger person, its diagnostic specificity and therapeutic implications may be quite different.

As a case in point, consider the diagnosis of diabetes mellitus, based upon tests of carbohydrate homeostasis such as the glucose tolerance test. In a healthy young adult the blood glucose normally returns to the fasting baseline within 3 hours of a meal, and 95 per cent have concentrations below 140 mg/100 ml at 2 hours (Fig. 11–4). However, glucose

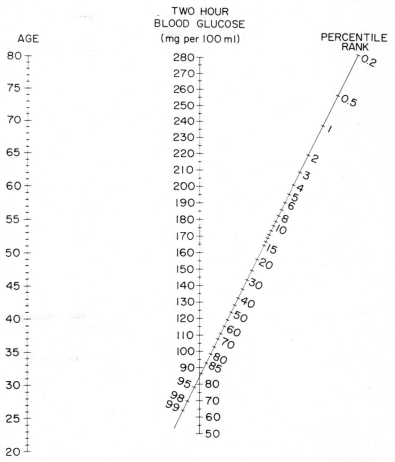

Figure 11–4 Nomogram for determining percentile rank of an individual's two hour postprandial blood glucose level as a function of age. This nomogram is used to judge performance on an oral glucose tolerance test. A straight edge connecting the subject's age with his blood glucose concentration two hours after the injection of 100g glucose will intersect the percentile rank line. A rank of 50 per cent is an average performance, and a rank of 2 per cent is relatively poor, since it indicates that 98 per cent of subjects of the same age will perform better than that individual. (From Andres, R.: Relation of physiological changes in aging to medical change of disease in the aged. Mayo Clinic Proc. 42:679, 1967.)

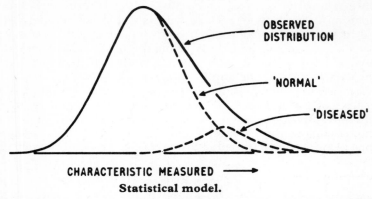

CHARACTERISTIC MEASURED ——▶
Statistical model.

Figure 11–5 Curve of the frequency distribution of a hypothetical quantitative characteristic, such as blood pressure, serum cholesterol, or post-oral glucose blood sugar levels. The asymmetrical upper tail of the curve may reflect the presence of two populations, one normal, the other diseased; however, the considerable overlap between the populations often makes the decision as to whether a given individual is diseased or normal highly arbitrary and subject to considerable error. Most such distributions become more widely spread and skewed in older populations, thus further blurring the distinction between normal and abnormal among aged persons.

tolerance universally declines with age, to the point where more than half the population of age 75 exceeds that same figure of 140 mg/100 ml. Does half of the elderly population have diabetes mellitus, or does the glucose tolerance test become a relatively nonspecific diagnostic index of disease among the elderly?

This diagnostic dilemma applies to many tests of physiological function, as the effects of age blur the distinction between the "normal" and "diseased" subpopulations in the distribution curves for various parameters (Fig. 11–5). These include chemical indices like blood glucose and urea, as well as physical characteristics, such as blood pressure, nerve conduction velocity, and maximal heart rate achievable during exercise. In practical terms this means that aging introduces problems of both diagnostic sensitivity and specificity (more of both "false positives" and "false negatives").

The problem of diagnosis among the elderly is complicated even further by yet another dimension, assessment of the cost of diagnosis. It is rather easy to estimate the economic costs involved. Each diagnostic procedure has its associated dollar cost, and the aggregate total can be staggering given the recent proliferation of expensive tests such as coronary angiography and gastrointestinal endoscopy, and the large proportion of the elderly who might be suspected of having atherosclerotic cardiovascular or gastrointestinal disease. Perhaps more subtle but equally important are the noneconomic, human costs of such procedures. Many diagnostic tests are themselves stressful and carry their own risk. Nearly all such risks are greater in the elderly, and few experienced health practitioners are unfamiliar with the chain reaction of progressive complications initiated in the frail elderly patient by a procedure which would be innocuous in a younger patient. Furthermore, nearly all such procedures are degrading to some degree and require adaptation to an unfamiliar environment. For a young, relatively robust person, the stress of such a test might be trivial. For an elderly patient in precarious physical and mental health, such a test might prove terrifying and disastrous.

Finally, if a given disorder is diagnosed, what is the efficacy and what are the risks of treatment? The "cost/benefit" ratio or therapeutic index of most conditions diminishes among the aged. Not only are the benefits of treatment often difficult to detect but also the side effects and practical problems are increased. This is especially true for chronic conditions and prevention of their long term consequences, as illustrated by the common problem of hypertension. First, the prevalence of hypertension increases with age (Fig. 10–8), and among the elderly treatment of all those considered hypertensive by the criteria of a systolic blood pressure exceeding 160 mmHg and/or diastolic of 90 mmHg would present a major public health undertaking. Second, the risks of treatment are increased among the elderly. Any geriatrician is familiar with the precipitation of postural hypotension and falling spells by diuretics prescribed for hypertension in the aged patient. Third, the treatment of hypertension is critically dependent upon careful, long term adherence to daily medication, in turn dependent upon good patient understanding and motivation. Problems of this kind are difficult enough to deal with in the young; among the elderly, social and economic as well as physiological considerations often make them impossible. Consider, too, the difficulties of estimating the benefits of antihypertensive treatment in the elderly. While the long term complications of high blood pressure, notably stroke and heart attack, are epidemic among the sick elderly, its high prevalence among the healthy in this age group makes it difficult to determine which person will and which person will not benefit from treatment. Besides, given the long latent period between the identification of cardiovascular risk factors such as hypertension and their atherosclerotic complications, treatment initiated in old age may be too late to exert a beneficial effect. Treatment also may be unnecessary where compensating factors coexist, such as a low beta (low density) lipoprotein or high alpha (high density) lipoprotein cholesterol level. It also may be irrelevant if greater problems in other spheres, such as deficient immune function leading to serious infections or malignant disease, limit life expectancy more than does the hypertension itself.

In this sense it may be difficult to assign a specific cause of death in an elderly patient. Did she die of a heart attack? Or of the complicating pneumonia? Did she die of a fractured hip? Or of the complicating pulmonary embolus? Since most aged patients carry multiple diagnoses in their medical charts, and additional problems lurk just beneath the clinical horizon at any given time, the death of an aged person may seem almost random regardless of its proximate cause. This is suggested by the semilogarithmic form of the tail of the human survival curve above 92 years of age (Fig. 11–6), resembling at this age the survival curve of water glasses in a cafeteria.

Given this matrix of conflicting considerations, the geriatric practi-

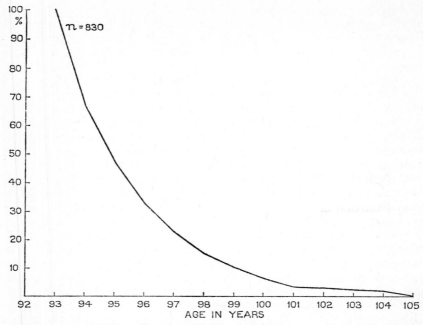

Figure 11–6 Semilogarithmic form of the tail of the human survival curve above 92 years of age. (From Ageing: The Biology of Senescence, by Alex Comfort. Copyright © 1956, 1964 by Alex Comfort. Reprinted by permission of Holt, Rinehart and Winston, Inc.)

tioner must exercise careful judgment in initiating any diagnostic or therapeutic action. Even requiring the patient to leave his home to attend a clinic or hospital may be contraindicated, and among the elderly house calls retain their old-fashioned rationale. The physician caring for elderly patients must above all practice the "art of medicine," wherein human considerations and common sense may be as important as scientific knowledge. This is in no way meant to diminish the importance of medical knowledge in assessment of the problems of the elderly patient. Quite to the contrary, since a small improvement in function may mean the difference between a bedfast institutional existence and an independent life in the community for such a patient, practitioners must unceasingly seek to discover reversible causes of disability. What it does mean is that diagnostic and therapeutic zeal must be tempered by knowledge of the special problems of the elderly patient.

One practical approach to diagnosis in the elderly has been the development of age-specific norms. A nomogram may be used to determine the percentile rank of the 2 hour postprandial blood glucose level specific to the patient's age (Fig. 11–4). While this technique does much to reduce the overdiagnosis of diabetes among the elderly, it does not answer the question, "How does one diagnose diabetes in the aged patient?" or its critical corollary, "At what blood glucose level should treatment for diabetes be initiated?" Once again the answers to these questions are particularly difficult in the aged patient, since therapy to reduce blood sugar carries an increased risk of hypoglycemia in this age group. Hence the critical place for clinical judgment in the diagnosis and treatment of diabetes in the elderly.

Psychosocial Changes

NANCY ROBINSON

Attitudes and practices with respect to the aged, the ill, and the weak are determined largely by the society's survival needs and its cultural traditions. In nomadic hunting societies, where survival depended upon rapid, efficient movement of small groups from one seasonal hunting ground to another, drastic methods of relieving the groups' burden of aged persons were adopted. Industrialized Western societies deal with the aged in ways which are less obviously cruel.

A chronologically aged, healthy person usually has needs and behavior patterns that do not differ greatly from those of younger persons. However, given the prevailing preoccupation with youth, physical activity, and attractiveness, and the severely economically disadvantaged position of the elderly in Western societies, three different approaches have been advanced as the best method to adapt to old age. These are *disengagement* — retirement from usual activities into a sedentary pace of living, to the ghetto of a retirement community when and where it is economically feasible; *maintenance of activity* — based on the premise that the best old age resembles middle age as closely as possible, with no special age segregation and no planned changes of behavior associated with aging; *maintenance of utility* — effective functioning is based, in large part, on the conviction of one's usefulness (when no contribution is possible, living loses its meaning). Consideration of these alternatives makes it obvious that none of them represents an optimal, realistic, accepting approach to old age, nor a recognition of the individual differences which are as characteristic of the elderly as of younger persons.

Socioeconomic Factors. The importance of socioeconomic factors is underscored by our definition of the elderly as "past the age of retirement," commonly taken in the United States to be between age 65 and 70. It is important to remember that retirement age is arbitrary and that retirement itself is a new institution; only the very rich and the disabled retired in the earlier days of our nation. Some people are "old" at 65; some much sooner, some much later. In eastern European countries, women usually retire at age 55 and men at age 60. For nonemployed women, the age at which their husbands retire may be much more meaningful than their own age of "retirement."

In our inflationary economy, a great many of the elderly are on fixed incomes which gradually decline in value. Those who were previously among the socioeconomically marginal may find poverty no new experience, but many who were not previously poor become so after retirement. Economic security is an important factor in the maintenance of good morale in old age, and the financial wherewithal greatly increases the alternatives and comforts available. Money effectively prevents some of the psychological and social misery of old age.

Family and Interpersonal Relationships.   As people grow older, their families and friends become preoccupied with their own problems, change jobs, move, become ill, age, or die. Often older people find it difficult to maintain interpersonal ties, and making new friends is exceedingly difficult. A distinction can be made between the aged isolate (one who can live alone in pleasure and comfort) and the aged desolate (one, who having lost family or friends, remains inconsolable and desperately in need of replacements). Those deprived prior to retirement appear to be less well prepared to tolerate the adversities and changes of old age than are those with educational and occupational advantages. The best predictor of adjustment after retirement remains the individual's adjustment before retirement.

Most marital couples face dissolution through the death of one partner significantly before the other. Both because of the greater longevity of women and because the woman is usually the younger of the pair, protracted widowhood is very frequent. Although financial problems are common, as we have seen, widows unaccustomed to handling family finances often are convinced that they are suddenly poverty-stricken even when quite the opposite may be the case. The grieving process in an older person may last much longer than in a younger one, who realistically has new activities and new friendships to fill the void left by the deceased partner.

Coming to terms with one's own life constitutes, for Erikson, the foremost task of the aging period. Erikson expresses this task as developing *ego integrity*, maintaining a sense of wholeness and adequacy, being satisfied with the way one has lived one's life. Without ego integrity, there is *despair*, wishing it were possible to live one's life over again differently, and knowing that it will never be possible. Individuals with ego integrity are able to face death calmly. (See Chapter 12.)

Cognitive Changes.   As we have seen, tasks which require speedy reactions and flexibility of thought processes begin to decline gradually even in the middle years of adulthood, but performance on tasks which call for breadth and depth of experience, such as the use of general information and vocabulary, often do not decline until persons become quite elderly. In general, persons of higher intelligence tend to hold up best in cognitive tasks. When learning deficits are observed, it is important to check first to see that sensory acuity problems are not at fault. The elderly individual may be shy to admit that she or he has been unable to read or focus upon the television screen, or has been unable to hear a question. There is reason to suspect that when cognitive abilities do show a sharp decline, brain damage or other health related problems may have occurred. Longitudinal studies have found excessively high death rates among those showing sharp declines in any of a number of cognitive measures, so that the phenomenon has come to be known as *terminal decline*.

Given a comfortable pace of exposure to new situations, and simple tasks to be mastered, old people may learn only a little less well than younger ones. As soon as interfering factors are introduced, however — a speeded up presentation, extraneous noise, a difficult task or a series of simple ones, or the need to change the material in some way (for example, to reverse a series of numbers before repeating them) — then a noticeable drop in efficiency is apparent. Because life often presents complicated learning situations, poor learning becomes rather common.

With respect to memory functions, the elderly seem to have considerable trouble with tasks requiring them to dredge up information they know, much more difficulty than with tasks requiring them merely to recognize information they have learned. The difficulty is with retrieval, as though the information is stored in their memory bank but indexing or finding it is difficult. Competence depending on unassisted recall thus declines with age. (See Figure 9–3, p. 188.)

COMMON PROBLEMS

Behavioral

NANCY ROBINSON

One of the major problems with growing old in North America is that it tends to happen as an afterthought. Financial and physical problems combine to force many older people into dependent roles, exaggerated by living far from stores and services; by environmental barriers such as curbs, stairs, and rapidly changing traffic lights; and by caretaking practices at home or in nursing facilities that fail to give sufficient reinforcement for adaptive, self-care behaviors.

The aged appear to be at particularly high risk for mental disorders, but statistics about this risk are difficult to evaluate. A study in Baltimore revealed a weighted rate of 28 per 1000 for persons above 65 years of age, compared with 6 per 1000 for those 35 to 64 years. However, deviant behavior among old people is often well tolerated by others and perhaps accepted as normal, until having been neglected, the problems result in destructive behavior and the older patient is brought into the mental health system. When this occurs, there is frequently an over-response, with full hospitalization for prolonged periods, if not on a permanent basis. Ambulatory or preventive care of the aged's mental health is often neglected, with only 2 per cent of all psychiatric and mental health center outpatients being in the 65+ age group. In contrast, approximately half the occupants of nursing homes have at least 1 psychiatric diagnosis, and two thirds receive psychotropic medication. Currently, approximately 4 per cent of the age group over 65 are in custodial care, yet if proper support were available, it is estimated that at least one third of these people could live in the community.

The etiology of behavioral and emotional disorders is often complex in the elderly person. In the past, there was a tendency to overplay the role of brain dysfunction and damage to the exclusion of social, psychological, and economic factors. Brain changes do occur with aging, attributable to degenerative processes in the brain cells, atherosclerotic cerebral vascular disease, or a combination of both. However, when careful attention is paid to rehabilitation and therapy, the response of the aged patient may be highly gratifying.

Specific behavioral disorders in the aged are often qualitatively similar to those of younger age groups. They include the following.

Depression.   Depressive reactions are very common in old age, while manic reactions are less common. Depression may be found in association with organic mental symptoms as well as in relatively pure form. One such form which often appears in persons not previously subject to depressive episodes is therefore sometimes referred to as an *involutional* affective disorder. Often reaching psychotic proportions, this reaction is characterized by depression, hypochondriasis, low self-esteem, guilt (especially about sexual behavior), and often florid paranoid ideation. Depression in the aged may be reactive to loss of spouse, friends, home, income, or social status, but may persist for long periods. Not infrequently, it leads to suicide, which is increasingly common with age among males. (See Table 11–1.)

Schizophrenic Disorders.   The incidence of schizophrenia increases with age. It is undetermined whether this represents age related expression of a lifelong predisposition, a longstanding process which simply has gone undetected, or a specific effect of the aging process. Paranoid process may flourish in isolated persons, especially in the hard of hearing, who may misinterpret or fail to discern what is said and grow excessively sensitive, irritable, and suspicious.

Alcoholism.   Abuse of alcohol is more common among the younger segments of the elderly age group. As with coronary artery disease, its declining prevalence in the aged may reflect the effect of selective early mortality among younger alcoholics, or (less likely) an actual decrease in alcohol consumption and dependence with the approach of old age.

TABLE 11–1   SUICIDE RATES IN THE U.S. for 1970
BY AGE, SEX, AND RACE (per 100,000)

Age range	White males	White females	Nonwhite males	Nonwhite females
15–19	9.4	2.9	5.4	2.9
20–24	19.3	5.7	19.4	5.5
25–29	19.8	8.6	20.1	6.0
30–34	20.0	9.5	19.4	5.6
35–39	21.9	12.2	13.9	4.5
40–44	24.6	13.8	11.4	4.1
45–49	28.2	13.5	16.5	4.0
50–54	30.9	13.5	11.3	5.1
55–59	34.9	13.1	12.3	1.8
60–64	35.0	11.5	8.4	2.8
65–69	37.4	9.4	11.5	3.2
70–74	40.4	9.7	8.2	3.9
75–79	42.2	7.3	5.7	3.1
80–84	51.4	7.2	22.9	3.2
85–plus	45.8	5.8	12.6	6.4

SOURCE: *Vital Statistics of the United States, 1970, Volume II, Mortality, Part A.* Rockville, Maryland: U.S. Public Health Service, 1974.

Chronic alcoholism over a period of years produces chemical deficits and imbalances which cause irreversible encephalopathy, with a typical pattern of symptoms called the Wernicke-Korsakoff syndrome. This includes disorientation, confusion, memory disorder, confabulation (filling in gaps in memory with plausible guesses), impulsiveness, and inflammation of the peripheral nerves.

Acute Brain Syndrome. Persons with acute brain syndrome show transient but severe mental impairment including confusion, memory loss, disorientation, and disordered thinking. This is often at least a partially reversible condition and is usually related to acute febrile, debilitating, or exhausting illness.

Senile Dementia. Old people may develop psychotic behavior that is characterized by delusions, memory defects, and general disorientation. Whereas single episodes of cerebral thrombosis, hemorrhage, or embolism give rise to focal rather than diffuse damage unless there is cardiovascular, pulmonary, or other system disease, senile brain changes are presumed when there are no focal neurological signs or history of stroke. Controversy currently exists as to whether senile dementia is a single disorder which is part of a continuum with Alzheimer's disease (presenile dementia, occurring before age 65) with a common viral etiology, or a descriptive category encompassing several specific disease entities. In either event, the individual can often be helped by a concerted effort to counteract the confusion and disorientation by reminders and reteaching of orienting information. A reality orientation which over and over restructures the experience of the elderly person, such that he or she has the information needed to cope with a simplified environment, may reduce the withdrawal, depression, and confusion so often seen as a result of mild declines in central nervous system function.

Nutritional and Metabolic Disorders

The nutritional and metabolic disorders of old age proceed from socioeconomic as well as physiological factors. On the one hand, given the traditional emphasis placed upon food as the antidote to illness, the frailty of old people has led to overestimates of the prevalence of protein, vitamin, and mineral deficiencies among the elderly in Western society. However, the prevalence of these deficiencies and the consequences to health and function are greater among the aged than among younger persons. Having less money to spend on food (and the greater cost of shopping at small nearby shops or having food delivered) often means less food is eaten. Salt restriction required for persons with heart failure may diminish palatability and increase food cost. Dental problems may restrict the menu and lessen intake as well. Since cooking for oneself represents less challenge and provides less gratification than cooking for a spouse, meals are often eaten from cans or boxes, and consequently, less is ingested. Depression also commonly decreases appetite. Finally, because caloric expenditure is reduced as the isolated old person withdraws into her home or apartment caloric intake is appropriately curtailed. Therefore, since minimum daily requirements for protein, vitamins, and minerals do not decline appreciably with age, their generous surplus intake in active young persons in affluent Western societies no longer applies in the elderly, and many old people subsist in a state of chronic marginal deficiency. While such a marginal state may not noticeably interfere with function under ordinary circumstances, processes such as infectious disease or thyrotoxicosis that increase nutritional requirements, or acute depression or gastrointestinal disorders that diminish intake, may precipitate overt nutritional deficiency syndromes. These most often are present in the form of *nutritional anemias*, such as the microcyte anemia of iron deficiency or the macrocyte anemia of folic acid deficiency. Nutritional status illustrates the contrasts between the healthy and the sick elderly; while overt nutritional deficiency is rare among the healthy elderly, it may be common and is indeed a frequent presenting problem among the sick. Hence one's impression of the prevalence of such disorders is likely to be heavily influenced by the kind of old person one most often encounters. To the community social worker or even the general practitioner who encounters many healthy elderly or those with minor ailments, nutritional deficiency among the aged may seem uncommon. To the geriatrician who cares for the multiply disabled or chronically ill, such deficiency may seem very common.

Obesity.   Obesity among the elderly is less prevalent than among the middle aged, and those who have survived into old age despite obesity, notably women, may be relatively immune to its deleterious cardiovascular consequences. Weight loss, rather than weight gain, is the more common nutritional problem of old age. It is important to stress, however, that these generalizations may not apply to the individual patient, whose disability may be aggravated by overweight. This is readily illustrated by the elderly person with osteoarthritis, in whom not only the pain of the disease but also the consequent immobility may be significantly improved by weight loss. Similarly, weight loss in the obese elderly diabetic may obviate the need for insulin or oral hypoglycemic therapy. As in younger persons, however, long term success at weight loss is rare in the elderly, understandably so, given their reduced caloric expenditure. Hence weight loss in old people is more often a harbinger of grave illness such as depression or malignancy.

Diabetes.   Symptomatic diabetes mellitus becomes increasingly common in old age, being more than twice as prevalent at age 70 as at age 50. The true prevalence of the disease remains uncertain, largely owing to the problems in diagnostic specificity previously described. It is especially common in those with chronic obesity (its prevalence related more to the duration than degree of obesity) and in relatives of diabetics (who are themselves usually obese if their diabetes was of adult onset). Since neuropathy and the microvascular features of the disease (notably retinopathy and nephropathy) increase with the duration of known diabetes, the macrovascular (atherosclerotic) sequelae, in themselves exponentially related to aging, are more common causes of morbidity and mortality among those with diabetes of old age onset. Nevertheless, longstanding diabetes is an important cause of visual defects in the aged, as it is in the total population, in which it represents the third leading cause of blindness. Unfortunately, apart from the prevention of keto-acidosis (rare in the obese patient) or the syndrome of nonketotic, hyperosmolar coma (a particular hazard in the elderly patient because of decreased mobility and diminished access to oral fluids), and treatment of the symptoms of polydipsia, polyuria, and polyphagia, antidiabetic therapy affords no clear protection against the late micro- and macrovascular complications. Consequently, major attention in the elderly diabetic should be directed toward avoidance of accidents, especially those involving the feet, where both blood and nervous supply may be impaired by the disease, and prevention of other stresses, such as dehydration and infection, which can trigger a rapid progression to major clinical problems.

Gallstones. Cholelithiasis (*gallstones*) represent the result of another common metabolic disorder, the excretion of bile supersaturated in cholesterol. (See Chapter 10.) Gallstones are very common in old age, and the complications of cholecystitis or jaundice due to obstruction of the common bile duct by a stone which has escaped the gall bladder occur frequently in the elderly. However, not all persons with cholelithiasis develop complications, and the risks of surgery, though small, increase in the elderly. Consequently, the frequent detection of gallstones in the asymptomatic elderly patient (or one with relatively nonspecific gastrointestinal symptoms) poses a particular dilemma for the physician. Should a cholecystectomy be performed on an elective basis under optimal surgical conditions, so as to prevent cholecystitis and the necessity of emergency surgery with its inherently greater risk? Or should one await the emergence of intolerable symptoms? This question remains unresolved, and various physicians adopt different approaches, depending upon their own background and experience as well as the peculiar circumstances of each case. However, recent trends in medical practice, tempered by physicians' increasing awareness of the susceptibility of the aged patient to surgery and the stress of hospitalization, have swung toward more conservative, expectant ("wait and see") management.

Osteoporosis. This is another common disorder among the elderly which is often considered to be of nutritional origin. While dietary mineral deficiencies may contribute to the problem, more certain causes relate to the inexorable loss of skeletal calcium with aging (Fig. 10–1), coupled perhaps with disuse atrophy and the sex steroid status of the individual. The fractures that complicate osteoporosis represent the end stage of a degenerative process beginning in early adulthood, when the peak mineral content of bone is reached. Hence such fractures are most common in those with the lowest peak levels and those who survive the longest. From both standpoints women are at greater risk. *Osteomalacia,* a condition caused by the lack of vitamin D, may also be present with the complications of a demineralized skeleton in old age. Its cause is more clearly nutritional, but the problems of fat malabsorption (vitamin D being fat-soluble) and lack of sunlight (the vitamin being manufactured in skin exposed to the sun) are more often at fault than dietary deficiency. Thus even a condition with apparently a single etiology, vitamin D deficiency, can be multifactorial in the aged patient.

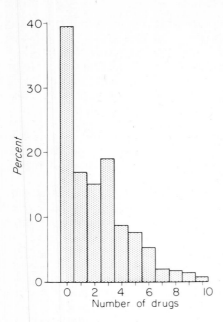

Figure 11-7 Percentage of 70 year olds taking different numbers of drugs. (Adapted from Svanborg, A.: Seventy year old people in Gothenberg, a population study in an industrialized Swedish city. II: General presentation of social and medical conditions. Acta Medica Scandinavica Suppl. 611, 1977.)

Chemical Agents

Alcohol.   Alcohol remains an important source of toxicity among the elderly, and with increasing affluence and alcohol intake among the population as a whole, it is likely to represent an even greater problem in the future. However, frank alcoholism and the medical problems of hepatic cirrhosis and pancreatitis are relatively uncommon among the elderly (most such alcoholics have succumbed by about age 55). Nevertheless, problem drinking is seen among certain elderly people, especially in situations of loss or loneliness, and the substitution of alcohol for food as a source of calories aggravates the already marginal nutritional status of the older person.

Drugs.   Drug overdoses in the elderly are common but most often iatrogenic, resulting from the failure of physicians to reduce doses to adjust for the age associated decline in hepatic and renal function, the prescription of confusing drug programs, age dependent idiosyncratic reactions (such as the paradoxical, stimulating effects of barbiturates in many old people), or from drug-drug interactions in persons on multiple drug regimens, particularly common in the elderly (Fig. 11-7). Perhaps the most frequent contribution of the geriatric specialist to the successful outcome of a referred case is the withdrawal of one or more drugs. The improvement can be little short of miraculous: the sleepy may wake up, the sleepless may sleep, the confused become lucid, and the bedfast become mobile and independent once again.

Some drug overdoses are intentional, and the elderly commit suicide with alarming frequency (the eldest one eighth of the population accounting for a third of "successful" suicides). (See Table 11-1). The reasons for the high incidence of suicide among the aged include not only the increased prevalence of serious mental disorders, notably depression, but also the reaction of the elderly to loss of function, self-esteem, and the companionship of spouse and peers; the prospect of lingering, often painful diseases such as cancer; and the pervasive feelings of rejection by society. Many of these feelings can be prevented or assuaged by changes in the immediate environment of the patient or in the attitudes of society. However, with the increasing number of people entering the "old-old" category and more open discussions among physicians, lawyers, clergymen, philosophers, and laymen regarding the right of an individual to choose his own time and means of death, the possibility of passive (negative) or even active (positive) euthanasia is more frequently considered by the incurably ill patient.

Trauma

Accidents are a serious menace to life and limb in older people. More than 3 million persons 65 years and older seek medical attention each year in the United States because of accidental injury. Most such accidents occur in and around the home, though traffic accidents are common, especially those involving the elderly pedestrian. Falls are particularly common, and fracture of the vulnerable femoral neck is a frequent cause for hospitalization and orthopedic repair, notably among those in the "old-old" age group.

Infectious Disorders

Viral Illnesses. The respiratory tract is the major site of serious viral disease. Influenza is frequently fatal among the elderly, particularly among those with coexisting cardiac or pulmonary disorders.

Bacterial Illnesses. The respiratory and genitourinary tracts are the chief sites of involvement. Pneumonia was once called "the old man's friend," since it was such a common terminal event in the old person with multisystem disease. Chronic and intermittently acute urinary tract infections are common in the elderly of both sexes, especially in men with bladder neck obstruction due to benign or malignant prostatic neoplasms. Tuberculosis remains an important cause of morbidity and mortality among the elderly, as improved hygiene and nutrition in the population at large has left only the weak and heavily exposed at significant risk.

Immunologic Disorders

Aging is associated with a decline in isoimmunity (reaction to foreign agents) and an increase in autoimmunity (reaction to self). Diseases common among the elderly attributable to autoimmunity include pernicious anemia, Addison's disease (adrenocortical deficiency), and

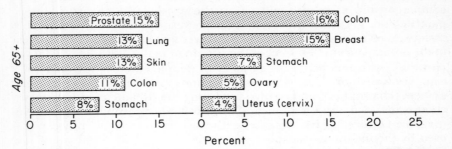

Figure 11–8 Death from various types of cancer as per cent of the total in males (left) and females (right) above age 65. (Adapted from Mortality from Malignant Neoplasms, 1955-1965. Part I. Geneva, Switzerland, World Health Organization, 1970, pp. 78–101.)

thyroiditis, since all are associated with circulating autoantibodies to the tissue from which the deficient chemical component is normally secreted. Evidence of the decline in isoimmunity is the reduction of immunity to past tubercular infections (with frequent conversion of a formerly positive to a negative tuberculin skin test) and hence the greater susceptibility of the elderly to reinfection or reactivation of latent tuberculosis. Neoplastic disorders may also reduce isoimmunity, especially those affecting the immune system such as lymphoma or multiple myeloma, both of which are more common in the elderly. Finally immunosuppressive drugs, including corticosteroids, may be used in treating autoimmune, inflammatory, or malignant disease in the elderly, further impairing resistance to infection.

Neoplastic Disorders

The incidence of most cancers increases with age (Fig. 11–8) and approximately half of all deaths due to malignancy occur in those over 65. In elderly men, prostatic hyperplasia becomes almost universal, and histologic evidence of malignancy is very common at autopsy. However, malignant dissemination is less frequent, and many elderly men die *with* but not *of* prostatic cancer.

COMMON CAUSES OF MORBIDITY

An axiom of medicine is that common diseases are multifactorial.

This complexity is magnified among the elderly, where multiple common defects often coexist in the same person. In practical terms this means that the disorders of the elderly are often not proper diseases in a medical sense, but simply a convergence of problems, each of which may be trivial when considered individually, but which in sum total can threaten the independence or life of the patient. Of particular importance in this age group is the possibility of a minor stress triggering a chain reaction of complications which can lead to death or chronic disability, as illustrated in Fig. 11–9.

As a reflection of the optimal, practical approach to the elderly patient, assessment is best made through systematic evaluation in 4 equally important dimensions: physical, mental, social, and functional status. The problem list in each of these categories is just as likely to include the death of a spouse or the recent breakdown of central heating as specific disease entities. Chief among problems of the elderly are the three "I's": Mental Illness, Instability/Immobility, and Incontinence.

Mental illness of the aged has been described earlier. Instability is caused by the multitude of neurological, ophthalmological, cardiovascu-

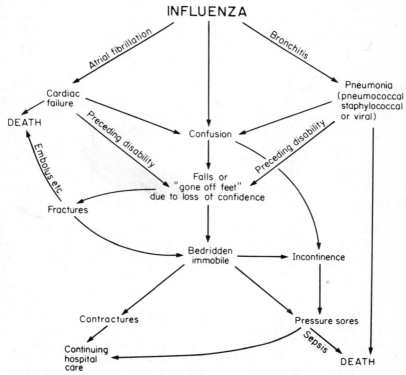

Figure 11–9   Cascade of disasters triggered by minor illness. (Adapted from Coni, N., Davison, W., and Webster, S.: Lecture Notes on Geriatrics. Oxford, Blackwell Scientific Publications, 1977.)

lar, and musculoskeletal problems just described. Immobility is either the advanced stage of instability (when the patient has "gone off his feet" owing to intolerable unsteadiness and fear of falls) or the result of additional insults such as fractures or stroke. Incontinence proceeds not only from mechanical problems such as prostatic urinary obstruction but also often from neurological disorders, frequently of central origin in the patient with a stroke or dementia. Needless to say, the end-stage geriatric patient frequently demonstrates all three "I's," and these disabilities not only cause the greatest burden upon the health care delivery system but also represent the greatest obstacle to effective treatment and placement of the aged patient. Few health care agencies are anxious to add a bedridden, incontinent, and frequently disoriented person to their patient population. While such reluctance is understandable, especially when staffs are already overextended and financial resources inadequate, the challenge and satisfaction associated with efforts to return such a patient to independent life in the community are matched by few opportunities in health care delivery.

While degenerative musculoskeletal diseases are among the commonest causes of morbidity among the elderly, cardiovascular diseases dominate the list of common causes of death, accounting for two thirds of the total (Fig. 11–10). In addition to coronary artery disease (see Chapter 10) other manifestations of atherosclerosis, such as cerebrovascular disease, become prominent in the aged. Cerebrovascular thrombosis, embolus, or hemorrhage, grouped generically under the acceptable term of "stroke" (or cerebrovascular accident) reflects the accumulation of arterial changes secondary to both atherosclerotic and hypertensive disease. Together with dementia and cancer they represent the most feared diseases of old age. Strokes are often fatal, accounting for 200,000 deaths per year in the United States, 80 per cent of which occur in persons over 65. The 8 out of 10 who survive may be left with serious impairments to movement, speech, thought processes, and emotional stability. Over 2 million survivors of stroke are presently alive in the United States. Many are chronically disabled, imposing an economic burden on family and community. Whereas earlier detection and treatment has been shown to reduce the cerebrovascular and renal complications of hypertension among the middle aged, the same favorable benefit/risk ratio has not yet been demonstrated among the elderly, and a narrow or even negative ratio can be predicted in this age group. Hence stroke is likely to remain a major cause of morbidity and mortality in the aged for the foreseeable future.

Peripheral arterial disease, causing intermittent claudication (cramping calf or thigh pains with exercise) and, in extreme cases, gangrene of the toes or feet, is another atherosclerotic complication which is common in the elderly. Most common, of course, is coronary heart disease. This may present as sudden death, angina pectoris, arrhythmia, myocardial infarction, or congestive heart failure. Hypertension contributes both to coronary atherosclerosis and directly to congestive heart failure by increasing peripheral arterial resistance and hence the work load of the left ventricle. Frequently elderly people present simply with edema of the lower extremities, and it is difficult to determine whether local factors (such as venous stasis due to varicose veins) or cardiac failure is at fault. If the latter, has there been a myocardial infarction (often clinically silent in the elderly), or is hypertension, thyroid disease (hypo- or hyperthyroidism), anemia, or some other factor causing the cardiac decompensation? Predictably, several factors often contribute while several others may be present but not clearly contribute. In this situation definitive delineation of the pathophysiology may not be possible, safe, or even important to obtain.

Chronic obstructive pulmonary disease, manifested as chronic bronchitis, fibrosis, and emphysema, is a very common cause of disability in this age group. Since it is 4 times more common in men than in women, it contributes importantly to the sex differential in longevity which makes old age a peculiarly feminine epoch. Predisposing factors include cigarette smoking and urban and occupational air pollution. At an organ level, the disease involves a breakdown of the normal connective tissue framework of the lung, presumably reflecting both basic age related changes and chronic inflammatory reaction. This disorder is a source of great discomfort and frustration, since it restricts activity. Progressive changes lead to death from superimposed bacterial infections, right ventricular heart failure, and/or severe hypoxia *per se*.

Morbidity among 70 year olds is summarized in Figure 11–11.

COMMON CAUSES OF DEATH IN OLD AGE

Death in old age reflects the high prevalence of serious disorders and the vulnerability of the aged to decompensation when subjected to inevitable environmental stresses. Major causes of death are depicted in Figure 11–10.

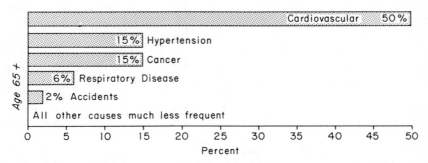

Figure 11–10   Common causes of death in old age (above age 65) as per cent of the total. (Adapted from Vital Statistics of the United States, 1968. Vol. II, Mortality, Part B. Rockville, Maryland, United States Department of Health, Education and Welfare, 1971, pp. 114–126.)

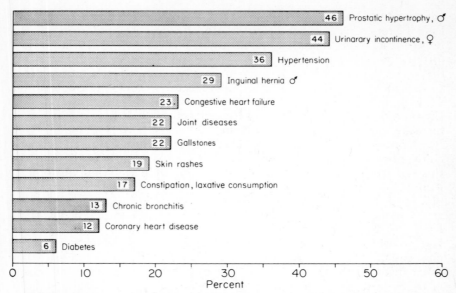

Figure 11–11 Prevalence (per cent of total population) of certain symptoms or diseases among 70 year olds in Gothenberg, Sweden. (Adapted from Svanborg, A.: Seventy year old people in Gothenberg, a population study in an industrialized Swedish city. II: General presentation of social and medical conditions. Acta Medica Scandinavica Suppl. 611, 1977.)

PREVENTIVE HEALTH MEASURES

Preventive medicine among the elderly shifts from more long term to more immediate concerns. While measures to reduce premature morbidity and mortality from atherosclerosis and malignancy are appropriate concerns for the health professional who treats young and middle aged adults, the geriatrician is more concerned with preventing accidents and preserving critical functions which permit continued independence. At what age this shift in emphasis occurs is not clear-cut, especially in individual cases. For the physiologically youthful man of 75, treatment of hypertension and even weight loss might prolong a vigorous lifestyle. Encouraging exercise of appropriate kind and intensity (walking, cycling, perhaps even jogging) is always salutary and may pay great dividends not only from a physical but also from a psychological and social standpoint. However, in general, greatest emphasis should be placed upon measures which improve the quality and not simply the quantity of life for the elderly. To paraphrase a famous remark by President John F. Kennedy, we must add life to their years, not simply years to their lives.

Many persons, not just health professionals, can contribute to the prevention of illness and disability in the elderly. Family members provide love, loyalty, human contact, and personal service. Neighbors and church or social group members help in similar ways and in turn receive personal satisfaction and mutual assistance. Community workers help to organize special events or programs for the aged and serve as advocates in government circles. Architects and builders contribute through construction of safer and more appropriate living environments or, often better, renovation of the old person's long-accustomed home (rails by stairs or bathtub, better lighting, central heating, etc.). Teachers design and conduct courses in adult education to be given at community schools and colleges or via radio or television. Social workers address the needs of the individual old person, in so doing taking advantage of family and community support systems. Nurses visit the home or care for the ambulatory elderly in clinic or day hospital, where dentists, physical and occupational therapists, speech therapists, psychologists, and physicians often make their most important contribution. The hospital is used only when these other measures fail (and stays in hospital are kept to minimal duration). The nursing home or long-stay ward, though sometimes unavoidable, is the court of last resort. Even here every effort is made to encourage independence and keep the patient out of bed. All too often this reluctant progression from independence to dependence is violated for reasons of expediency (e.g., hospitalizing the old person with bronchitis when a house call and support by family or neighbors could suffice). Sadly this may lead to chronic institutionalization to the detriment of society, the health care system, and, most importantly, the old person herself.

SPECIAL COMMENTS

Geriatrics defines the special attention to the care of the elderly by health professionals. A homily appropriate to geriatrics might introduce this epilogue: "Grant me the skill to change what is changeable, the patience to accept what is not, and the wisdom to know the difference between the two."

It is often surprising to young health professionals to discover that the elderly patient does not often expect to be cured. She may not even expect (or wish) to live much longer. In those circumstances the patient is often wiser than her physician, who may consider death a defeat and a blow to self-esteem. Especially among the elderly, whose illnesses are so often chronic, the image of the physician as life saver or miracle worker is particularly inappropriate. Perhaps for that reason the care of the elderly has been relatively neglected by the medical profession, even in such socially sensitive countries as the United Kingdom, where geriatrics has been recognized as a separate medical specialty for over three decades.

What, then, is the future of geriatrics? First, geriatrics can only grow in importance as the populations of Western countries age and their elderly consume an ever increasing proportion of health care resources. Second, if physicians continue to be attracted chiefly to younger patients with more definable and potentially more reversible disorders, the care of the aged will pass ever more into the hands of nurses; social workers; physical, occupational and speech therapists; physician's assistants; and other paramedical personnel. Third, since multifactorial, multidisease, and multiproblem situations are the rule in geriatrics, the contributions of multiple professions will usually be required for optimal health care delivery. Hence the effective geriatrician must become more a team leader, coordinator, and administrator than colleagues in the medical or surgical subspecialties. As a corollary to this development, the opportunities for nonphysicians are enormous in geriatrics. Hence multidisciplinary teamwork is the watchword in geriatrics, each member of the team making his or her distinctive contribution in synergism with professional colleagues from other disciplines.

REFERENCES

Andres, R.: Relation of physiologic changes in aging to medical change of disease in the aged. Mayo Clin Proc, *42*:413, 1967.
Birren, J. E., and Schaie, K. W. (Eds.): Handbook of the Psychology of Aging. New York, Van Nostrand Reinhold, 1977.
Brocklehurst, J. C.: Textbook of Geriatric Medicine and Gerontology. London, Churchill-Livingstone, 1973.
Brocklehurst, J. C. (ed.): Geriatric Care in advanced Societies. Lancaster, MTP, 1975.
Brocklehurst, J. C., and Hanley, T.: Geriatric Medicine for Students. New York, Churchill-Livingstone, 1976.
Comfort, A.: A Good Age. New York, Crown, 1976.
Coni, N., Davison, W., and Webster, S.: Lecture Notes on Geriatrics. Oxford, Blackwell Scientific Publications, 1977.
Hodkinson, H. M.: Biochemical Diagnosis of the Elderly. London, Chapman and Hall, 1977.
Kalish, R. A.: Late Adulthood: Perspectives on Human Development. Monterey, California, Brooks/Cole, 1975.
Ostfeld, A. M., and Gibson, D. C. (Eds.): Epidemiology of Aging. U. S. Department of H. E. W., Publication No. (NIH) 75–711, U. S. Government Printing Office, 1974.
Rossman, I. (Ed.): Clinical Geriatrics. Philadelphia, J. B. Lippincott Company, 1971.
Svanborg, A.: The Gerontological and Geriatric Population Study in Göteborg, Sweden. Acta Med Scand Suppl 611, 1977.

12

Death and Dying

CAROLINE E. PRESTON

Ours has been characterized as a "death-denying" society. Often, we have gone to absurd extremes to avoid the acknowledgement of our own mortality and that of others. In recent years, the mechanisms of death avoidance have been under attack, and rationalizations for it are eroding. Death as the crucial determinant of our humanity has been the topic of curricula or content in many university programs and community or church conferences, and the focus of much significant writing and research. It is unclear whether or not programs aimed at desensitizing us to fears of death achieve this goal. What *is* becoming clear is that health professionals can no longer feel comfortable or function effectively by avoiding questions about death and dying.

Conflicts generated in many who serve and care for dying patients can be intense. The tendency to avoid interaction and to withdraw emotional or physical support from such a patient and loved ones is an understandably human failing, but a grievous one, because communication at that time is desperately needed. Kübler-Ross identifies dying as a process with several stages, beginning with the initial denial and isolation, and progressing to anger, to bargaining, to depression, and finally to acceptance. She regards the persistence of hope as a necessary condition for the accomplishment of the work of mourning one's own or another's death. Hope, she claims, may be different for the dying than the living. Hope for the dying may not necessarily be the expectation that the dying process will be reversed, but rather that this process will not erode one's dignity, and that the suffering will be bearable. The temporal relationships of these stages in the dying process, according to Kübler-Ross, are represented in Figure 12–1.

In the experience of dying vicariously with patients, one must set aside what has been called "the satisfaction of rescue fantasies" that often determines the choice of a healing profession in the first place. In attending death and dying, one must also cope with his or her own death fears and the fear of the deaths of loved ones. The justification for avoiding dying patients is often that the patients have too little time left

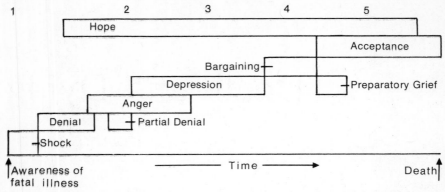

Figure 12–1 The above chart conceptualizes the stages an individual often goes through as death and dying approach. This is an adaptation from Dr. Elizabeth Kübler-Ross (see references). In giving her permission for the use of this chart, Dr. Kübler-Ross had the following pertinent comments: "I think you have to emphasize that the goal of a therapist is not to push people through the stages of dying, but rather help them to die in dignity, which means to die in character. This means that people who have been fighters and rebels throughout their life are more likely to regard it in character if they are allowed to fight until the end, and are certainly not sedated at the end of their life to simply fit into a pattern and to give the illusion that they are in the stage of peace and acceptance. You should also emphasize that these stages are only put together for teaching purposes and that most patients are in two or three stages together or simultaneously, and often go back and forth."

to warrant our investments and energies. A more logically tenable argument could be made that precisely because so little time remains, the dying patients should have their days and hours as bearable and enriched as possible.

Health professionals vary widely in how they communicate probable terminality to patients and their families, or whether they communicate it at all. Some state categorically, "I never tell my patients they are going to die," while others invariably confront the patient and everyone concerned with at least the possibility that the condition may be fatal. In my own experience, it does not become an either/or question at all, if one takes one's cues from the patients. By their questions and comments, by their verbal and nonverbal actions they will tell us when, how, and what they need to know about their immediate or remote futures. If, for example, a diagnosis is made clear to a patient and the patient does *not* indicate any concern about the prognosis or future course, one can be reasonably sure this patient is not yet ready to speculate realistically about the implications of the condition. But this initial reaction should not make one insensitive to other or later cues that the patient has achieved the readiness to look squarely at the future and discuss this honestly with the physician, staff, and loved ones.

In my own counseling and therapy with older patients, I find many who welcome the opportunity to talk openly and freely about the imminence of death. Some of our liveliest group discussions have centered on such issues as the high cost of dying in today's world of life-sustaining gadgets, the dispatch of cremation versus the prohibitive shortage of real estate for coffin burials, being on the brink of death, and the harshness of returning to full consciousness, often to pain. Many older people claim no fears of death but rather fear the potential loss of or change in the essential integrity of their being.

We have followed patients of all ages with potentially terminal illnesses over a period of 6 months, as summarized by Peter Hashasaki in an unpublished report in 1973–74. Our approach to these patients was one of concern about the kinds of problems confronting people in the course of coping with serious illnesses. We asked how they perceived their futures and understood their prognoses, but did not mention the possibility of death unless or until this was brought up by the patients themselves. In the course of frequent interviews, only 2 of the 25 patients both young men, ignored our cues to talk openly about their impending deaths.

To people of any age, actual death seems much less fraught with concern than the dying process. What we fear most is not when we will die, but how. Most authorities are in agreement that today, no one need reach such a point of despair and anguish as to be driven to suicide or to require a contrived death. Anger or depression, or both appear to be the salient motive for most suicides, and help in dealing with these feelings is paramount for patients who ask us or themselves, "Why can't I die?"

Concerning negative euthanasia, which lets people go by withholding life preserving treatments, Fletcher, in Williams, 1973, argues this is already a *fait accompli* in modern medicine. "Every day in hundreds of hospitals across the land decisions are made clinically that the line had been crossed from prolonging genuinely human life to only prolonging subhuman suffering and when that judgment is made respirators are turned off, life perpetuating intravenous infusions stopped, proposed surgery cancelled and drugs countermanded. . . . Arguing the pro and con about negative euthanasia is therefore flogging a dead horse."

The pros and cons of positive euthanasia, which involves the initiation of life shortening measures, are more complex (see Williams, "To Live and to Die: When, Why and How"). Some compromise of conflicts around this issue is achieved by proponents of "benemortasia," which translates as "a good death." The ethic of benemortasia avoids the proscription against murder which is leveled against proponents of positive euthanasia and emphasizes the amelioration of suffering and promotion of well-being for the dying.

Supporters of benemortasia recognize that comatose patients pose special problems. As one writer sees this question in Ramsey, 1970, "The best we can do is to develop some rough social and medical consensus about a reasonable length of time for keeping 'alive' a patient's organ system after 'brain death' has occurred. Because of the pressure to do research and to transplant organs, it may also be necessary to employ patient advocates who are not physicians and nurses. These patient advocates, trained in medical ethics, would function as ombudsmen."

Attitudes toward euthanasia among patients themselves are apparently significantly different depending upon the age of the people asked about their preferences concerning contrived death. In one survey of middle-aged people done by Levisohn in 1961, 80 per cent answered "yes" to the question, "Would you welcome euthanasia if you were incurably ill?" From our interviews with veterans' home and nursing home patients, with a mean age of 72, range 60 to 95, again we found most people very willing to talk about the issue of preferences for positive or negative euthanasia. About half of our subjects rejected both positive and negative euthanasia, one quarter rejected positive but favored negative euthanasia, and about a third favored both positive and negative euthanasia. From these results we speculate that life may indeed become more precious as the awareness of death deepens. Cappon's study of dying patients, published in 1962, reflects a similar ambivalence about death in dying patients "who neither universally welcomed induced dying nor rejected intercessions on behalf of their deaths." The conclusion drawn from the results of this study was that "the sicker the patient, the more unwilling he was to give up life."

Assistance to patients who are dying revolves around helping them deal with their "livingness" rather than their "dyingness." Jeanne Benoliel, writing in Feifel, 1977, conceptualizes dying as a "journey" and cites four purposes for assisting in this process: "to facilitate normalization of living according to the patient's preferences throughout the process of dying; to maximize opportunities for the patient to participate in decisions affecting living and dying; to foster and encourage open communication between the dying person and those who are important to his or her life; and to help the patient find an 'appropriate death.'"

Pattison describes an appropriate death as a style of dying that is adaptive to the specific person: "We seek to assist the dying person to view his or her own death and live out his or her dying in a manner consonant with his or her own pattern of coping mechanisms, definitions of the meaning of death and life context. Thus the criteria for an appropriate death will be fulfilled in different ways by different people."

Weissman, in 1974, provided the following criteria of an appropriate death:

(1) The person is able to face and resolve the initial crisis of acute anxiety without disintegration.

(2) The person is able to reconcile the reality of his or her life as it is to his or her ego ideal image of the life he or she wanted it to be.

(3) The person is able to preserve or restore the continuity of important relationships during the living-dying interval and gradually achieve separation from loved ones as death approaches.

(4) The person is able to experience reasonably the emergence of basic instincts, wishes, and fantasies that lead without undue conflict to gradual withdrawal and the final acceptance of death.

The increasing determination of people to control how and where they die has sparked the hospice movement. This began in England with the work of Cecily Saunders, a British physician, and is spreading in this country. The movement is dedicated to the creation of settings where all efforts are directed toward helping people die with dignity and grace. Such care may be provided either in a hospital or in the dying person's home and familiar surroundings.

Cecily Saunders writes eloquently of her philosophy in caring for the dying person:

The treatment at St. Josephs (an English hospital where dying patients are cared for) is designed to relieve pain. Yes, one *can* do that, to enable the patient not only to die peacefully, but to live fully until he dies, neither swamped with distress, nor smothered by treatments or drugs and things we are doing nor yet enduring in sterile isolation."

The timing of medication is adjusted by Cecily Saunders according to the rhythm of pain so that patients never need to ask for medication or to dread mounting levels of discomfort. Peacefulness and serenity in dying are the goals of the hospice movement.

REFERENCES

Alsop, S.: Stay of Execution. Philadelphia, J. B. Lippincott Co., 1973.

Cappon, D.: Attitudes of and toward dying. Canad Med Assoc J, *87*:693, 1962.

Feifel, H. (Ed.): The Meaning of Death. New York, McGraw-Hill Book Co., 1959.

Feifel, H. (Ed.): New Meanings of Death. New York, McGraw-Hill Book Co., 1977.

Group for the Advancement of Psychiatry: Death and Dying: Attitudes of Patient and Doctor. Vol. 5. Group for the Advancement of Psychiatry Conference, Symposium No. 11, 1965.

Kastenbaum, R., and Aisenberg, R.: Psychology of Death. New York, Springer Publications, 1972.

Kubler-Ross, E.: On Death and Dying. New York, MacMillan Co., 1969.

Kubler-Ross E.: Questions and Answers on Death and Dying. New York, McMillan Co., 1974.

Kubler-Ross, E.: Death: The Final Stage of Growth. Englewood Cliffs, N. J., Prentice-Hall, 1975.

Levisohn, A. A.: Voluntary mercy deaths. J Forensic Med: *8*:57, 1961.

Lifton, R. J., and Olson, E.: Living and Dying. New York, Bantam Books, Inc., 1975.

Mitford, J.: The American Way of Death. New York, Great Fawcett World Library, 1973.

Pattison, M.: The Experience of Dying. Englewood Cliffs, N. J., Prentice-Hall, 1977.

Pearson, L. S. (Ed.): Death and Dying: Current Issues in the Treatment of the Dying Person. Cleveland, Case Western Reserve Press, 1969.

Preston, C.: The Aged and Euthanasia. In Pattison, E. M. (Ed.): The Experience of Dying. Englewood Cliffs, N. J., Prentice-Hall, 1977.

Preston, C. E., and Williams, R. H.: Views of the aged on the timing of death. The Gerontologist, Vol. II, No. 4, Part 1, 1971.

Ramsey, P.: The patient as Person. New Haven, Yale University Press, 1970.

Scherzer, C. J.: Ministering to the Dying. Philadelphia, Fortress Press, 1967.

Weisman, A. D.: On Dying and Denying: A Psychiatric Study of Terminality. New York, Behavioral Publications, Inc., 1975.

Weisman, A. D.: The Realization of Death. New York, Jason Aronson, 1974.

Williams, R. H.: To Live and Die: When, Why and How. New York, Springer-Verlag, 1973.

13

Some Overviews of Life

GROWTH
DAVID W. SMITH

As a closing overview on growth, it is of interest to review a few charts depicting growth from birth to old age. The data for these charts were obtained from the references listed at the end of this chapter. For height (Fig. 13–1), there is the initial rapid infantile growth followed by a gradual deceleration prior to the adolescent spurt. After the plateau of the young adult there is a gradual decline into old age. Most of this decline is vertebral, since the long bones tend to maintain their length.

The weight curve is rather different, as shown in Figure 13–2. After the rapid infantile period is over there is gradual acceleration of weight growth in midchildhood followed by the adolescent spurt. Then, instead of a decline, there is a long term gradual increase which peaks in the 40's to 50's in women. This increase in middle age adult weight is not muscle! Muscle is declining in the 40's and onward. Some of the increase may be explained by increase in the breadth of bone. For example, you may note the increase in facial breadth in middle aged individuals versus young adults. However, the great majority of this additional adult weight is adipose tissue. Figure 13–3 shows subscapular fat thickness which is greater in the female than the male from early childhood, and increases until middle age. Incidentally, adipose tissue tends to decline in the limbs by middle age. The centripetal regions are the last to go.

The chart on head circumference growth (Figure 13–4) dramatically illustrates the thesis that different tissues have different growth patterns. The majority of brain growth is complete by 3 years of age. The mild adolescent growth spurt is at least partially related to the increase in thickness of the calvarium and enlargement of the frontal sinuses at adolescence. There is only a very slight decline in head circumference with old age.

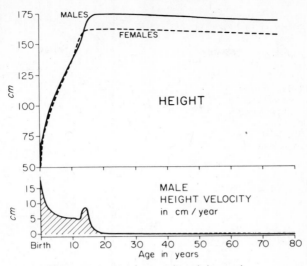

Figure 13–1 Height growth and degrowth.

At least a few tissues keep on growing throughout life. One of these is the ear, as shown in Figure 13–5. The cartilage of the nose also continues to grow and the nose becomes both longer and broader — a fact that must have been known to Carlo Collodi, the creator of Pinocchio.

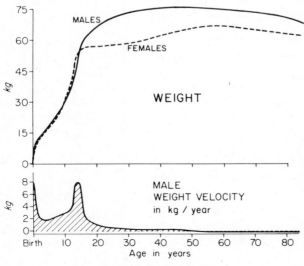

Figure 13–2 Weight growth.

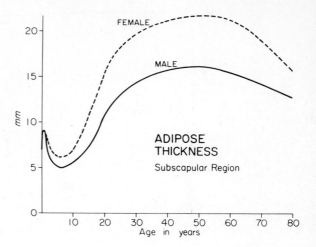

Figure 13–3 Adiposity increases in early infancy, decreases through mid-childhood, increases to a peak in the 40's and 50's, and then progressively declines.

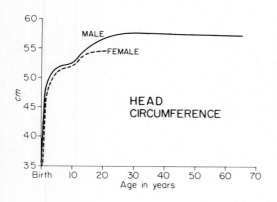

Figure 13–4 Head circumference growth, which largely reflects brain growth.

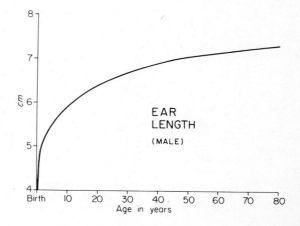

Figure 13–5 Ear cartilage, which does not mineralize, continues growing throughout life.

PHYSIOLOGICAL AND METABOLIC CHANGES
EDWIN L. BIERMAN

Not all physiological systems and functions decline with age. In an automobile, different systems may age and fail at different rates depending on the designer's blueprints and the environmental insults to which the car has been exposed. Similarly, the major systems within the body may lose their functions at different rates, also depending upon the varying genetic blueprints and environmental experiences of the individuals. Through natural selection, evolution has assured that for the ordinary individual, these rates of failure are not so out of synchrony as to interfere with reproduction. However, the rates of functional failure may differ substantially when an individual has passed the childbearing years, there being little natural selection for fitness beyond that age.

Some of these physiological changes may be due almost entirely to intrinsic aging, such as the progressive change in renal function with age (Fig. 2–7). Other changes observed with aging may be largely due to the impact of environmental factors; perhaps the change in lung expiratory capacity with age (Fig. 13–6) reflects the lifelong ex-

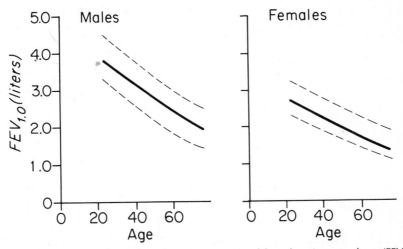

Figure 13–6   Relationship between age and 1 second forced expiratory volume ($FEV_{1.0}$) in males and females in an American community (Tecumseh, Michigan). The solid lines are 50th percentiles; the dashed lines are 20th (lower) and 80th (upper) percentiles. (Adapted from Epstein, F. H. et al.: Prevalence of chronic diseases and distribution of selected physiological variables in a total community, Tecumseh, Michigan. Amer. J. Epidemiol. 81:307, 1965.)

posure to air pollutants and cigarette smoke in the bulk of our population. Other changes may reflect the summation of environmental impact and intrinsic aging; for example, the progressive increase in blood pressure with age in Western societies (Fig. 10–8) is almost negligible in primitive cultures that have never been exposed to salt. Likewise, the gradual increases in circulating cholesterol and glucose levels with age (Figs. 10–9 and 10–10) are minimized in less westernized cultures that maintain totally different lifestyles and dietary habits.

Other physiological and metabolic functions may not change at all with aging. Examples include basic metabolic rate or oxygen consumption, which when expressed as a function of lean body mass is virtually unchanged with age. Also, the oxygen carrying capacity of the blood (hemoglobin concentration) remains stable with aging (Fig. 10–5).

Thus, biologic or functional age is a composite, and for any individual it may be quite different from his chronological age. Just as bone age in children is a functional parameter of biologic aging as distinguished from the chronological age, so can an index of biologic aging be developed for adult and older individuals. However, it is likely that a battery of tests, rather than a single measurement, will be required to evaluate physiological age. Such knowledge is essential if we are to evaluate any type of therapeutic intervention designed to alter the rate of aging, or to make social decisions such as appropriate retirement age based on more than chronology alone. Since some individuals are senile at 40 and others are tigers at 80, we need to measure this functional difference more appropriately and precisely.

We should not end on the pessimistic note in the description of the ages of man in Shakespeare's *As You Like It,*

> "The sixth age shifts
> Into the lean and slipid pantelone
> With spectacles on nose and pouch on side;
> His youthful hose, well-sewed, a world too wide
> For his shrunk shank, and his big manly voice
> Turning again to childish treble, pipes
> And whistles in his sound. Last seen of all,
> That ends this strange eventful history,
> Is second childishness, and mere oblivion,
> Sans teeth, sans eyes, sans taste, sans everything."

but rather end with Tennyson,

> "Old age has yet his honour and his toil;
> Death closes all: but something ere the end,
> Some work of noble note, may yet be done,
> Not unbecoming men that strove with Gods."

PSYCHOSOCIAL-BEHAVIORAL CHANGES
NANCY ROBINSON

As we have seen, psychosocial growth proceeds by fits and starts throughout the life span with eras of more rapid and slower change interspersed. The most rapid changes of all occur during infancy and the preschool years, during which the totally dependent newborn becomes an individual exhibiting systematic thought, complex speech, finely tuned perceptual motor skills, and a wide variety of interpersonal relationships. The elementary school years are a relatively quiet period of ripening and growing which erupt into the highly dramatic period of adolescence. From then on, most lives reflect alternating periods of crisis and calm, the precise ages of attainment having less to do with biology than one's sense of self, one's intimate partner(s) or their lack, one's educational and job progession, and one's health. Some authors suggest that the years of crisis are 18 to 25 (early young adulthood), 40 to 50 (transitional middle age), and 65 to 70 (retirement); others suggest different periods. The point is that crisis and calm cycles of adulthood tend to be individualized, often private, unlike the public and observed crises of children and youth.

The health professional is in a privileged position to observe the pains and pleasures of growth, and to aid in minimizing the former and optimizing the latter. Many persons reveal concerns to the primary health care providers that they reveal to no one else. Primary care health professionals constitute the single helping group in contact with all members of the society, whatever their age and economic circumstance. Sensitive professionals are good listeners and astute observers. They are continually impressed with the multitude of major and minor pressures and behavior problems which normal individuals experience in the course of a lifetime. Often they can observe minor problems before they fester into major ones, detect serious behavioral processes before they are full-blown, and remain available at times of crisis. Distinguishing between normal and abnormal problems, knowing just when to intervene and when to wait, and understanding when to take action themselves and when to refer to mental health specialists are seldom easy judgments, but may make a significant difference in the lives of an entire family. At the same time, however, experienced professionals come to understand that even without expert help, most people weather their difficulties with a positive outcome. The human spirit is remarkably resilient and forgiving.

REFERENCES

Damon, A., Seltzer, C. C., Stroudt, H. W., and Bell, B.: Age and physique in healthy white veterans at Boston. Aging and Hum Develop, 3:302, 1972.

Smith, D. W.: Growth and its Disorders. Philadelphia, W. B. Saunders Company, 1977.

Smith, D. W.: Recognizable Patterns of Human Malformation. 2nd ed. Philadelphia, W. B. Saunders Company, 1976.

Stroudt, H. W., Damon, A., and McFarland, R. A.: Heights and weights of white Americans. Hum Biol 32:331, 1960.

Stroudt, H. W., Damon, A., McFarland, R. A., and Roberts, J.: Weight, height and selected body measurements of adults. United States. 1960–62. Public Health Service, publication No. 1000, Series 11, No. 8, Washington, D. C., U. S. Government Printing Office.

Tanner, J. M.: Physical Growth and Development. In Forfar, J. O., and Arneil, G.C.: Textbook of Pediatrics. London, Churchill Livingstone, 1973.

INDEX

Page numbers in *italic type* refer to illustrations and tables.

267